The Messenger

JOHN AND ROBIN DICKSON SERIES IN TEXAS MUSIC
Sponsored by the Center for Texas Music History
Texas State University
Jason Mellard, General Editor

The
Messenger

The Songwriting Legacy
of Ray Wylie Hubbard

BRIAN T. ATKINSON

Forewords by Jerry Jeff Walker and Hayes Carll

Texas A&M University Press • College Station

SEAN
TRACEY

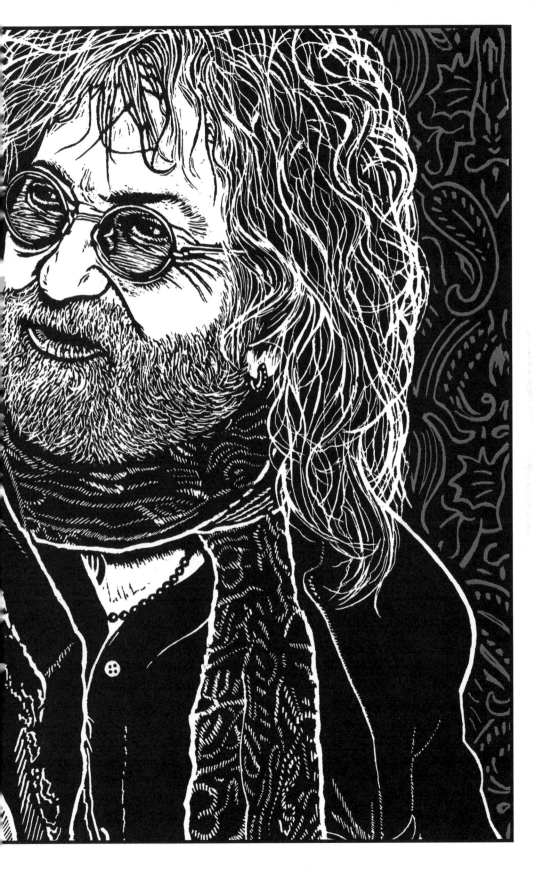

Library of Congress Control Number: 2019943261

ISBN 13: 978-1-62349-778-1 (cloth: alk. paper)
ISBN 978-1-62349-779-8 (ebook)

Image on previous page by Sean P. Tracey, Mosquito Studios, Denver, Colorado, based on a photograph by Mary Keating Bruton.

For Jenni, my favorite

Contents

BRIDGE
Name-Dropping (The Songwriters Behind the Songs)

VERSE FOUR
Without Love

Foreword

I met Ray Hubbard at the old Rubaiyat in Dallas, Texas, in 1964. That coffeehouse was the folk scene. Up-and-coming singer-songwriters like Bill Moss, Allen Damron, Michael Murphey, Donnie Brooks, and Segle Fry would all take turns playing there. Then I popped in off the road. I looked like the real deal to city kids with my beat-up hat, beat-up guitar, and all I owned in a beat-up satchel. I had some songs. So did they. We felt we had an affinity for performing.

We loved it. I met these players, heard new songs, got a better stage presence, and learned better delivery in coffeehouses. Then Damron drove me to Austin the first time in his Caddy. I've never forgotten that ride. There were no rules in the Austin music scene. You had the right to express yourself. Otherwise, take your cute rhymes, go to Nashville, and stand in line with your hand out. We had to dig deeper here and be more honest (even if we lied a little). We all encouraged each other and listened intently to what was being said by our witty friends.

I finally tried my hand in Greenwich Village, and Donnie Brooks got me in touch with David Bromberg to play my old songs. That meeting led to "Mr. Bojangles" and me buying a Corvette and heading south. I was on a mission to find a band of compadres like the one that Bob Dylan had found in Toronto with Ronnie Hawkins. I was looking for that when I ran into Ray Hubbard again in Red River, New Mexico. He was playing at a place called the Outpost, and I was staying at the Lazy H dude ranch north of town.

While we were having a grand old time, buying people drinks and getting change, Damron showed up and said he'd been in in Taos, New Mexico. He heard I was up in Red River. Damron said, "You ought to be back in Texas. Your friend Hondo Crouch has bought this old 1800s town and now has a place to be Hondo in." I went the next morning. I started playing with the guys back in Austin who became the Lost Gonzos. Ray and I had a common friend in Bob Livingston, who was in my band at that time. Then I decided to get married in Luckenbach. Hondo was the best man, and I decided to record a live concert in the town where I had the most fun and loved the most to be in.

I needed a couple songs to fill out the album *¡Viva Terlingua!* that we recorded there in Luckenbach. Livingston said, "Hey, Hubbard has written this crazy pushback song called 'Redneck Mother,'" and he played enough to pique my interest. We called Ray and got the skinny on the song, but he said there ain't much to it. So we spelled out *m-o-t-h-e-r* to stretch it out. Bob did his best redneck impression to start it off on the recording. Then he said, "This song is by Ray Wylie Hubbard." They played that version of "Redneck Mother" years later to the astronauts to wake them up one morning in outer space. Fun stuff, our lives! Oh, by the way, Ray has been called Ray Wylie Hubbard ever since that recording. Even in Russia.

Jerry Jeff Walker
June 2018

Foreword

"Redneck Mother" was iconic. Ray was most identified with that song for decades and probably still is for lots of people. It's hard to live down stuff you've done and songs you've written. I'm sure "Redneck Mother" will get a mention in his obituary, but to me, the song's not even on the radar. I've watched him evolve, grow, and move so far beyond that for almost twenty years. It's like a different lifetime now. As a songwriter, I think anybody who cares about songwriting will see Ray as somebody who has invested and bought into writing about his life and making great music. He followed his muse and wasn't afraid to push himself. I think his legacy will be that he was somebody who brought joy to people through music.

Ray explores his spirituality and mysticism, his own history and family, and the world at large through his music. He has a lot to say. It'd be a shame if all that was overlooked because of one song, but sometimes that's how it works. I played him [Carll's 2008 Americana Music Association Song of the Year] "She Left Me for Jesus" and asked his advice. I knew what a blessing and a curse that song was. It could become an albatross you have to carry around. Ray said, "Sometimes when you let that cat out of the bag, it's really hard to get it back in." He knew from experience. Ray has pushed me as a songwriter, and he's also helped directly by encouraging the good songs. His seal of approval is a big thing. He'll praise you [for] something you're not necessarily expecting, and that gave me more motivation to not play it safe. I respected him and wanted to show him that I was worthy of being in the same room as a writer. Watching him work all these years has been an inspiration that I lean on a lot. When I get stuck, I think, *Here's what Ray does. Let me try that.* He's a treasure and has had a fascinating life. Ray's been an artist in every sense of the word. He has stories for days that he can tell and people can tell about him. He has influenced artists and non-artists alike, and he's provided comfort and hope for people. He's entertaining, inspiring, and one of my favorite human beings. Ray would be at the top of the list if I were gonna read about somebody's life.

Hayes Carll
November 2017

Preface

Hayes Carll initially crossed paths with Ray Wylie Hubbard at the Old Quarter in Galveston, Texas. "When I met Ray, I said, 'I want to do what you do,'" Carll says. "'I want to be in show business.' He said, 'Well, carry my amp to the van.'" The moment foreshadowed a long, deep, quick-witted friendship they've shared ever since. After all, Carll summoned Hubbard onstage to sing their cowritten "Drunken Poet's Dream" when he appeared on *Austin City Limits* for the first time in 2013. (Hubbard, for whatever inexplicable reason, has never been asked to perform on the long-running television program.) That night underscores a primary reason this book exists: for far too long Hubbard has been overlooked in the conversation about great Texas songwriters. He shouldn't be passed by. As several dozen songwriters within these pages proclaim, Hubbard has created a catalog over the past four decades deserving mention among monumental tunesmiths such as Guy Clark, Steve Earle, Lightnin' Hopkins, Kris Kristofferson, Mickey Newbury, Billy Joe Shaver, and Townes Van Zandt.

Important note: *The Messenger: The Songwriting Legacy of Ray Wylie Hubbard* touches on but does not thoroughly dissect Hubbard's early years in the Outlaw Country movement in Texas throughout the 1970s. Jan Reid's *The Improbable Rise of Redneck Rock*, Rick Koster's *Texas Music,* Jason Mellard's *Progressive Country: How the 1970s Transformed the Texan in Popular Culture, Pickers and Poets: The Ruthlessly Poetic Singer-Songwriters of Texas*, and countless others have already extensively covered the topic. Readers can answer most questions in those texts. Instead, *The Messenger* focuses most specifically on Hubbard's captivating second act, in which he has reinvented his career and life as a sage and sober mystic and guiding light for younger songwriters. Frankly, grace and gratitude hold more interest as years have passed.

The Messenger frames a structure I originally envisioned for my first book *I'll Be Here in the Morning: The Songwriting Legacy of Townes Van Zandt*, a narrative based almost entirely on primary source interviews. The model was inspired by George Plimpton's oral biography *Truman Capote: In Which Various Friends, Enemies, Acquaintances, and Detractors Recall His Turbulent Career* (Nan A. Talese/Doubleday, 1997). (You can find further context in *The Messenger* in interviewee biographies near the end.) I simply edited these interviews for accuracy, clarity, and length. I occasionally cut and pasted sections of an interview to improve flow and edited out peripheral words and phrases when necessary (such as if an interviewee said, "You know," or "I mean" repeatedly). Otherwise, my fingerprints on the following interviews are minimal. As can be assumed, I never deliberately changed words said by an interviewee except to correct factual errors or add clarity. Those passages are bracketed.

Acknowledgments

As always, very special thanks to the John and Robin Dickson Series in Texas Music, Thom Lemmons at Texas A&M University Press, and Gary Hartman, Jason Mellard, and the Center for Texas Music History for making this idea a reality. Jenni Finlay serves as my partner in all crimes and went one further as research assistant on this book. She simply makes everything seven times better. A special thank-you to my parents, Ted and Ruthanne Atkinson, who have offered endless encouragement throughout all my days. Additionally, Texas music spirit animal Walt Wilkins deserves big thanks for his excellent ideas and photographs. Ditto Jack Ingram for connecting essential dots. Big thank-you to all the singers, songwriters, and players who offered their time to talk about Ray Wylie Hubbard. Some I wished to interview remained unavailable despite several requests, but nearly everyone jumped at the chance. Ray Wylie is clearly beloved among musicians in Texas and far beyond. Most important, thank you to Ray Wylie and Judy Hubbard for their cooperation as this book came together.

Finally, thanks to my personal advisory board: Janet Berger, Mary Keating Bruton, Chris Fullerton and Lindsay Preston, Mike and Michelle Grimes, David Holmes and Mary Miken Holmes, Jennifer Menchen, Tamara Saviano, Troy Schoenfelder, Sean Tracey, and Marianna Whitney. Additionally, thanks to Lagunitas Brewing Company and to everyone who has supported Squeaky String Productions, Eight 30 Records, Red Burgundy Films, Barefoot Recording, Catfish Concerts, Magdalene Catering, and everything else Jenni and I dream up. Our lives are richer for the experiences.

The Messenger

●-●

Prologue

I got a Silvertone around eighth grade, but the guitar wouldn't stay in tune. My fingers hurt when I messed with it, so I forgot about it. Then I went to Adamson [High School in Dallas] in tenth grade and met Rick Fowler in class. We went to a talent show assembly and Michael [Martin] Murphey, who was a cheerleader, came out with a guitar and said, "Here's a song I wrote." A lightbulb went off in my head. "Wow, that's a songwriter." Fowler had a guitar, so I went and dug out that old Silvertone, and he showed me a couple chords. Then I saved up some money and bought a Harmony Sovereign guitar.

Rick had given me Bob Dylan's funky first album [1962's *Bob Dylan* on Columbia Records], and I really liked it. I went, "The guy can't sing, but his writing is cool." So through Dylan I discovered Woody Guthrie, Cisco Houston, Jimmie Rodgers, and Leadbelly. All of a sudden, I got me some desert boots and a corduroy coat, and I was a folk singer. I didn't really start writing songs at that point, though. Wayne Kidd, Fowler, and I were in a group called Three Faces West,[1] and we did a lot of Murphey songs. We'd see Murphey when he'd come back and play at the Rubaiyat in Dallas. We'd hang out, and he'd show the songs to us. We played "Worried Man [Blues]," "Greenback Dollar," a whole folk repertoire back then.

Rick and I did what we called the Texas Twosome for three weeks in a summer in New Mexico and Colorado. We saw a poster at the end of the school year that said, "Talent needed for a New Mexico ski resort." Rick said, "We need to try out for this." I went over to this guy T. A. Painter's house. He said, "Yeah, I'd like you guys to do this and play each night at this barbecue joint." We were seventeen and high school seniors. We went up to Red River and played at the ski resort each night for the people eating barbecue. Then we came back, and I went to Arlington State [College]. I was gonna be an engineer. I went into my first physics class and went, "Nope, this isn't for me." I changed my major to English. I didn't know how to speak physics, but I did know how to speak English.

Rick and I rented a cabin. We used to have these guitar pulls up in New Mexico across from this redneck bar called D-Bar-D in 1966 or '68. The Vietnam War was going on, and hippies were happening. There was hostility if you had long hair, and the country was very split between the rednecks and the hippies. Merle Haggard had "Fightin' Side of Me." So we were at this hootenanny one night and [needed beer]. There was a bar in Red River called the Red Onion, a pretty safe musician bar, but everyone said, "Don't go in the D-Bar-D. There are rough rednecks." Red Onion was about a mile away, and I didn't want to drive. I said, "Well, hell, how bad could it be?" I walked into the D-Bar-D, and it was like the jukebox stopped. Everybody looked at me. I went up to the bar and said, "I'd like a case of Coors." The bartender said, "You got an ID?"

About that time, this old woman, whose name I think was Tilly, said, "How do you call yourself an American with long hair like that?" I said, "I don't remember calling myself an American. I just remember asking for a case of beer." She said, "That's my son over there, and he don't like long hair." We got into this really tense situation. Finally the bartender came up and said, "Here's your beer, son. Now get out of here." A guy said something like, "I don't care if you beat him up, you just can't do it in here." I walked out with the case of beer and saw an old pickup truck with a gun rack, Oklahoma tags, and a bumper sticker.

I got back to the cabin. Rick Fowler, Bob Livingston, and maybe B. W. Stevenson were all sitting around. I said, "I almost got killed getting this damn beer." They said, "It's your turn to sing a song." I picked up a guitar and hit a G chord and said, "This old woman over there was born in Oklahoma." I just made it up. Then Livingston left. He went to California to play bass with Michael Martin Murphey and came back to Texas to play bass with Jerry Jeff [Walker]. They were playing somewhere one night and Jerry broke a string. He said, "Bob, play a song." Bob has an incredible memory and probably knows ten thousand songs. He sang "Redneck Mother," and people were laughing and singing along. Jerry said, "What the hell is that?"

So Jerry started doing the song. They were recording [Walker's landmark 1973 album] *¡Viva Terlingua!* in Luckenbach. Bob called me and said, "Jerry wants to record that song, but it needs a second verse." We'd always just do the first verse and chorus and then spell out *m-o-t-h-e-r*. I wrote the second verse on the phone and said, "There it is." For some reason, when they did the song, Bob said, "This song is by Ray Wylie Hubbard." I think the record label told Jerry to take that off the song, but Jerry said, "Nah. Leave it on there." I'd been Ray Hubbard up to that point. I got a middle name when Livingston said that I wrote the song.

¡Viva Terlingua! was the definitive Progressive Country record.[2] Even if it didn't have "Redneck Mother," it was the defining record for the movement. It had really cool songs and attitude. It got my name out there, but it was a blessing and a curse. "Redneck Mother" was the only thing I was known for, and I didn't even have a record out at that time. I'd go to these joints and people would say, "Play 'Redneck Mother.'" I'd play "Redneck Mother," and say, "Here's another song I wrote." They'd say, "Play 'Redneck Mother' again." I didn't get a career until I was in my forties, but I'm sure "Redneck Mother" helped get me some notoriety.

[The Cowboy Twinkies started when] we were up in Red River, but we'd been playing down at Ray Kennedy's joint the Chequered Flag in Austin as Three Faces West. I looked on their mailing list calendar and saw Tony Joe White was gonna play on a Wednesday night. I called Rod and said, "Can I come open for Tony Joe White?" I had just heard "Polk Salad Annie" on the radio. He said, "Yeah, sure." I talked to Rick and Wayne and said, "After we close Tuesday night, I'm gonna go to Austin and open for Tony Joe. I'll be back Thursday." My guitar playing wasn't that good at the time. I was a strummer.

Somebody said, "There's a kid who works down at the Pizza Hut. He plays guitar." I went down there, and there's this guy washing dishes. I said, "Hey, man, you wanna go to Austin next Wednesday and open for Tony Joe White?" Terry ["Buffalo"] Ware said, "No, I'd rather stay here and wash dishes." We got together and rehearsed. We played the gig on Tuesday with Three Faces West, and we left there around eleven o'clock. We drove straight to Austin, got there at three or four in the afternoon, and met Tony Joe. The two of us opened the show for Tony Joe, and we hung around there for a while. We left there at midnight and got back to Red River at three or four in the afternoon and played that night.

At one point, Terry and I were playing as a duo at a little folk club in Dallas called the Rubaiyat. [Former Dallas Cowboys defensive end] Pat Toomay came and heard us and said, "There's a country and western bar in Fort Worth and you'll probably need a band." I called up Terry and said, "Hey, man, we can play this gig. There's probably pretty decent money, probably five hundred bucks, but we need a bass player and a drummer." He was in Norman, [Oklahoma]. They drove down. We started learning these songs in my parents' living room for the gig the next night. I said, "We need a name for the band. Ray Wylie Hubbard and . . ." The bass player, Dennis [Meehan], said, "I always wanted to be in a band called the Twinkies." I said, "Since we're playing a country bar in Fort Worth, we ought to be the Cowboy Twinkies."

I drank and took pills a lot in my twenties and thirties. Somebody would come up and say, "You wanna go fast?" "Yeah, I wanna go fast." "Take this." You could drive to Colorado and not go to sleep. I was into drinking, pills, and later cocaine. I thought cocaine was the answer to my drinking problem. I guess I really went off the deep end when my dad died. I got into blackout drinking and daily drinking. It was not good.[3] I'd tell myself I'd just have two beers, but I'd go way beyond that. My dad had left me some money, and it was gone. I was going with a girl who was trying to get me into recovery. She was giving me little hints like "You're a bad drunk."

I didn't really know Stevie Ray [Vaughan], but I'd run into him at Riverside Studios. He'd gotten sober and was speaking to some people at a meeting. After the meeting, I took some time to talk to him and got a little hope that maybe I didn't have to live like this. I went into recovery and started doing what I was supposed to do on a daily basis. It's still foggy. I really don't remember how it happened, but it was powerful to me that he took the time to help me. It's like I was in a plane crash, baggage was everywhere, and all I had in my head was the black box running all the time. Guilt. Shame. Remorse. Resentment. I was forty-one years old, and I'd burned every bridge I'd slept under. What did I really want to do?[4]

I had all the fun I could stand because it wasn't fun anymore. It was time.

I got sober on my forty-first birthday. I didn't really have a career at that point. I was a bar-band guy with a pretty bad reputation. Gruene Hall [in New Braunfels, Texas] wouldn't hire me because I didn't show up for a gig—or maybe because I did show up. I said I really want to be a real songwriter about a year after I got clean and sober. At that point, I knew I had to play guitar better because all the songwriters I liked knew how to fingerpick. I ran into a guy named Sam Swank at some party. He was over in a corner playing "Deep River Blues." I called him up later and asked, "Will you teach me how to do that?" I decided to write songs not to see what I could get from them. I wasn't going to write them because I had a publishing deal or to try to get anybody to record them. I wanted to write what I hoped would be cool, valid songs. I really started getting into that when I was forty-two.

"The Messenger" was the first song I wrote when I got into fingerpicking and learned these patterns. Someone at an AA meeting gave me *Letters to a Young Poet* by [Prague-born poet Rainer Maria] Rilke. There was a phrase in there where he was talking about fear and the line just came out of me: "Fears are like dragons guarding our most precious treasures." I went, "Ah." The idea was that I was a messenger, and I would write songs to give a message to people. I'm wearing old boots with high Cuban heels. They're old boots. My jeans were torn. It was a story about this guy, this persona I could put on and be that messenger: "I'm not here looking for God, not looking for sex. I don't need water or roses. I'm here to tell you, here's the message: Our fears are like dragons guarding our most precious treasures."

It started out real acoustic fingerpicking with those songs, and then I got into checking out Lightnin' Hopkins and thought, I'd really like to learn how to play this lick. I got into John Lee Hooker, Lightnin', and what I call the "dead thumb" groove thing. It was really a good marriage to have the lyrical and even humorous depth and weight in folk music with a deep groove. I felt like having that groove was good, but I laid down lyrics on it that weren't just "I woke up this morning and had the blues." I keep trying to learn new things like fingerpicking, open tuning, slide guitar, and mandolin. You get things to come in the door that weren't there before with new things. If I hadn't learned open D tuning, I wouldn't have gotten "God Looked Around" [the opening track to Hubbard's 2017 album *Tell the Devil . . . I'm Gettin' There As Fast As I Can*]. If I hadn't learned slide, I wouldn't have gotten "Three Days Straight" [from 2001's *Eternal and Lowdown*]. I'm an old cat, but learning new things keeps me on my toes. There's still a lot to learn.

I don't think I'm really consciously writing about spirituality when I'm working on a song. It just happens because that's the life I'm in. I live based on spiritual principles. I try to have some communication. I'll be writing a song and all of a sudden a line will come up that has to do with God, the devil, Buddha, or John Lee Hooker, but I'm not sitting down to write a gospel tune. There's the song "Prayer" [also from *Tell the Devil...*]. I think somebody had passed away. I remembered my grandmother used to say, "All we can do is pray." Well, that's not all we can do, but it's the best thing we can do. So, I sat down and had all these little thoughts I wanted to contribute. Maybe somebody will hear that and go, "Oh, okay." It's hard to pray and be a son of a bitch at the same time.

The music was gonna be another character in [the Hubbard-written movie] *The Last Rites of Ransom Pride* like *Oh, Brother, Where Art Thou?* In once scene, these Chinese twins are smoking opium, and I said, "We need a song about opium." Okay, right here this fellow's gonna be dying, and it'll be a long-pan scene. I need a song that is like "Knockin' on Heaven's Door," so I wrote "Black Wings." I needed a song for the credits. Well, "A. Enlightenment, B. Endarkenment, Hint: There Is No C." I figured out then that if you have an idea or a title, you can write a song about it. I thought, Yeah, I know how to do this. I need to bring this same mindset to writing commercials.

The snake farm has been there in New Braunfels [Texas] for thirty, forty years. I'd probably driven by ten thousand times. I'd just read Flannery O'Connor's letters, and she said in there, "Never second-guess inspiration. It's okay to rewrite." So I was driving by the snake farm and went, "Ew. It just sounds nasty." I thought, Well, it is. It's a snake farm, a reptile house. It ain't a hospital. I went: "Snake farm, just sounds nasty / Snake farm, pretty much is / Snake farm, it's a reptile house / Snake farm, ewww." I didn't doubt it. The next thought was, What do I do with this? That was the inspiration, but the craft is what to do with it.

What if it's about a guy who doesn't like snakes, but he's in love with a woman who works at the snake farm? What kind of woman would work at the snake farm? Well, she'd drink malt liquor, like [popular Welsh new wave band] the Alarm, and dance like Little Egypt. You just describe the woman this guy's in love with. One of my favorite lines is "there's nothing to do in the winter." You know, they're all hibernating. I had the chorus by the time I got home. When I got home, I said, What would her name be? Ramona, of course. You have this image, and it was pretty easy to personify the woman who would work there.[5]

[When] I came out of this honky-tonk fog I'd been in, I said, "Okay, by god, I'm gonna try to do this," and I got real into guitar and trying to learn fingerpicking like Mance Lipscomb, Lightnin' [Hopkins], and Jessie Mae [Hemphill], the dead thumb technique where you keep that low E-string going. I'm not a full-tilt blues or rock guy. I've never been a country or folk purist. I've been influenced by all that music. I feel fortunate to have seen Lightnin', Mance, and Freddie King, but also Ernest Tubb, Gary Stewart, Bill Monroe, Ralph Stanley, the 13th Floor Elevators, and the Moving Sidewalks. Love it all. Right now I feel like I've got that foundation in folk music, and I can take those lyrics and throw them on top of a deep groove.[6]

I really do need to thank my wife, Judy. She said, "Write whatever you want to write. You make the records you want to make. I'll try to sell the damn things." So for a songwriter, that's a good place to be. I'm not writing songs thinking about their future. I'm not writing songs because I've got a publishing deal. I'm not writing songs because I'm trying to get somebody to cut them. I'm writing songs because I go, "Oh, damn, there's a snake farm."[7]

You know, I've never thought about my songwriting legacy. I guess I've written some pretty cool songs that nobody else seems to be writing. I've written about Charlie Musselwhite, Spider, Snaker, and Little Sun, and Jessie Mae. I mention Tony Joe White and cool guitars and amps.[8] Somewhere in there I realized that songwriting was inspiration plus craft. Inspiration is the great "Aha, that's a great idea for a song." Craft is to make it fit the laws of music. I learned to keep learning new things. Once I became aware of what the fears and doubts were in my head, I could do the opposite and start to improve.[9] I guess as far as legacy, I hope it's that I wrote some cool, badass songs. Some sold and some didn't. Most didn't.[10]

   Ray Wylie Hubbard

Introduction

Ray Wylie Hubbard simply shifted shape with sobriety. The Dallas, Texas, native, a successful yet hard-living country singer during the Cosmic Country boom throughout the 1970s, discovered the doorway toward fulfillment early into his fourth decade when he swapped alcohol and drugs for unforeseen secular and spiritual depth. Legendary blues guitarist Stevie Ray Vaughan guided the journey. "He was the first guy I'd ever met who'd gotten sober and didn't turn into a square," says Hubbard, who was born on November 13, 1946, in Soper, Oklahoma, but raised in Dallas, Texas.[1] "I got a little bit of hope that maybe I didn't have to continue living like that from Stevie. He said that without the alcohol and drugs he could really play the guitar. That stayed with me."[2]

The tatterdemalion troubadour's rebirth—launched with *Lost Train of Thought* (1992) and most focused on follow-ups *Loco Gringo's Lament* (1995), *Snake Farm* (2006), *The Grifter's Hymnal* (2012), and *Tell the Devil . . . I'm Gettin' There As Fast As I Can* (2017)—continues blossoming today. Sharp storytelling shapes his star. "Ray Wylie Hubbard's someone you might not have heard of, but I've loved him for a while," legendary Beatles drummer Ringo Starr says. "'Snake Farm' is really great and interesting."[3] "Ray has a great groove and really puts it in the pocket," echoes pioneering independent artist Terri Hendrix, who toured Europe with Hubbard and iconic instrumentalist Lloyd Maines near the millennium's turn. "There's a saying in music: The easier something appears, the harder it is to play and write. Any easy guitar part is actually really difficult, and sparse music really has to be in the pocket. Very few people can do that. I would consider Ray's a simplistic musical style that's really hard to nail."[4] Hubbard effectively whittles songs down to marrow.

His punch ("Rabbit," "Kilowatts") and precision ("All Loose

Things," "Dead Thumb King") overcame a significant obstacle: "Up Against the Wall Redneck Mother." The songwriter's early landmark, a defining Cosmic Country calling card made famous by celebrated singer Jerry Jeff Walker, has haunted his every shadow for more than forty years. "The song probably should have never been written, let alone recorded, let alone recorded again," Hubbard says. "You know, people will come up to me and say, 'Ray, what's the most important thing about songwriting? Is it the words or the music?' I'd have to say that the most important part of songwriting is right after you write a song, ask yourself, 'Can I sing this for twenty-five years?' I'm serious. I'm really serious."[5]

Walker's guitarist Bob Livingston cemented Hubbard's youthful legacy on 1972's ¡Viva Terlingua! by introducing "Redneck Mother" with seven words that simultaneously boosted Hubbard's stock and froze his ascent: "This song is by Ray Wylie Hubbard." Hubbard recorded "Redneck Mother" on 1978's Off the Wall (and the song appears on 1998's Live at Cibolo Creek Country Club as "The Obligatory Encore"), but Walker single-handedly hung his albatross. "A long time ago in a land far away called West Texas and East New Mexico, if you was a long-haired hippie musician, Cosmic Cowboy type, it was dangerous," Hubbard says when introducing the song. "This is before Willie Nelson sang at the Armadillo World Headquarters in Austin, Texas, bringing hippies and rednecks together, creating the hip-necks."[6]

Substance abuse notoriously fueled the movement. Most notably, legendary singer-songwriters Guy Clark, Waylon Jennings, Kris Kristofferson, Mickey Newbury, Willie Nelson, Billy Joe Shaver, and Townes Van Zandt wrote fast and lived faster during that time. Hubbard orbited the same circle. "Ray Wylie Hubbard's a great songwriter," Kristofferson says. "I remember going to his show, and there were two girls fighting over him. I mean, they were really fighting. One started pulling the shirt off the other, and I was thinking, All right. I had to stop the other one because she was hitting her right in the face. I said to Ray, 'You sure stir up a lot of weird emotions there.'"[7]

Hubbard followed Ray Wylie Hubbard and the Cowboy Twinkies' self-titled debut (1975) with three solo albums—Off the Wall (1978), Something About the Night (1979), and the tellingly titled Caught *in the Act* (1984)—while developing a reputation as class clown and party animal. He eventually crashed and burned. "Jersey had Springsteen, California had Jerry Garcia, and Texas had Ray Wylie Hubbard," explains the narrator in a promotional video recorded for Hubbard. "Ray was knocking them dead at honky-tonks, road-houses, and arenas two hundred nights a year, but by the mid-eighties the honky-tonk hero badge was getting old. He wasn't happy. Ray knew he needed to slow down and catch his breath. His demons were catching up with him."

Hubbard sobered up. He swallowed his pride and took guitar lessons. Endlessly paged through historical and spiritual texts for personal and professional inspiration. Narratives emerged from deeper wells. Vivid vignettes—timeless songs such as "The Messenger," "Mother Hubbard's Blues," "Drunken Poet's Dream," "Stone Blind Horses," "Mother Blues," "In Times of Cold"—appeared on subsequent albums. Accordingly, fans today look toward Hubbard as a literate songwriter on par with the most celebrated. "'Redneck Mother' has its charm," says legendary instrumentalist Gurf Morlix, who produced several Hubbard albums and played guitar in his touring band for years. "His throwaway song about getting beat up turned into an anthem, but his writing today and how literate his songs are even as they go deep in the mud stand out among songwriters. He's more unique than Bob Dylan."[8]

Hubbard frequently balances sacred ("New Year's Eve at the Gates of Hell") and secular ("Chick Singer Badass Rockin'") with an everyman's grace ("Dust of the Chase"). "[Spirituality] shows up in the songs," Hubbard says, "but I still enjoy being a smart-ass." Others from the past two decades such as "Screw You, We're from Texas," "New Year's Eve at the Gates of Hell," "Loose," "Wild Gods of Mexico," "Henhouse," "Coricidin Bottle," and "Down Home Country Blues" back the claim. "My friend Ray Wylie Hubbard," longtime Eagles guitarist Joe Walsh says, "is brilliant."[9] Songwriter Paul Thorn, who covered Hubbard's "Snake Farm" on his album *What the Hell Is Goin' On?* (2012), doubles down: "Ray's gonna go down in the ranks standing by the great ones like Kris Kristofferson and Billy Joe Shaver. He'd be right beside them on the Mount Rushmore of great songwriters."[10]

Additionally, Hubbard has mentored countless younger songwriters and served as a spiritual beacon for the past quarter century. "Everyone's trying to seek out lyrics like his," rapidly rising songwriter William Elliott Whitmore says. "Ray really made me want to be more studious. I've always taken pride in my writing, but you can always do better. He proves that. If you want to do well, you have to be able to stand up and compare yourself to guys like Ray Wylie Hubbard. He makes me want to do better."[11]

Artistic integrity ultimately charts his legacy. "I think Ray will be remembered as a folk singer, a songwriter who wrote with the stuff that started people out in coffeehouses, especially the ones who came after Bob Dylan and had to survive in this room that he took all the air out of," explains iconic singer-songwriter Steve Earle. "It's a hard job, and we're all still doing it. Ray will be remembered as someone who believed like Guy did that songs aren't finished until you play them for people. I think he'll play every song he writes that he likes for an audience. That's the purpose and the reason you create. He'll be remembered as a singer-songwriter."[12]

Verse One
Redneck Mother

Ray Wylie Hubbard Band, Motherlode Saloon, Red River, New Mexico, 1969. Left to right: Paul Pearcy, John Inmon, Ray Wylie Hubbard, Bob Livingston. Courtesy Bob Livingston.

The Cowboy Twinkies were a fun folk-rock band, but we didn't have that many songs. We would also do [Led Zeppelin's] "Communication Breakdown" and [the Surfaris'] "Wipe Out." We'd been playing here in Austin, and Willie [Nelson] moved down from Nashville. Jerry Jeff [Walker] was here, and we were playing the same places as them. I still thought of myself as a folk singer, but with the band we were doing folk rock. Michael Martin Murphey made it all fit together. It wasn't really country music. It was songwriters: Jerry Jeff, Rusty Wier, Steven Fromholz. I was just fumbling around trying to be a writer in my twenties.[1]

—RAY WYLIE HUBBARD

Bobby Bare

Ray Wylie's the only person I know who recorded a song with half a word: *mother*. I met him down in Texas after I recorded "Up Against the Wall Redneck Mother." I said, "I know what you meant by that." Everybody else did, too. I think Billy Joe Shaver brought the song to my attention. He told me that Jerry Jeff Walker had done "Redneck Mother," so I recorded it. I did the song at all my shows. I always fucked around with the spelling part with *mother*. In mine, *T* was always for tits, *H* was for huge tits, and *E* was for enormous Dolly Parton tits. Of course, *R* was for redneck.

I coproduced a television show with songwriters back in the eighties. We had on all the great writers, including Ray Wylie. My manager managed him for a while, and we've been friends ever since. Ray Wylie has written some great songs, and he keeps putting them out. I was gonna do "Snake Farm" on the record I put out earlier this year [2017's *Things Change*], but I didn't. I've done so many Shel Silverstein songs that "Snake Farm" isn't even a reach. Ray Wylie's got a sick mind. I love him, and I love his songwriting.

I find songs on the radio or someone draws my attention to them

Left to right: Noel McKay, Bobby Bare, and Brennen Leigh during the recording of "Snake Farm" for Eight 30 Records' The Messenger: A Tribute to Ray Wylie Hubbard, *Cinderella Sound, Madison, Tennessee, September 12, 2018. Photo by Brian T. Atkinson.*

like Billy Joe did with "Up Against the Wall Redneck Mother." Billy Joe was writing for my publishing company back in the seventies. In fact, he's the one who got me Paul Craft's "Dropkick Me, Jesus, Through the Goalposts of Life." I was gonna record a Paul Craft song that Linda Ronstadt had done, and Billy Joe said, "Have you heard that song called 'Dropkick Me, Jesus'?" I said, "Wow, great." Billy Joe got it and played it for me, and I recorded it and not the other. You know it must be special if a songwriter draws your attention to someone else's song.

Billy Grammer had recorded "Detroit City" before me, and I heard his record on the radio. I thought, That's the greatest song I've ever heard. I was living in L.A., and I stopped on Sunset Boulevard. I tied up work traffic for three minutes listening to the song on the radio. I didn't care if I was blocking traffic. I recorded "Detroit City" as soon as I got back to Nashville. I knew it had been out before and didn't have visions of a big hit record. I recorded it for love. I didn't even know they were gonna put it out as a single. You just love a song, and you gotta do it.

Interpreting a song's like watching a movie. You have to see the picture. The whole story runs through my mind even now when I do a song. I see the picture in my brain, and I love to sing it as straight as I can so everybody can get the story. You've gotta pronounce your words clearly. You can't mumble. I love Mary Gauthier's writing. Boy oh boy. I recorded her song "I Drink" [on *Things Change*]. If you have a great story song like "I Drink" or "Redneck Mother," you have to get it out there plainly. You know that guy in the song. Hell, I've known that guy all my life.

Ray will be remembered for his whole catalog. I could listen to ["Mother Blues"] and that story about his Les Paul guitar and that girl forever. We all did that playing in those joints. We were in it for the pussy. Anybody who says that they weren't is lying. Ray Wylie could capture that like nobody else. Shel Silverstein was great at it, too. His song "Rosalie's Good Eats Café" is nine minutes that captured a story. You know, Shel wrote verses to that while he was jogging. I've got eighty more. I could do three more nine-minute records. That's what a great writer does. Ray Wylie's a great songwriter and a great guy. I had a hip replacement after Ray Wylie had his replaced, so I called him on the phone, and he talked me through it. He's a good, honest man, the kind of guy you'd like to hang out with—funny, funny, funny and cynical.[2]

Michael Martin Murphey

Ray Wylie and I went to high school together. I was a senior when he was a sophomore. We knew each other when we played around Dallas in bohemian coffeehouses because we weren't old enough to go into a bar or club. As a child, I never listened to much rock and roll. I listened to gospel, bluegrass, hard-core country, and folk and was influenced a lot by Woody Guthrie, Christian, and gospel music. Ray was in a band called Three Faces West, and they played at the Outpost in Red River, New Mexico, a very small little pizza and Coca-Cola place. I was in college then, and they were in late high school. They were all drivers who would take people on Jeep tours and were just having a good time being kids in Red River. It wasn't an attempt to rule the world with a band.

I was either playing solo acoustic or with Bob Livingston when

Michael Martin Murphey was hugely influential in Ray Wylie Hubbard's early development as a singer and songwriter. Hubbard's band Three Faces West frequently covered his songs and followed his footsteps on the touring circuit. Murphey's hits include "Wildfire," "Carolina in the Pines," and "Don't Count the Rainy Days." Courtesy Lance Cowan and LC Media.

I was at UCLA and would come home for Christmas or summer vacation. We'd play gigs, hang around Red River, and go sit in with those guys. I'm pretty sure that's where they first heard me play "Wildfire" and other songs, and they started performing those songs. As they got better known, they'd come down to Texas and play shows at the Rubaiyat in Dallas, the Chequered Flag in Austin, and the Kerrville Folk Festival.[3]

I was around Ray during the Urban Cowboy period quite a bit. Anything even touching on country music was big in Texas then. We were playing at Gilley's [the Dallas honky-tonk that served as the location for the movie *Urban Cowboy,* starring John Travolta]. By then Ray had become a name because he'd written "Redneck Mother," which was a really funny and popular song among the redneck cowboy and hippie cowboy crowds from the time it came out on Jerry Jeff Walker's album *¡Viva Terlingua!* It's really typical of what we kids in the church in Texas had to go through if we played in honky-tonks where there was drinking involved.

We all know that drinking and drugs took over Ray Wylie's life. I quit hanging out with him at one point because he was just too crazy with drinking and taking drugs. He was over the line, and that made me uncomfortable. I've always been a Boy Scout and a straight arrow. Ray was always the class clown of the Texas music scene, so "Up Against the Wall Redneck Mother" isn't that surprising a song from him. He has a lot of satirical songs about Texas culture and Texas people.

Being straight built some walls between me and the Texas music scene. I regret those walls in some ways, and I don't regret them in others. I think a lot of people who were heavily involved in that grew up and realized the bad effects it was having on them. I remember when Jerry Jeff quit drinking and doing drugs. He started jogging through Zilker Park [in Austin, Texas] and up and down the waterways and bicycle paths of Lake Austin. That was a big change for him because the whole thing was based on the party mentality of "let's get drunk and play some redneck music." There's nothing wrong with a party, but when it becomes self-destructive, it's something you've gotta look at. I left Austin by early 1975 because drugs were taking over the town.

Ray's songwriting has been fantastic since he got sober, but he

was writing great songs before then. There are no rules for creativity. Ernest Hemingway was probably flat drunk or hungover
when he wrote some of the best novels in history. Did it make it
easier for some of those people to write? I don't know. Maybe it
did. I won't judge that. I only judge self-destruction on the basis
of how much destruction it does to you, not on your work. I think
Ray has always been a great songwriter who has written great stuff
before, during, and after getting sober.

Texas Monthly did a story on who exactly originated the Austin,
Texas, music scene [a few years ago], and I was in a conference
with Ray. Getting back together with Ray about that point was absolutely great. I had heard that he had really turned his life around,
but I hadn't really talked with him that much. I lost track of him,
and I was thrilled to catch up with him. After we got out of that conference, we probably spent an hour with each other, and I called
him on the phone and talked with him a few times. I'm absolutely
amazed at the turnaround he did. It took an incredible will.

I think Ray Wylie is one of the most influential songwriters.
He may not have had as many hits as others like Kris Kristofferson, but the way he writes songs is very poetic. He has a lot of
influence on other songwriters. We found out about each other's
work back in the day by getting together at parties and passing
the guitar around. We didn't have the Internet to share a video of
our latest song. Ray Wylie's my hero as a writer. It's not a contest,
but he's a great writer. Ray very gently and very gentlemanly had
a very influential role in the poetic lyrics that have come out of
Texas.[4]

Jerry Jeff Walker

I think Ray was still playing at the Outpost when we cut "Redneck
Mother." I went to see them play there, and my famous old Roy
Smeck Stage Deluxe, a Gibson guitar that they put out in the fif-
ties, was hanging on the wall. I street-sang with it in New Orleans.
I saw it on the wall and said, "Oh, there it is." I had sold it off to get
a handmade guitar in Dallas. A guy there named Ed Holt made gui-
tars, and we were all buying them, our first real guitars. I got out to
Red River somehow, and Hubbard owned the Roy Smeck.[5] I said,

*Left to right: Willie Nelson and Jerry Jeff Walker at Cheatham Street
Warehouse, April 22, 1975. Walker launched Ray Wylie Hubbard's career
two years earlier by including Hubbard's "Up Against the Wall Redneck
Mother" on his album* ¡Viva Terlingua! *Courtesy Jenni Finlay archives;
photo by Hal Odem.*

"Ray, can I borrow that guitar for a night?" I did. I was playing it,
and I wrote a song called "That Old Beat-up Guitar."

I came back and said, "I wrote a song." Then I played three-quarters of it. I stopped and said, "If you trade your old Roy Smeck that
you're not even playing for my Guild, I'll sing the last verse." Everybody in the room said, "Do it, Ray. We want to hear the last verse."
Well, that verse is the same as the second verse, but it's in the present tense instead of past. That was the only difference, but I still
got the guitar. Hubbard said, "All right." We made the switch, and
that tied us together. I think I even introduced the song that way
on the record [1972's *Jerry Jeff Walker* on Decca/MCA Records]: "I
lost a guitar, and it belonged to a man named Ray Wylie Hubbard.
I traded for it. Here's the last verse."

Austin was the reason the [Progressive Country movement]
happened. We all came back around 1970, and Austin was the

cheapest city to live in. You had thirty thousand college kids going to school at [the University of Texas] then. They filled the bars, bought tickets, and allowed us to have cover charges. It was different than Nashville. We could afford to live here, and it had a nice climate. Everybody was wearing suits, riding in buses, and making that wall of sound with the same musicians on every record in Nashville. They wondered why they all sounded the same. Austin allowed us to live and make music the way we wanted to.[6]

I had been living in Key West, Florida, and drifted back. I was having entirely too much fun and not getting enough creativity done. I wanted to put a band together that played and sang my music and did harmonies. People in Austin didn't care whether it was a hit song or something you just wrote. They could sit around, have a beer, listen to it, and judge whether they liked it or not. If they applauded really hard, you probably done good. If they yawned, you probably weren't doing so good. I liked that. The Texas artists I know are pretty hard on themselves. They'll be their own worst critics. If I'm going in to hear another person playing or dancing or whatever their art is, I'm sure they're doing their best, and they're probably trying to please themselves more than they have to. That's what I like about it here.[7]

Kids could tell the difference between good and bad. If you had a personality, you could communicate with them and have fun. It was a good base, and it helped that I had "Mr. Bojangles" and shortly thereafter cut [Guy Clark's] "L.A. Freeway," [Gary P. Nunn's] "London Homesick Blues," and "Redneck Mother" within a couple albums. Hubbard and I stayed in touch. Bob Livingston was our link. Livingston was my bass player in the [Lost] Gonzo Band, and he also played with Hubbard. He went back and forth. When we went out to Luckenbach to record ¡Viva Terlingua!, Livingston told me about a song that Hubbard wrote called "Redneck Mother." The rest is history.[8]

I flew out to New Mexico about 1970 to spend about a month on a dude ranch with some friends and play music. The Texas folk singer Allen Damron had passed through and told me that Hondo Crouch had bought Luckenbach, Texas, to make it his own little place to do stories and regale people. He said that I should check it out. When I did move back here in 1971, I headed down to Luckenbach to see what Hondo got for himself. As the scene got more and more active around Austin and Willie took off and then Michael Murphey, Rusty Wier, and I were flying out more to do dates, coming back off the road, it felt good to go out to Luckenbach. We'd get an infusion of the funk, sit around, and watch old men pitch washers and stuff. We just depressurized from the road. It was nice to lay back and keep abreast of how far away from that we were when we traveled away on jets.[9]

We had planned on taking a pass at six or seven songs when we went to record at Luckenbach. Bob told me that Ray Wylie had this song about getting even with some bubbas out in Red River. He knew a little of the chorus: "Up against the wall, redneck mother / Mother who raised her son so well." I said, "That'd be fun to do. Let's give that a shot." We called Hubbard and got what little he had down. He only had two verses. We said, "That's good enough." We decided to spell *mother* like they do in "Respect": *r-e-s-p-e-c-t*. We stretched it out by doing that. Little did we know it was gonna become an anthem.

The audience responded pretty well to everything we did at

The Motherlode Saloon as the bar looks today, Red River, New Mexico, January 27, 2018. Photo by Walt Wilkins.

Inside the Motherlode Saloon today, Red River, New Mexico, January 27, 2018. Photo by Walt Wilkins.

Luckenbach for *¡Viva Terlingua!* They were loud, screaming, hollering. We had already cut nine songs during the week at the dance hall. All we had to do on Saturday night was get some lively stuff. We did "Sangria Wine," "Redneck Mother," "London Homesick Blues." We were just making sure we got our parts right because we hadn't played some of these before. We knew "Redneck Mother" would work better in front of a live audience than it would to do it dry, and it went over well. It was a wild and woolly ride. I wanted to get the band out of the studio where the surroundings would influence them and not the studio.

Every little thing is focused on in the studio. It's like open-heart surgery. Your instruments aren't good enough. Your vocal doesn't sound quite as nice as you wanted. You're playing to an engineer who looks at you like *Hmm*. I wanted us to be interacting with a crowd. The big picture was the album inviting you to a party in the Texas Hill Country for an evening. [Former Texas governor] Rick Perry told me that he was stationed in the military in Germany, and he had his buddies over. They drank longneck beer, listened to it, and it was like they were in Texas. That's what we were trying to accomplish. Most people only made live albums if they were doing their hits. We were with MCA Records in California, and they said they sold seventy thousand copies of the live record. We sold fifty [thousand] in Texas. It was working because FM stations were playing cuts off this album. It was fun stuff. That tuned everybody into it. Everybody moved to Austin because it looked like a fun place to live.

Ray with the Cowboy Twinkies was like seeing Ray now, but the band was better. He had a better band because the guys needed money, and the money you made went farther back then. You could get a pretty decent musician for fifty bucks. Now you have to pay five hundred bucks. Bob Livingston and John Inmon played with him. Bob would keep me updated on what was going on here and there because we got the Gonzo Band a record deal after ¡Viva Terlingua! Once I heard they had a deal for sure, I figured I was gonna have to find another band. They did it about a year by themselves before it all fell apart. By then I had another band together. So we got kinda separated, but I'd get reports and stop in and see what's going on.

We're survivors down here. There must be something to us because we're still playing. You play until you get enough gigs, and then you're outta here. You're not played on the radio because you were that good twenty years ago. If you die, they'll play you on the radio for about twenty-four hours a day for a week. Then it dwindles off. So what legacy is there? If you want gigs, you keep playing while you can. When you can't anymore, you're done. I'm as much tied to "Redneck Mother" as Ray is. I have to play it every night at some point.[10] [Walker's wife] Susan said before we cut "Redneck Mother," I was a singer and a songwriter. I became a barman yahoo after that. I said, When everybody's drinking around you and having a good time, how quickly it all catches up to you and whirls you around. The next thing you know, the bills aren't paid and you're in a fix. You have to pull it together.[11]

Michael Hearne

I had heard about Ray from people I knew in Red River, New Mexico. My uncle Bill and aunt Bonnie Hearne had told me about this

Michael Hearne,
song swap with
Susan Gibson,
Poor David's Pub,
Dallas, Texas, May
2018. Photo by
Dave Hensley.

band Three Faces West with Hubbard, Rick Fowler, and Wayne Kidd and their concert venue called the Outpost. Then they broke up and Ray started [the Cowboy Twinkies]. I would see them in Dallas, where I was born and raised. I used to see all those guys play like Hubbard, Michael Martin Murphey, and B. W. Stevenson. They were the original Texas music guys. I would go to Fannie Ann's on Greenville Avenue and hear Ray and the Cowboy Twinkies play with Buffalo Ware. Sammi Smith used to sit in with them all the time. She had a hit with [Kris Kristofferson's] "Help Me Make It Through the Night." It was always fun when she sang with Ray.

The Cowboy Twinkies were a rocking band, and Hubbard was a cool cat. I was very impressed with him. Fannie Ann's always had people in there partying and having a good time. I was one of them even though I was only eighteen or nineteen at the time. I also used to go to a club called the Rubaiyat starting when I was seventeen because my aunt and uncle played there. People like Uncle Walt's Band and Murphey played there, and I used to play there as well. I play with Shake Russell now, and I was about seventeen when I saw him play there for the first time. Dallas was a great atmosphere for me to grow up in and be around all that great music and have access to a place like the Rubaiyat.

The Rubaiyat was one of the only listening rooms in Dallas back in the day, an amazing little place. They served beer, wine, and coffee. I saw Steve Martin perform there once with his banjo and balloon tricks. That was before [Martin's breakthrough 1979 film] *The Jerk*. He was just coming on the scene. He was playing small clubs that would let him work for the door. I did an open mic there when I was seventeen. I lied and told them I was eighteen. This was back when you could drink at eighteen. I just wanted to be around that environment. I'd get my acoustic guitar out, get up onstage, and people would listen. The Rubaiyat was great for acoustic music.

Hubbard's a great songwriter. I like the line in "Portales": "Hand woven love songs and sadness / Is all I sing when I think of you." He has a way with words. The whole vibe of that song got me and struck me as being cool. I went to see Hubbard and the Cowboy Twinkies one time, and they played this old Tom Rush song "Driving Wheel" [written by David Wiffen; Hubbard eventually recorded on his 2005 album *Delirium Tremolos*]. They turned that into a long, rocking jam.

I heard Shake for the first time when I was seventeen years old. He was playing bass with the Ewing Street Times. I heard him sing "Deep in the West," and I was hooked. I've been through the gamut since then. I've lived in Taos, New Mexico, for thirty-five years and have my own festival called Michael Hearne's Big Barn Dance Music Festival. Hubbard played there once about five years ago. His guitar wasn't working. He borrowed mine to play. That was pretty cool. Ray's evolved into a different Ray than I knew back then. He was party Ray. Now he's artistic Ray. It's obviously paying off, and I'm really proud of him. He's a hero for sure, and we've become good friends, especially in the last few years. He's helped me a lot with my personal issues over the past few years. Ray's a blessing. I think Ray really respected Bill. I can see that laugh on his face when I tell him Bill Hearne stories.[12]

Bill Hearne

I met Ray in 1965. My aunt and uncle took me every summer to
Red River, New Mexico. Ray, Rick Fowler, and Wayne Kidd were
college guys. They had a trio with a gig at the ski chalet playing for
the barbecue supper. They had wine, barbecue, and a show after-
ward. I was seventeen years old and crazy about country music,
and I was mesmerized. Of course they had to do stuff they didn't
want to do, like stock country songs, but they slipped in Murphey
tunes and their own songs. I remember meeting Rick Fowler first
and then Ray. The folkies didn't cut off the end of their strings when
they changed them back then. I asked Ray why they wrapped the
strings around the tuning head, and he said, "To hold our cigarette."
Ray had a crazy sense of humor.

I moved to Austin for school in 1968. My real education began
then, and it wasn't in the classroom. It was the education of life.
There was this folk club called the Chequered Flag, the cool, hip
place to play. Murphey, Jerry Jeff, Townes, Guy, and Rusty Wier
played there when they came to Austin. I met [my wife] Bonnie
[Hearne], fell in love, and started hanging out there together. We
saw that Three Faces West would be coming one weekend. They
toured during the winter, and they were trying to make it as a trio
doing original songs. I was impressed and introduced myself to
Ray. He said, "Man, you look familiar. Were you ever in Red River?"
"Yeah, I remember a trio in the ski area at the barbecue joint." "My
god, that's you. You were the only one paying attention." I was into
it. I guarantee I was sitting in the front row.

They had started the Outpost coffeehouse in 1970. Wayne asked
Bonnie and me to come up in 1970. We rode the bus from Austin
to Red River because I'm legally blind. We played the whole first
week of August 1970 as their opening act. We'd open, they'd play,
and we'd all get up at the end together. It was a rousing success,
and they asked us back to do the whole summer in 1972. That was
a crazy summer. Ray's struggles with alcohol and dependency are
well known. We came up in mid-June and stayed until Labor Day.
We opened for them the whole time, and we got some gigs across
the street at the roadhouse D-Bar-D, which is now called the Motherlode. We would do our opening set for them and then run over
to the Motherlode and play from 9:00 p.m. to 1:00 a.m. Ray and

*Bill Hearne.
"Whenever I come
to Santa Fe, I make
a point of checking
to see where Bill
Hearne is playing,"
longtime Ray Wylie
Hubbard supporter
Eliza Gilkyson
says. "His music is
evocative of all that
I love about New
Mexico and the
West." Courtesy Bill
Hearne.*

Rick took care of our rooms at the little cabin where Bonnie and I stayed. It was one of the best, greatest fun summers I've ever had. We didn't make any money, but we sure had a good time.

I think Ray wrote "Redneck Mother" that summer. We didn't see them a lot during the day. They drove Jeep tours. A couple years later, Ray left Three Faces West and went out on his own. Rick and Wayne formed a group called Texas Fever with Bob Livingston and a drummer named Michael McGarry. I didn't see Ray for a long, long time. We'd just cross paths every now and again. Bonnie and I had moved to Red River in 1979 and played there for twelve years at the Alpine Lodge. Back in the 1970s, we'd congregate there after the Outpost and jam.

Ray came by there in 1987. He was back in Dallas, and I knew that his mother had died and his father was not doing well. He told me that he quit drinking. We all had known that he had sunk to rock bottom. He said in [Hubbard's 2015 memoir *A Life...Well, Lived*] that he was a folk-rock star, but he was really nothing but a drunk. He finally realized it, and Stevie Ray Vaughan had helped him. He joined AA. I couldn't be more happy for him. He came over personally to tell Bonnie and me that he had quit. He found his way, and he stayed with it. Thank goodness.

Ray wrote some great songs back in the late 1960s and 1970s.

Bonnie and I used to sing "Portales," one of my favorites. I think that was his heyday even though he had his demons and lost his way. He wrote another I like with our buddy Jimmy Johnson called "Bordertown Girl." As you know, "Redneck Mother" has been an albatross, but wild and crazy really sums up how it was in Red River in '71 and '72. Ray stayed away from Red River for a long time. I think he had too many weird memories, but he's made peace with it now. He played the Motherlode maybe last winter or the one before. The town's changed a lot and has gotten more conservative. Ray's a good man, and I couldn't be happier that he met a wonderful lady in Judy. She's done a tremendous amount for him. I'm mighty proud to know Ray and call him a friend. He loved Bonnie. I know Ray's heart was there for her funeral service.[13]

Rick Fowler

Ray and I went to school together in the early days, and we started a folk trio in high school that brought us to Red River, New Mexico. We got friendly with these people who ran a place called Frye's Old Town. They'd put on these mock gunfights every afternoon where we'd play characters and shoot blanks. Ray would get shot, and he'd fall back into this saloon with just his feet sticking out. He had a whole stash of comic books back there that he'd read for the rest of the gunfight because all people could see was his feet. We sang Westerns like "Old Paint" at the gunfights. That was the summer of 1965, which was the first time we were up there.

We got a summer job in Red River after we graduated from high school working for this place called Chuck Wagon Dinners. We'd answered an ad they put in the Dallas papers. We would put on our show while people were eating barbecue. Turned out that they were more interested in having kitchen help than entertainment. They would send notes up to us, "Wrap the show up. Dishes are piling up in the back." We fell in love with Red River, and we spent the next summer traveling around calling ourselves the Texas Twosome. We didn't have any gigs. We'd go into a town, find a coffeehouse, audition, and play. It was probably the best summer of my life with that first taste of freedom.

We had started writing a little bit, but the songs weren't great.

*Album cover for Three Faces West's self-titled and only album
(Outpost Records, 1971). The band—Ray Wylie Hubbard, Rick
Fowler, and Wayne Kidd—included one Hubbard original
("He's the One") with cover songs by Michael Martin Murphey
("West Texas Highway," "The Seasons Change"), Jerry Jeff
Walker ("Mr. Bojangles"), the Doors ("Light My Fire"), and
several more. Photo by Brian T. Atkinson. Courtesy Ray Wylie
and Judy Hubbard.*

We got a trio together that we called Three Faces West, and eventually we opened the Outpost in Red River. We made an album
back then [1971's *Three Faces West* on Outpost Records], and there
were a couple originals. I remember one Ray wrote called "He's
the One," which went, "He's the one who made me number two."
Three Faces West comes from an old John Wayne movie (director
Bernard Vorhaus's *Three Faces West*, starring Wayne, Sigrid Gurie,
and Charles Coburn in 1940). The name sounded good to us and
fit because we were very much a folk group in the early days. Our
influences were the early folk people like the Kingston Trio, Bob

Dylan, Phil Ochs, Tim Hardin. We would do the Outpost in the summers, and then we were in school. Ray was going to North Texas University, and I was going to Texas Tech University.

We had a comedian friend who had a radio show in Dallas in the sixties. He was doing stand-up and had a big house in the Hollywood Hills. We went out there in 1970 after we graduated. He had a giant basement where we stayed with our sleeping bags. We were playing clubs around Hollywood, Pasadena, and Huntington Beach. There were a lot of folk clubs there at that time, and we did pretty well. B. W. Stevenson came out and stayed with us. Then there was a big earthquake in 1971. B.W. freaked out and went back to Dallas, where he was playing a club called the Rubaiyat. There was someone from RCA there, and he got a record deal after trying to make it in Hollywood.

We pretty much moved back after that. Ray and I started another band called Texas Fever with Bob Livingston and a drummer named Michael McGarry. He played for Beto and the Fairlanes for a while back in the seventies. We had a booking agency in Denver, and we played folk clubs all over. Texas Fever was folk-rock, and we got a little more electrified. Three Faces West was really a more traditional folk group in the sense that there was a bass player, two guitars, and I played five-string banjo. We were doing original songs and Michael Martin Murphey songs. We carried those into Texas Fever and added drums. I think we played a couple years maybe.

Ray and I were Jeep drivers in Red River when he wrote "Redneck Mother." We'd take people up on these scenic trips and show them the ghost towns. We'd sit around the bunkhouse and play music. I remember Ray working on "Redneck Mother." We were worried about doing it live in our show at the Outpost because it was such a conservative family place back then. There was a lot of tension between the longhairs and rednecks, and saying "kicking hippies' asses" was a little risque back then. We did it, though, and it was always a big hit from the start.

Ray was always fun. He's a great character, his own man. He was always writing songs and also always just writing in general. I think he had it in mind to play music for the long haul even back then. Ray said he moved back to Dallas when he discovered beer and electricity. We replaced him with another guy and kept Three

Faces West and the Outpost going for five, six years. Ray had his band the Cowboy Twinkies when he went back to Dallas, and he did really well. Jerry Jeff's version of "Redneck Mother" launched Ray's career. People didn't pay attention to who wrote the song and probably would just have assumed that Jerry Jeff wrote it had Bob not said, "This is a song by Ray Wylie Hubbard." That was a big break for Ray. That opened doors for him.[14]

Bob Livingston

I was going to Texas Tech in 1969, and I had a little club called the Attic in Lubbock where frat rats hung out. A girl walked up to me after one show and said, "Hey, there's this gig in Red River, New Mexico. You'd basically be playing for room and board and tips. It's all summer long. I can give you a couple weeks to think about it." I said, "I don't need a couple weeks. I'll take it." I split and went to Red River. A guy walked up to me one night when I was play-ing and said, "You need to hear this band down the street called

Bob Livingston, Waltstock & Barrel Music Festival, Fredericksburg, Texas, April 2018. Photo by Dave Hensley.

Three Faces West." So I go and see the show, and it blew my mind.

They were a couple years older than me, and they were really great. They had their patter and bits between songs, and they really poured those over their set list. They did a couple shows a night, which were always different. They came out after the show. The guy who had me come down to the show said, "This is my new boy, Bob. Bob, why don't you play them that 'Early Morning Rain'? Sit on a stool here." I'm sitting there singing very earnestly: "In the early morning rain..." I look up after, and Rick, Ray, and Wayne are rolling their eyes and sniggering. I knew I'd done something tragically unhip, but I didn't know what.

The other two guys went away and Hubbard says, "Come here, son. I need to give you some advice. Number one, never sit down when you sing. Always stand up. You command the room when you're standing up. People pay attention. You have energy. Number two, don't ever do 'Early Morning Rain.' If you're gonna do a Gordon Lightfoot song, pick one that everybody doesn't do." You know, basically don't do [John Denver's song popularized by Peter, Paul, and Mary] "Leaving on a Jet Plane." Go deep into an album and find something [more obscure]. Of course, Three Faces West did Lightfoot songs. I've told people that story and they've said, "Shit, they did 'Early Morning Rain.'"

Three Faces West played Mike Murphey songs like "Wildfire." Murphey called me one night, and I said, "I met Ray Hubbard. Those guys play your songs, and I love them." He said, "We need to meet." So I moved to California, got a record deal, and started playing with Murphey. They gave me some money, and I bought a Datsun pickup truck and a Martin guitar. Both our record deals fell through, and we came back to Texas and cut *Geronimo's Cadillac*, which was twenty-six songs in two days. Murphey was such a stern taskmaster. After the sessions for this major record, Hubbard calls me and says, "What are you doing?" I said, "Well, we just finished cutting this record." He said, "Ah, well, Wayne is quitting the band, and we need a bass player. Would you consider it?" "I would." I quit Murphey. Ray's new band was called Texas Fever, and they had just gotten a new drummer named Michael McGarry. Murphey was paying me hardly anything, like fifty to seventy-five dollars a night. Ray said, "Look, we'll split this four ways."

Bob Livingston (left) and Ray Wylie Hubbard, Billy Bob's Texas, Fort Worth, Texas, 1980s. Courtesy Bob Livingston; photographer unknown.

We're talking about gigs from five hundred to fifteen hundred dollars each. So for the first time in my musical life, I made money with Texas Fever. I roomed with Ray on the road. He had already written "Redneck Mother" in Red River, but he wouldn't play it with Texas Fever. He was afraid. He thought he would get beaten up because we were playing all these funky places up and down the Midwest. I thought it was the perfect song to sing, so I learned it. Then Murphey called me up and said, [legendary Leonard Cohen, Bob Dylan, and *Geronimo's Cadillac* producer] Bob Johnston wants you back in the band. I quit Ray and went back to Murphey to tour behind *Geronimo's Cadillac*.

At the same time, Jerry Jeff Walker shows up in Austin, and we make two records. At some point when I'm playing with Jerry Jeff, we were in Seattle. He breaks a string onstage. He says, "Hey, I'm gonna change this string. Why don't you do something?" I did "Red-neck Mother." The place went bozo. People started pouring beer on their heads and singing along. Jerry Jeff was surprised, and he took note. The second night he didn't break a string, but he said, "Do that song again." Then I'll never forget the third night. We were at the Palomino [Club] bar in North Hollywood. Guys like Robert Duvall and Will Sampson, the Indian from [director Milos Forman's classic 1975 film] *One Flew Over the Cuckoo's Nest*, were there for their dose of country music. Jerry said, "Hey, let's do that song, but this time I'm gonna sing it." So he did sang, and I did the spelling part.

We recorded *¡Viva Terlingua!* in Luckenbach all week. Then we were gonna do a live show in the barn there. Jerry Jeff says, "Man, every country song has three verses, but 'Redneck Mother' only has two and that weird spelling thing. It's gotta have a third verse." So I called Ray up on the pay phone. "Man, we're gonna cut your song." He said, "You're kidding." "No, but it's gotta have a third verse." He made up some funky third verse right there on the spot that Jerry Jeff didn't use. "You know there wouldn't even be any rednecks / If redneck mothers weren't around to go their bail / Jerry Jeff and Ray Wylie and David Allan Coe and all the other Merle Haggards / never went to jail."

Everyone knew the words and went crazy by the second or third chorus. That song got Ray Wylie's name out there. Who knows how it would've proceeded if my shout-out to him hadn't happened. They would've found out he wrote it [eventually], but thousands of people bought the record. He calls the song an albatross, but he uses that to his advantage. Now, he says, "If you write a song, you better be prepared to sing it for the rest of your life. I don't know if I'm prepared to do that, but twice a year I go to the mailbox and get a nice check."

The Lost Gonzo Band quit Jerry Jeff to go out on its own in 1977. We were on MCA Records and toured for about two and a half years. We played the Cotillion Ballroom in Wichita, Kansas, with Ray and the Cowboy Twinkies one Sunday night in 1979. Our truck broke down. We were starving and desperate. I have a wife and two kids, and I can't figure out how to make money with this Gonzo Band. Our manager was putting us in far-flung places, and

we were making a meager, meager salary from the record company, which already dried up. Ray and the Cowboy Twinkies had
a big fight and broke up. I went home and quit the Gonzo Band.

Ray called me. "What are you doing?" "Man, I'm doing nothing.
I'm thinking about becoming a house painter." He said, "I have a
couple gigs in Dallas. Could you come play bass?" "Yes, I could." I
played that weekend, and it was fun. I made money. He paid me
really well. Then he called me the next Monday. "Bob, I think it
worked really good. Could you put together a band for me?" Of
course, it was Paul Pearcy on drums from the Lost Gonzo Band and
the great guitar player John Inmon. They both jumped. We went
up and started playing. John brought his brother Jim, who became
road manager and sound guy.

We went from a van to a bus. We ripped out the guts, built crude
bunks, and it was so funky. We split money five ways: Hubbard got
two-fifths, and John, Paul, and I got a fifth. Ray would play Whiskey
River Friday night and then the next morning at a studio opening. Then he'd play a gig at Northcross Mall. Then he'd go across
town that night and play the American Cancer Society benefit or
another club. We were making the best money I've ever made as
a musician, and Ray was the fairest of all bandleaders. We put out
an album with that four-piece called *Something About the Night*
(Renegade Records, 1979). Ray got Bruce Springsteen interested,
and they were talking. Everybody thought, "Boy, this will be a big
jump for Ray. He's gonna be opening for Springsteen." None of that
happened. He couldn't ever really get into the mainstream even
though we always drew a big crowd.

Ray and I had written a song called "Hold On," which was really
"Hold On for Your Life." Ray forgot about it immediately, but I always
played it. We recorded it with the Lost Gonzo Band in 1976, but
we lost our record deal and it never came out. We had a manager
Michael Borofsky, who also managed Jerry Jeff and Joe Ely. We were
in New York, and he said, "I have this band from Scotland called
McKendree Spring, and they're doing a new record. They're looking for songs. I said, "Yeah, I've got a song." The head of the band
comes down to the bar. I grab a guitar and play him "Hold On." He
said, "That's cool. We'll cut it."

ART IS FOR MAN'S SAKE

THE TOO BITTER

SUPPORT THE ARTS FOR YOUR SAKE

222 E SIXTH   472-1335

RAY WYLIE HUBBARD, long-remembered originator of "Redneck Mother," comes to the Too Bitter January 3 & 4 along with respected back-up members John Inmon on guitar, Bob Livingston on bass and Paul Pearcy on drums for a special rock 'n roll performance. Included in the Texas-sized musical event will be hits from Hubbard's recently released LP, "SOMETHING ABOUT THE NIGHT." Ladies will be admitted free Thursday.

ONCE UPON A TIME . . .

. . . there existed in the Southwest the TOO BITTER: a rock 'n roll club, a concert hall, a theatre for the performing arts, and, since 1974, the foremost center of creative activity in San Marcos. Presented by THE FREEWATER BOOKIN' CORPORATION, the 800-seat club featured live entertainment 7 nights a week including national recording artists such as Harvey Mandel, Rusty Wier, Head East, Rick Derringer, Doug Kershaw, Canned Heat, Blood, Sweat & Tears, The Flying Burrito Brothers, Wet Willie and David LaFlamme to mention but a few.

Additionally, the TOO BITTER was foremost in the area for helping local musicians find an audience. Five years ago, fledgling bands such as Fools, Too Smooth, Electromagnets and Denim performed their first gigs for SWTSU students at the TOO BITTER. Over this period of time, San Marcos was exposed to superb musical entertainment and spontaneous, long-to-be-remembered rock 'n roll nights, all of which added to the TOO BITTER'S growing reputation for unequaled good times.

The San Marcos club was closed by Freewater Bookin', Inc. on November 17, 1979 and re-opened at its new location in Austin on December 5, 1979. The unique atmosphere of the original club is preserved in its new home in the renaissance area of Sixth Street. And so also preserved is the dedication to presenting the best in live entertainment, delectable mixed beverages and memorable nights . . . right down to the bitter end.

JANUARY CALENDAR

50¢ DRINKS 8-10	NO COVER FREE SUDS	NEW WAVE NIGHT LADIES FREE	$1.99 NIGHT	LADIES NIGHT LADIES FREE		25¢ DRINKS 7:30-8:30
SUNDAY	**MONDAY**	**TUESDAY**	**WEDNESDAY**	**THURSDAY**	**FRIDAY**	**SATURDAY**
		1 CLOSED — NEW YEAR'S DAY	2 CHAZER — FULL MOON 99¢ NIGHT	3 RAY WYLIE HUBBARD	4 RAY WYLIE HUBBARD — RICK STEIN — ALBUM SIGNING	5 HEYOKA & SPECIAL GUEST GULLIVER — LASER ● LASER
6 HEYOKA — DISCO DESTRUCTION	7 DOGS AT PLAY	8 THE NƎXT	9 ONE HAND CLAPPING	10 BETO Y LOS FAIRLANES — Please, no dancing on tables	11 the legendary . . . BUGS HENDERSON & SPECIAL GUEST	12 BUGS HENDERSON
13 CRYSTAL IMAGE & RABBIT — NO COVER	14 $2.00 ADMISSION	15 THE SKUNKS	16 TRAVELER & SPECIAL GUEST — 99¢ Cover	17 BETO Y LOS FAIRLANES	18 EXTREME HEAT	19 EXTREME HEAT — Extremely Good Music
20 CALL CLUB	21 DOGS AT PLAY	22 Rockin' Devils	23 SIRIUS — Rock 'n Roll at its brightest . . .	24	25 the ERIC JOHNSON GROUP	26 the ERIC JOHNSON GROUP
27 FREEDOM MACHINE	28 TALEWIND	29 CALL CLUB	30 TRAVELER	31 TALEWIND	CALL CLUB, 472-1335	

Poster from the Too Bitter, Austin, Texas, announcing two Ray Wylie Hubbard record release shows for Something About the Night *(Renegade Records, 1979). "Ray Wylie Hubbard, long-remembered originator of 'Redneck Mother,'" reads the photo caption, "comes to the Too Bitter January 3 & 4 along with respected back-up members John Inmon on guitar, Bob Livingston on bass and Paul Pearcy on drums for a special rock 'n' roll performance." Photo of poster by Brian T. Atkinson.*

Flash-forward twenty-five years, and the phone rings in my office in Austin. "Are you Bob Livingston?" "Yes." "Did you write a song with a guy named Ray Hubbard?" "Yes." There's this rap artist named Lloyd Banks. The way I figure, he and his brother were hanging out in New York. They ducked into discount record bin and looked at all the records for ten cents. They pull out this one and that one and take them home. They put this thing on. The first thing they hear is "Hold On." They go, "That's a cool groove. Let's sample it." So they sample the song, basically just the descending line I wrote, and it went through the entire song called "Warrior."

Eminem produced it for Interscope Records, which is why they were being really careful about searching the author down. In this case, they find us. I call Hubbard, and we get together. We become quarter songwriters on this song. I remember the woman calling and saying, "You need to get your publishing shit together because he's gonna be the next 50 Cent." They sent us the demos. Ray Wylie called and said, "Have you heard the demo? Bob, you and I need to get straight who wrote what line. Are you the one who wrote, 'Get out of my face nigger / I'm gonna kick your ass?' Because I'm pretty sure I wrote, 'I'm gonna ride you like a dog, you bitch.'" These horrible words were the new lyrics, and they sold almost a million records in the first quarter. I guess it would be our bestseller.[15]

Terry "Buffalo" Ware

Three Faces West were playing at the Outpost in Red River, New Mexico, in the summer of 1971 when the rock and roll band I was in played at the skating rink. Ray came out and heard my band on his night off, and we heard Three Faces West on our night off. Three Faces West were great. I had never heard anything quite like them with their really cool folk music. They had a great following and influenced many people during that time. Ray was really funny. He's always been that way. His stage banter was great even then. I started playing with Ray when I moved to Red River after I graduated from college a year later. He was still in Three Faces West, but he was gonna leave them after the summer season was over. We made a couple trips to Austin when I started playing with him.

I moved to Red River in May 1972, but I got my draft notice in early November and came back to Oklahoma to take the physical. I failed. I worked for my dad for a couple months and then moved back to Red River. Ray was the first person I ran into. He said, "Hey, you wanna play?" I said, "Yeah." We were traveling around working as a three-piece with a bass player. Then the bass player left, and Ray and I played as a duo. In the fall of 1973, we got a gig in Dallas where a band was needed. I got a couple guys from Norman, Oklahoma, to go down and play. We got the drummer from the Dallas gig and another bass player, and that's how Cowboy Twinkies came together.

Ray wrote most of the Cowboy Twinkies material. Our main musical influences were coming from his country and folk background. I played primarily rock and roll, and my influences were the Beatles, Chuck Berry, Jimi Hendrix. Ray and I wrote [the closing track on 1975's *Ray Wylie Hubbard & the Cowboy Twinkies'*] "Belly of Texas" in Red River. Ray had the lyrics. I contributed chord changes. He had just written "Redneck Mother" when I first met him. Of course he'll never shake that song. There was another verse to it that nobody sings anymore. It went something like, "You know there never, ever would be no rednecks / If redneck mothers weren't around to throw their bail / To raise Carl Bob Billy Joe / and all the Merle Haggards that went to jail."

Cowboy Twinkies played from about fall of 1973 through 1979. Our original bass player quit in the early part of 1978, and we started just going by his name then. Ray Wylie Hubbard and the Cowboy Twinkies was a specific group of people to us. We got a different bass player, a guy who played keyboards, and fiddler named Dave Gant. Dave went on to be Garth Brooks's musical director since Garth's first record came out. I played the straight man a lot with Ray. We never worked on it, but we had a natural chemistry. We played again mostly as a duo in the late 1980s through the late 1990s. We always had a musical and personal connection that worked really well. We're still good friends.

Sobriety changed him musically. He says he was in a honky-tonk fog before he sobered up. He got a lot more serious about his writing at that point. Actually, he hadn't been writing all that much before. He reached back to his early roots on *Loco Gringo's Lament*. Those songs are really strong. You can tell that those songs really draw on his early country-folk and country-blues influences. Ray also got a lot more serious about his guitar playing after he sobered up. He did fingerpick a fair amount when I first met him, but then he got away from that [during the Cosmic Cowboy years]. Finger-picking is his strongest suit as a guitar player.

Working with [producer and instrumentalist] Lloyd Maines on *Loco Gringo's Lament* was great. He ran the sessions real business-like. They were relaxed, and he played along with us. He didn't just sit in the control booth and direct things. He sat down and played acoustic guitar, steel, and Dobro. I love working with him. *Dangerous Spirits* was pretty much the same. Lloyd produced that as well. The thing that was different on that record was we did some overdubs in Nashville. We took the tapes there after we recorded in Austin. Kieran Kane and Mike Henderson came in and played on a track. Kevin Welch was still living in Nashville and came in. We mixed both those albums in Nashville.

Terry "Buffalo" Ware, Norman Music Festival, Norman, Oklahoma, 2014. Photo by Vicki Farmer.

Ray's redefining himself again today. He says it's all grit, groove, and tone now. Lyrically, he still comes from a different place than most people. I like it, but it is quite a departure from *Loco Gringo's Lament*. I think Ray will be remembered for his lyrics and particularly songs like "The Messenger" and the spiritual and poetic way he writes. "The Messenger" has a really nice melody, and I like the chord structure, the whole idea of the lyric. I remember the first time I heard it. We were opening a show for Guy Clark at a theater in Fort Worth. Ray showed it to me in the dressing room. He said, "I have this new song, and I wanna do it tonight." We played it back there before we went on, and I said, "That's a cool song." I remember Guy saying that he particularly liked it. That song has always stuck with me.[16]

Tommy Alverson

I wanted Ray to do those old Cowboy Twinkies songs again after he went off drugs. I had the original Twinkies album, and there was a place in downtown Arlington called the Mine Shaft where I

Tommy Alverson, Waltstock & Barrel Music Festival, Fredericksburg, Texas. Photo by Dave Hensley.

went to see him in the seventies. He was always showing up at Willie Nelson's shows or vice versa during that time. I had no idea I'd get to record with him one day. I started doing "Bordertown Girl" with my band and then asked if he would come sing with me [on Alverson's 2004 album *Heroes and Friends*]. He was living in Dallas and came out to sing on the studio version. Then he came back for the fun, wild release party to do it live.

Cowboy Twinkies was a funny name, and [his banter] between the songs was funny, too. The Progressive Country scare was a great time for great music. I was just a fan back then doing covers of Ray Wylie, [Steven] Fromholz, Willie, Waylon [Jennings], and Rusty Wier and worked a day gig. It was a whole different deal when I started writing my own songs, but I still do all those other guys' songs. They were all folk singers at one time, and they all had their own niche. Fromholz was folky. Ray's band was more rocking, and he had an edge. They were really good. When you hear a song—whether it's the lyrics or the music or both—you know you like it. I really like those old songs, but the new songs like "Conversation with the Devil" are really good, too.

Ray's a survivor. He was always a very cool and funny guy to hang with, but he doesn't hang much anymore. He does his gig, and he's gone. Now he has Lucas and the band with him. When they're done, they're packed and gone. I really respect him so much for getting straight. I've never had a problem with drugs or alcohol, but I can't imagine going through that and coming out alive. He's the one who hung around and did what he wanted to do. That's what we're all trying to do. Anyway, when he drove over to do "Bordertown Girl," he did his part and said, "Adios." I said, "What do I owe you?" He said, "Nothing." He did it because he wanted to.[17]

Tom Russell

I moved to Austin, Texas, from Vancouver, British Columbia, where I'd started in low-end Skid Row honky-tonks. I took a Greyhound around America in 1972 and went through Nashville. I landed in Austin. You could feel the difference right away. Austin was definitely hip, Beat outsider, literary in a real West Texas way with Guy Clark, Townes Van Zandt, Steve Fromholz, B. W. Stevenson, occa-

sionally the Flatlanders, and of course Willie Nelson, Jerry Jeff
Walker, Rusty Wier, Billy Joe Shaver. Ray Wylie Hubbard wrote
"Redneck Mother," but he had a great repertoire beyond that.

Ray Wylie certainly would attract your attention. He was always
very funny in that dry Texas way. Those guys all had their own Texas
humor that soaked into the songs. Ray's in-between-song patter
was always really cool. This guy had been there, and he took you
to that place so you wouldn't have to go there yourself and bleed.
I don't think I actually met Ray until the nineties, although I saw
him a bit when I lived in Austin in the seventies. He was already
a legend by the time I hit Austin because Jerry Jeff had recorded
his song, and he was one of those guys who just had that laid-back
"Texas cool." I only saw him a few times, but he was funny as hell
and with that accent you couldn't fake, coming out of the earth
somewhere up near the Oklahoma border.

He twirled off great lyrics and humor. He had that North Texas
bluesy edge with savage punch lines. He seemed like he was singing in your front room with no tricks and not trying to bullshit anybody. There aren't many great songwriter-performers like him out

Jenni Finlay and Tom
Russell, Barefoot
Recording, Austin,
Texas, January 16,
2019. Russell recorded
"Dust of the Chase"
for Eight 30 Records'
The Messenger: A
Tribute to Ray Wylie
Hubbard. *Photo by*
Brian T. Atkinson.

there with real heart and grit. His songs are down-to-earth, grabbing acoustic blues without cliché, which is hard to do. I'm always inspired by folks who are real, and Texas is as real as it gets. Ray's a survivor who carries that long, sometimes painful, personal journey into the songs. He's done the work for us and always with humor. He's up there with the greats, the big boys: Willie Nelson, Guy Clark, and Townes Van Zandt.[18]

Kinky Friedman

Ray Wylie Hubbard and I are about the only two musicians from Texas with an inherent sense of humor. I remember finding Ray very funny onstage and off. That was a rarity. Others have a sense of humor, but they don't reveal it. You don't know that Willie Nelson is a really funny guy if you watch the show, but he could do a pretty good stand-up act. Ray Wylie and I are so funny that it's really a curse. I think it would have been a more financial pleasure for both of us if we had been serious, pompous-ass motherfuckers to start with. Although now I'm passing into what could be a real hot air for the Kinkster. I get hot every ten years. Ray and I did a lot of shit together, but the problem is that I've forgotten the first half of my life. I'm seventy-three now.

People get confused. I never recorded "Redneck Mother." They see me doing "They Ain't Making Jews Like Jesus Anymore," and they think they saw Kinky doing "Redneck Mother." That's always been true of the public. You do *The Tonight Show*, and they think they saw you on something else. The public and the media never quite get it right. They think the wrong person did that song. The only ones who ever get it right are Ray and Kinky, and sometimes I'm not so sure about Ray. That was pretty good. The last thing I said right there is the first thing that's made sense.

"Redneck Mother" was a watershed song, one that was fun, funny, and pushed the spiritual envelope a little. It really rang true. "Redneck Mother" was calculated just enough to not succeed as much as "Muskrat [Candlelight]" by Willis Alan Ramsey. It's not gonna be a mainstream commercial success, but it does avoid nostalgia. It's been a long time, and the song still holds up. I don't wish I would have written it, though. I think there's only one song I wish I'd written, and I can't remember the title of it. If you find it, let me know. It wouldn't probably be a Ray song. You can tell Ray has a mixed audience of people, a mixed race audience. He appeals to Jewish homosexuals as well as African Americans. He appeals to a lot of young people, which is good to see.

Ray and I weren't competitive. He was funny a lot of the time, and I think that'll always cost you. If you're gonna come on as "Weird Al" Yankovic, that's the way to go. Everything you do should be weird and funny. You should understand that you're never gonna be accepted as a serious writer. As Billy Joe Shaver would say, Ray Wylie and I are both serious souls who nobody takes seriously. There are some who do take us seriously, but they're probably living at the Shalom Retirement Village right now or the Bandera Home for the Bewildered. Are you getting all this? It's pure genius. What I'm saying is incredible. I didn't realize I was this spiritual.

Like all good songwriters, you've gotta be miserable to write a good satirical song like "Up Against the Wall Redneck Mother." If you're happy, you can forget about it. I suggest that anyone who

Kinky Friedman, Jenni Finlay Promotions and Conqueroo's second annual Rebels & Renegades showcase, Threadgill's World Headquarters, Austin, Texas, March 19, 2017. Photo by Brian T. Atkinson.

wants to write, whether it's satirical or not, should first make sure they're miserable. It isn't hard. I think Flaubert's recipe for happiness is that you have to have three things: You have to be stupid, selfish, and have good health. If stupidity is lacking, all is lost. You need those three elements. I think [Ingrid Bergman] stated it differently. She said the key to happiness is good health and a bad memory. That's pretty wise. Writing satirical stuff is really pointless.

Of course, today the audience has become the show. There is no real audience or show. It doesn't mean anything to be on the charts. Everybody has a CD coming out, and they have their little release party. Spotify and all that downloading take it away instantly. It's harder to get anything across. There's probably no such thing as a legitimate hit. Maybe there is, but you or I certainly don't know what [the singers'] names are, and they'll last for about fifteen minutes. Be miserable. If you're unhappy enough, you can write like Ray. Blaze Foley is another who wrote that way.

There are a lot of pretentious people out there, and they want pretentious people to write pretentious songs whether the songs are any good or not. Maybe we've just run out of talent in the gene pool of the human race, and that part is dry. You know, every town has a guy that can play like Stevie Ray Vaughan, but not quite. They're not Stevie Ray Vaughan. A chick can sing like Janis Joplin at karaoke because it's a karaoke world. It works for karaoke and for downloading stuff from one place to the other. I don't fuck with any of that high-tech shit, to quote Kris Kristofferson. Maybe I should. We'll see who's right. Many people say I'm wrong to not have email.

I read this story once where Sandra Bullock was doing this movie. She said that she checked for the first time on the Internet where people leave comments. She said that she cried because it was so nasty. Ninety-five percent of the comments were nasty, like "Look how fat she's gotten," "She never had any talent anyway," "She should be ashamed of herself for making this piece of shit." Everything was negative and nasty about her. She's an innocent type. I can see how someone might get irritated by Ray Wylie Hubbard or the Kinkster, but why would you write something nasty about her? She was right to never look at that shit again.

There are a lot of unfulfilled people out there. The Beatles were right. People are lonely, but they're also angry and unfulfilled. Doesn't make sense. If you're a four-hundred-pound woman, you're probably not gonna be an acrobat or Olympic star. If you're a guy who's never done nothing besides write nasty letters to Sandra Bullock, then you probably aren't gonna be a film director like you think you are. Not that you have to drive a cab and do everything in the world like Jack London, but I think it helps to have a little bit of experience.

Nostalgia is deadly. As Abbie Hoffman said, nostalgia is a sign of illness in a society or an individual. I'm wary of longevity, too. Longevity has ruined as many men as it's made. Look at Bill Cosby. Harvey Weinstein would have been fine if he had fallen off his perch a month ago. We would all be saying what wonderful movies he made. Cosby, too. We'd love him, but they lived a little too long. I don't know. I'm gonna be seventy-three in a few weeks, but I read at a seventy-five-year-old level. I saw Ray at Willie's last Fourth of July Picnic in Austin and he looked pretty well preserved. He's a guy who can really write, and there ain't that many of them. The hit songs of today sound like background music for a frat party.

Most people don't know Tom T. Hall. I've run into all these damn people, and they don't know the guy. I always say I love Tom T. Hall and both of his melodies, but he does tell a story. Some are pretty clever. Ray Wylie is clever, too. He can't help himself. That used to be an ingredient of good country music, and now that's gone. If you happen to get even one half-ass decent line in there, that's a song now. You won't find a complete song with a thought any-where. Roger Miller was what country music was all about and still should be about. Shel Silverstein was another great writer. [Mill-er's] "King of the Road" and [Silverstein's] "A Boy Named Sue" are well crafted.

It's a privilege to be Ray's and my age and still be playing and drawing a crowd. You can go someplace and there are people. That's pretty damn good. It's the opposite today. You get somebody you've never heard of starring in a movie for seventy-six million dollars. No one's ever heard of that person again three to six months later. That's what it feels like. It's a whole different ball game, like base-ball season this year. Everybody's hitting home runs. The ball's being thrown faster, and maybe it's juiced a bit. There are infield-

ers who never hit home runs who have hit twenty or thirty. Everyone's very young, homogenous, and sanitized. Then they're gone.
Culture has ADD today. For Ray Wylie Hubbard to be around for
multi-generations is remarkable.

Going from country to blues is a real strange thing to do. That's
akin to Bob Dylan [going electric] at Newport [Folk Festival in
1965]. I'd forgotten how much Bob Dylan was booed the first time
he went on tour with the Band [then known as the Hawks in 1966].
They were booed at every show, and [drummer] Levon [Helm] was
complaining, "What is the point of this shit if they end up booing
us at every single show?" Then he did another tour with the Band
years later [in 1974], and it was an amazing success. People were
holding up their cigarette lighters. Fuck 'em and feed 'em Froot
Loops. You can't worry about that. Ray's a serious soul, and it looks
like he's transitioned smoothly to blues. I find the blues stultify-
ingly dull myself. There are people who are not fucking bored by
it like Bob Dylan. He loves the blues, but I wouldn't go to a blues
show. Well, I might go, but I might blow my fucking head off.[19]

Ray Benson

Asleep at the Wheel played Flag Pole Hill in Dallas with Ray Wylie
Hubbard and the Cowboy Twinkies in the mid-seventies. I remember very well. I've always loved Ray because he's such a great storyteller, and the Cowboy Twinkies were a loose bunch of hippies
from the Dallas–Fort Worth area. They played very Cosmic Cowboy,
Progressive Country, Jerry Jeff Walker–like music. Ray was very
much the songwriter in the band, and "Redneck Mother" was their
anthem. The song accurately described the situation we were all
in. People nowadays don't realize that being a longhair trying to
play country music in Texas was sometimes a dangerous proposi-
tion, especially from 1969–1970 when the transition was happening.

"Redneck Mother" was like [Arlo Guthrie's] "Alice's Restaurant,"
a song that united everyone who knew the same situations like
being a longhair going into a redneck area and having to deal with
all that. Ray lives in that storytelling. I call him "Old One Chord,"
which is a compliment. Ray can get more out of one chord than
a lot of us can out of twenty. He's mined that niche very well. He

Ray Benson, backstage at Austin City Limits Music Festival, October 8, 2010, Austin, Texas. Photo by Brian T. Atkinson.

says when he found he could play what I call a suspended fourth, which is modal music, he really understood where he lives best. He does such a good job of looking at the seamier side of Texas.

We always thought that the snake farm [in New Braunfels, Texas] was a front for a whorehouse. There was a secret word that you have to tell the lady to get into the brothel, but I never found out. I don't know if that's true. What a great subject for a song. We've driven past the snake farm a thousand times in the past fifty years and never thought to write a song about it. After Ray got straight, he really focused on being Ray Wylie Hubbard, the great musical storyteller. He's a touchstone for the newcomers, the modern-day Texas singer-songwriter and bon vivant. There's a little intellectualism and a bit of redneckism in what he does and in the best way.

When you discover Ray, you go, "Wow. This guy has a different point of view." There's no one like him. That's been my case and his. As long as there's nothing like you, you're always number one. He'll be remembered for all of his songs, but there's nothing wrong with

"Redneck Mother," a time piece, really something to be very proud about. What he's done since has earned him the legitimacy in this business, but the crowd always sings along to "Redneck Mother." That's the greatest compliment. You obviously thank Jerry Jeff for the popularity, but it's perfect when you see Ray do it and he tells the story. That's the Ray Wylie Hubbard essence. Sure, he wrote this song, and Jerry Jeff got away with having a great hit record, but Ray's story makes it amazing. Ray makes it a theater piece.

One time we were playing in Dallas in the mid-eighties, and he was still using. I thought that was gonna be the last day I was gonna see him alive. He had really hit rock bottom. He was strung out, and I literally thought that was it. I'm so proud of him for getting straight and carrying on. Sobriety focused him on his strengths—storytelling. Sure, there are novelty songs like "Snake Farm" and "Screw You, We're from Texas," which are great and so well done, but he's a poet as a songwriter now.[20]

Steve Earle

I knew about Ray Wylie Hubbard before Jerry Jeff Walker recorded "Redneck Mother." I had heard about him from when I was fourteen hanging out at this coffeehouse in San Antonio called the Gatehouse. Ray never came down there to play, but I started running into older people who played Sand Mountain, the Old Quarter in Houston, and the Rubaiyat in Dallas. I aspired to play those places and was at the first Kerrville Folk Festival when it started in 1972. I probably saw Ray at Kerrville. There were some Three Faces West reunions around then, so I forget if I saw him with a band or on his own. I would always go and get in Kerrville however I could.

I liked "Up Against the Wall Redneck Mother," but by the time I started seeing him play on a regular basis, he was with the Cowboy Twinkies. They were a country-rock band, and Ray fingerpicked better than anybody else. I knew I was dealing with a folk singer from the way he played because that's how I started. Jerry Jeff was that, too, but that never really translated to electric guitar. He just got a Fender Stratocaster and beat the fuck out of it. There was something that stood out about Ray's guitar playing, and now it's [even better]. We did a guitar pull on the Cayamo cruise—Ray,

Lucinda Williams, Paul Thorn, and me—the year before last. That's where he comes from, sitting there and telling stories and playing guitar and singing. He could go down to the subway, busk, and make a living doing it.

We were all trying to be more country [in Texas in the seventies]. I mean, I wore cowboy boots my whole life. I was listening to the Rolling Stones, the Beatles, and Bob Dylan, but I was also listening to Johnny Cash and country music I felt was cool. Then there was [Austin's 99.3 FM] KOKE, and everybody's wearing Manny Gammage hats and Charlie Dunn boots if they can afford them. We all got more country, but I think the blues thing Ray did came even before that. He was a folk singer. You knew Lightnin' Hopkins and Mance Lipscomb just by having a fucking guitar and being from Texas. I think Townes Van Zandt[21] understood it better than anybody. He gleaned the essence of what Lightnin' did better than almost anybody I ever saw.

Ray's got the Mance fingerpicking thing down. I saw Lightnin' and Mance in the same room at the same time a couple times. I opened for Mance once at Sand Mountain. Ray, Guy Clark, Michael Martin Murphey, and those guys probably all saw Lightnin' and Mance on the same bill. People in New York and Boston maybe got that, but not nearly as often as the Texas folkies did. There are some places in the country that had coffeehouses, but Lightnin' and Mance didn't go there. Texas is a really fortunate place to have been if you wanted to see that.[22]

Writing a song with a beginning, middle, and end in reasonable time is job enough. I was directly apprenticed to Guy Clark, so I learned how to do it pretty quickly. It's not easy, but Ray does it. You're evoking emotion. If you don't, it ends up being journalism. It's not just about the information. You have to push buttons when you go through the process. I read a critic one time criticizing a movie by referring to it as "emotionally manipulative." Goddamn, I thought that was our job. I don't know why you would criticize an artist for being emotionally manipulative. Ray's good at it. He knows how to get the setting in in the first verse and introduce the character and then start describing the environment where you see it all.

[Evolution] is surviving and keeping yourself interested. I evolve

Steve Earle, Red Rocks Amphitheatre, Morrison, Colorado, 2004. Photo by Brian T. Atkinson.

by deciding I'm gonna make a bluegrass record or a blues one. Political records are easy. I knew what I was writing about when I did *Jerusalem* [2002] and *The Revolution Starts Now* [2004]. My next record probably will be pretty political, and I know exactly what I'm writing about. It's just all an excuse to make the next record. You've got to make art about something. It's all about you, but nobody's gonna relate to it if it's about you and only you. That's where [legendary comedian] Andy Kaufman failed. He thought that anything that made him laugh would make everybody laugh. You just keep reinventing yourself if you stay in this business any length of time at all because it's a matter of survival.

Talking about sobriety's tricky because there are rules and traditions. Why would it not impact songwriting? Who in their right mind thinks you can write a better song when you're fucked up than when you're sober? I never believed that. I had no fear that I was not going to be able to write when I got sober. I knew that the more fucked up I was, the worse my songs were. I was just trying to get fucked up and write songs. I did perform sober for the most part except at the end, where I would get sick if I was.

My songwriting got better when I got sober. I wrote "Ben McCull-
och" and "Tom Ames' Prayer" [both from Earle's 1995 "comeback"
album *Train a Comin'*] when I was twenty, and they're pretty good
songs. I did use drugs and alcohol then, but I didn't write anything
for four and a half years near the end [of my using]. The first song I
wrote when I got sober was "Goodbye." Eventually [addiction] does
what it does, and you will not write anything. I've never bought the
myth that there's any connection between getting high and writing. How can you create art if you're spiritually and emotionally
bankrupt?[23]

Verse Two
Drunken Poet's Dream
(THE BLANK YEARS)

Ray Wylie Hubbard & the Cowboy Twinkies *album cover, Warner Bros., 1975. Photo by Brian T. Atkinson.*

Ray Wylie Hubbard & the Cowboy Twinkies had lady singers and rope letters on the album cover. I called the lawyer who'd put this deal together and asked him what to do. He said, "I suggest you start drinking," and that's what I did for about the next twenty years.[1]

— RAY WYLIE HUBBARD

Chorus
The Messenger

Ray Wylie Hubbard at his home, Wimberley, Texas, November 14, 2017.
Photo by Brian T. Atkinson.

"The Messenger" happened over three or four hours. Judy
was pregnant at the time, and I went down and played it
for her belly. I used to do that a lot. If I would get stuck
on the song, I'd think of a band name. So the True Believers, Loose Diamonds, Hearts and Flowers are all in there.
Nobody's really acknowledged it except when I've told
them about it. They were just little tricks I enjoy doing.
After that, I wrote "Dust of the Chase" and "Without Love."
That's when I was on the track I wanted to be on.[1]

—RAY WYLIE HUBBARD

Troy Campbell

I was a drunk and a drughead when I met Ray Wylie Hubbard. My band the Loose Diamonds had made a sampler cassette called *Blue Days Black Nights* back in the early nineties before we made our record. Ray Wylie loved it. He reached out to us to do a gig. His big plan was to book a gig in Deep Ellum in Dallas at a big venue with the coolest band from Oklahoma, which was the Silver Tongued Devil, and us because we were the hot young band from Austin, and then he was gonna play. His plan was to charge people, and it was gonna be packed because it was during the University of Oklahoma and University of Texas football game. Everyone would come out. He'd make a fortune.

He didn't put into perspective that everything down the street was free. So we played at this big outdoor thing, and I'd never met him. We showed up at the gig in our van, which had a little secret compartment in the back. We had Christmas lights back there

Troy Campbell (left) and Michael "Cornbread" Traylor, Jenni Finlay Promotions and Conqueroo's second annual Rebels and Renegades showcase, South By Southwest, Threadgill's World Headquarters, Austin, Texas, March 18, 2017. Photo by Brian T. Atkinson.

so we could see the gear. We were all huddled back there, cross-legged smoking pot in the dark with the Christmas lights. He beats on the door for us to do soundcheck. We open the door and all fell out of the van like in a movie. We did soundcheck, and there was nobody there. He kept apologizing and saying, "Man, it's gonna be so packed." The place could hold about a thousand people, and there were probably a hundred. It was like a cartoon.

Everything he said at that show was so funny. I met his new wife, Judy, and she was such a cool lady. I was like, "What are they doing with us?" He told me how much he liked our music, and onstage he kept telling stories and jokes. I just fell in love with him. I'd never heard anybody that was that funny before, and he said he didn't drink anymore. I couldn't imagine anyone being that funny without drinking. So that gig was a big bomb, but I walked away thinking, That guy was awesome. We kept in touch. I sobered up soon after.

He still lived in Dallas at the time. He wanted me to do a writers round later with Christine Albert, him, and someone else. It was awesome, but I ended up hanging out in the back room. I'd just gotten sober, and we were in a bar, which made me really uncomfortable. Ray said, "Let's go back and have a little meeting." We sat there and talked. That was right around when I decided I wanted him to be my sponsor. I thought, Here's one guy who has what I want, which was the ability to have a sense of humor and not be drunk. Our car broke down on the way back home. I talked the whole time to my manager Robin Shivers and Christine for two or three hours about how I thought Ray Wylie was interesting—probably drove them crazy. But we've been best friends ever since.

I can say I've never been disappointed in him as a sponsor. There have been many times when I call him and his answer is not what I expect, though. I called him one time and was really, really mad because I didn't really have very many skills about how not to rage. I called him and was like, "Ray, I'm so fucking mad and these people—" He said, "Why don't you hold on to that anger for about three weeks and call me back." Then he hung up on me. I sat there fuming, and then I realized that I couldn't possibly hold on to that anger for three weeks. What he meant was *good luck with that.* So I called him back, and we started another conversation.

I called him from a red pay phone booth in the middle of Ireland one time. I remember shoving these giant coins into a pay phone there in Northern Ireland. I said, "I'm at this party, and things are getting really weird. I'm talking with these two women, and I think something's gonna happen." I was so freaked out because it was like a war zone. I wasn't drinking, but I felt drunk. He said, "Are you calling to brag or do you have a real problem?" He put it all into perspective. I just needed to hear his voice and for him to remind me that I'm probably an all right human being if I acted like one.

I usually call Ray thinking that what's going on is so hard and horrible, and he'll share his life story or another story or what's going on. He either disarms me or I just realize that I'm not alone. There's a therapeutic value in the relationship between two recovering addicts that's unparalleled. I felt that he knew what I was talking about, whereas other people didn't. I felt like I could listen to him. It's hard when you have this disease of addiction to just listen or feel like someone's listening to you. Ray Wylie taught me a lot about learning to trust myself and wear the world a little looser than I was, which was extremely tight.

I tricked a bunch of sponsors before finding Ray. I would find people who were fans of my music or thought what I did was cool. If they said, "Did you do the work?" I'd say, "Well, I was on the road." "That's so exciting." Then I'd change the subject. Ray would say, "Uh-huh." Then he'd get right to the point. I'd be like, "Oh, no." He's extremely busy, but he's always there. I could call and say, "I'd really like to talk to you." He'll call back even if it's the middle of the night. He'll start talking about how his day was rather than anything else, and I'll suddenly reframe what I was worrying about because he let me know that I had a friend. I wasn't alone. The Twelve Steps offer us the ability to not be alone. You come in sick and alone, and you're still sick [in recovery], but you find out you're not alone and you have somewhere to start. Sick and alone is the most powerless feeling.

I was in the studio with Stephen Bruton, who helped me get sober, like on my second day of sobriety. I told him, "Look, I won't be able to write any songs. I don't know what I'm gonna do." He said, "You wrote songs despite being a drug addict." I was writing songs then, but I was fucked up. I thought being fucked up wrote the songs. So now I'm not hungover and fucking around, and it didn't take me long to realize I had the time to write about those things I was burying. Ray turns anything into a song. He's industrious, and he knew that I was. He nurtured that. You have to look for the truthful story. I ended up making more music after I sobered up, and now I'm doing more work than I ever fathomed. I was just looking to make a couple records as a kid. Now I'm making everything you can imagine. I'll call Ray every once in a while and say, "I'm overwhelmed." He'll remind me: "Remember when you lived on a couch? That was thirteen years ago." Perspective. That wasn't long ago.

Ray is the most spiritual guy I know. He's funny and the one I can trust with my life, so I wanted him to marry my wife and me. He said, "How do you do that? You figure all that out and we'll do it." So I got on the Internet and ordained him. I called him and fucked with him. I said, "Ray, I did it. You're ordained." He said, "That's crazy, but all right." I said, "Yeah. It was twelve dollars to do the regular ordainment on the Internet, but for another dollar you got the Church of Satan. It comes with all these candles." He said, "What?" "It's Church of Satan, and you get these awesome black candles." He goes, "Please tell me you're joking." I kept it going for a while. That was the first time I really got him.

The only agreement was that I get him one of those minister collars so he'd look like a cowboy minister. He hadn't married anyone before, and I hadn't been to a real wedding ceremony like that. He forgot to tell everybody to sit down. They were all standing the entire ceremony. My mother-in-law and father-in-law thought he was a real minister. We never explained who Ray Wylie Hubbard was. We figured they wouldn't get it. They're from California. So at the end, they're asking him preacher questions and stuff. Judy made him wear the collar longer because she went to Catholic school and said it was hot.

The wedding was so cool. Roky Erickson sang "Starry Eyes," and Ray Wylie was the minister. I was like, "Half these folks have no idea that this is my dream. I've got my dream girl with my favorite people singing to me. How wonderful." Look how far I have come since I met Ray. I can't say enough about how wonderful it is for someone like that to have been in my life from then until now. I can look back on many, many times where that guy suddenly redirected me. Then I look back on his career. I watch how he thinks. He is a fast thinker, and that name Wylie really suits him. I've been sober for twenty-three years now.[2]

Jon Dee Graham

My first exposure to Ray was listening to "Up Against the Wall Redneck Mother" in high school. My older brother had come to the University of Texas for school, and he came home with all these records. One was the Cowboy Twinkies. I remember listening and thinking, This shit isn't really country. It's not rock and roll. It's really funny. It was the humor that drew me to it, but the music was super well played, too. I mean, that's Buffalo Ware on guitar. It was one of the first times that I could understand that a song could be funny without being a novelty song.

Ray's gone through this process of reduction in his songwriting in maybe the last ten years. The songs have musically gotten simpler and more contained, and the lyrics have gotten more elemen-

Left to right: Jesse Sublett and Jon Dee Graham, Continental Club, Austin, Texas, September 18, 2014. Photo by Brian T. Atkinson.

tal. Of course, "Snake Farm" is hilarious, but with the economy of language he tells a very complete story in three verses. I remember talking to him one time when we were working on some cowrite things. He was explaining that he had gotten things down to two chords, but his real goal was to get it down to one chord. He's there now.

Look at "Rabbit." That's one chord throughout the whole song, and you don't miss the others. Damn, this is *one chord*. Building an entire song with dynamics and parts and never have it leave the one chord? That's an incredible accomplishment. You talk about Buddhism and the Wylie Lama myth, and Ray's a pretty deep guy and he deflects a lot of things with his humor. When you really listen to the words, he uses few enough that it's easy to project your own meaning on the songs. In a lot of ways, he lays out a situation and lets you think about it.

I think we share that sense of economy in our songwriting lyrically. I don't like to tell the listener how to feel, and I don't like to tell them exactly what happened. I like to paint my pictures using as few words as possible. People will invariably fill in the blanks, and they all fill them in differently. I think Ray is keenly aware of that. Musically, we have in common what Stephen Bruton called the "monkey bone." You listen to music and feel it and go, "Hell yeah, that's my monkey bone." Ray's music hits you on the monkey bone. Man, he has that mastered. He lives there.

Impressionist painters took out the middleman of interpretation. They said, "This is what I see and how I see it." A lot of times, Ray's stuff is so simple that your mind just fills in the blanks. You know, there's a woman on the beach in a parasol. Your mind comes up with so many more details than [there are] in the actual painting. It's being able to catch some feeling or moment or thought and you don't have to explain it to them.

It was at least twenty years ago when I met Ray. He still played guitar with a pick and mainly straight. Then there were songs like "Without Love," where he'd put down the pick and fingerpick. I was like, "Man, how did you learn to fingerpick like that?" I came up through punk rock. That was not an attribute that you sought. It was really cool. When I asked him, we sat down and he drew me a little chart on a piece of paper, which I still have somewhere, a left hand with the four fingers numbered. He started writing this chart with these numbers: This finger plays this note, this plays that note. He said, "Go slow. It'll take you a while to get the hang of it, but then you get a little faster. Then you're fingerpicking." I believe he said Danny Barnes taught him that.

Ray was a decent guitar player when I met him, but now he's a son of a bitch. He's really good. He's honed in on what he wanted with these one-chord songs. He just went, "This is my goal. I don't know exactly how to get there, but I'm gonna." The way he plays guitar now is unlike the way he played twenty years ago. Changing midstream like that is really hard to do. I think he went from very clouded and without direction to crystal clear. He's absolutely filled with intent as far as what he wants to do in the time that I've known him. That's sobriety's gift right there. I don't know anyone who has worked as hard at it or has fought as hard to keep it as he has. He's a walking, talking billboard for it.

I don't think we know his legacy yet. In the last five years or so, he's running around with Ringo Starr. He's been on the Letterman show. If he died tomorrow, I think his legacy would be the last three records he's made. I don't think anybody looks at Ray right now and goes, "That's that 'Redneck Mother' guy." The first time I saw him play after I moved to Austin was at the old Hole in the Wall. He sang a couple songs, and then he did 'Redneck Mother.' It was obviously an onerous, painful job. When he gets to the part about spelling it out, he goes, "*M* is for 'My god, I'm sick of this song,' *O* is for 'Oh, no, I have to play it again,' *T* is for 'Think of all the money I could have made . . .'" It went on like that. The first time I got to talk with him substantially when we became friends, he said, "You know, be careful when you write a song because you might have to play it the rest of your life."

Ray and I met up for coffee somewhere five, six years ago. I was complaining, "Shit, I'm past fifty now. I've done this and that. I've done things I'm proud of, but my career's stalled. I'm like one step below where I need to be." He looked at me and said, "Jon Dee, some people are on the rocket to success. You and me, we're on the covered wagon to success. We're heading across the plains of the music business looking at the corpses and skeletons of those who came before us." Of course he made me laugh, but there's truth there.

Ray did it like that. He's sitting on the wagon. He keeps going and going and gets through another day.[3]

Danny Barnes

I went down to Austin in high school in the seventies and got familiar with guys like Doug Sahm and Ray Wylie Hubbard. We would go to the Armadillo, Raul's, Antone's, and those classic venues. Antone's had the real blues going on then. You could catch Lightnin' Hopkins and Albert King because those guys played there pretty regular. I saw the Ramones on a couple tours and Devo and the Clash at the Armadillo. I caught them as often as I could. I also saw Bill Monroe and Ralph Stanley. I liked the bluegrass, punk rock, and really hard-core blues. I probably saw Lightnin' twenty times in Austin.

Lightnin' was amazing and would play Antone's during the week. Antone's was down on Sixth Street across the street from the JJJ Tavern, a few blocks east of Congress. I think [Lightnin'] lived in Houston at the time, and he'd come through once a month. I'd see

Left to right: Ray Wylie Hubbard and Danny Barnes, former Texas Music Office director Casey Monahan's backyard, South by Southwest, Austin, Texas, March 2010. Photo by Jenni Finlay.

him at the Armadillo, too. There was a [state representative] named Ron Wilson who played bass with him some. He was a really good musician, and I think he played on a couple records. Lightnin' was the real thing. He played amplified and electric, but you could really hear the acoustic guitar base in his playing. He was plugged in and cranked up, so it was wailing.

My older brother was into Progressive Country. The hotels in Austin would have these folders on Progressive Country in them, so I was familiar with Ray from his records. I saw Ray play live five or six times back in the day. He always had such a great band and great songs and was touring. He was a good inspiration for folks who [were] trying to do stuff like that, and he was working hard back then. My perception was that he was on the road a lot. When you're seeing a guy like that live, you're watching the songs. I also always liked Mandy Mercier, who he had on fiddle. She was really good and a great singer herself.

Lloyd Maines produced the last two Bad Livers albums and mixed one when we were on Sugar Hill. I've also played quite a few sessions when he was producing other people. Lloyd has a really good [attitude]. There's a lot of stress when you're making a record because you're spending a lot of money. Maybe the band is fixing to break up. Maybe the record company's all over you because the last one didn't do so good. It can be tense. You have a band of four guys who basically put their whole lives into it, and the record needs to do good. People are afraid of being poor. Then you go into the studio, and it's the guy's space. You live there for twenty-four hours for two weeks, and then you never see the guy again. It's a giant algebraic equation with all these factors.

Lloyd's awesome, a real calming guy. You have this feeling: It's gonna be okay, and we'll get this all worked out together. I've been in a couple real jams, and Lloyd came in, made it work, and made it right. There aren't that many people who can do that. I learned a lot from him. Number one: What matters is getting it done, not talking about it. A lot of times you work with guys who will just talk on your time. It only counts if the problem goes away. Lloyd has a way of smoothing things over. "We're gonna make the record company, the band, and us happy, and we're gonna bring this in for a landing." Shit, you almost never deal with people like that.

Sobriety has influenced my songwriting a lot. Growing up in

the seventies and eighties in Texas, you always associated music with drinking. You'd get a record, and you'd start drinking before you'd even put it on. You drink to listen to music and to go hear music. Drinking was part of the fabric. You see those guys play, and they're all drinking beer. It's tough when you take something out of your life that's been a part of your life so long—especially if you've written songs in your drinking years that have done well. You think drinking and music went hand in hand, but I don't think they have anything to do with each other.

Sobriety puts the whammy on you. You're like a jockey who lost his lucky hat. You wonder if you'll be able to do anything. It freaks people out. You tend to get better about technical details about writing when you're sober, but it's not an absolute. Not everybody who starts drinking has a problem with it, and not everybody who doesn't drink does great. It's more algorithmic than linear, as most things in the universe are, but it's real tough to go back to writing. In the back of your head, you're always comparing and wondering and being afraid, but after you stick with it for ten years, you don't think about it. It definitely changes things, though. You used to go over to somebody's house and drink a beer. Now you go to the recording studio and they're drinking beer, but you're not. You play a concert. Everybody's drinking. Go backstage. Everyone's drinking.

Songs are like little movies. I've always liked ones that paint a picture. As time goes by, books, movies, records, plays tend to lay out the details more for you. Movies have a million edits now. They spell out how you're supposed to interpret it, but I like when it leaves [things] open enough where you can imagine a scene. John Hartford said a record is like a movie, and songs are the scenes. I learned to not look at the older songs as autobiographical about me, so that helped [put distance between me and the songs I wrote when I was drinking]. You run out of ideas after a record and a half writing about yourself anyway. You have to get things from novels and people you talk to. I don't know how Ray Wylie thinks about it, but that's how I do.[4]

Lloyd Maines

I worked on *Loco Gringo's Lament, Dangerous Spirits, Live at Cibolo Creek Country Club*, and *Crusades of the Restless Knights* with Ray.

Left to right: Shawn Camp, Jen Gunderman, Hayes Carll, Tamara Saviano, Glenn Fukunaga, Lloyd Maines, and Verlon Thompson, Cedar Creek Recording, Austin, Texas, January 4, 2011. Carll was recording "Worry B Gone" for This One's for Him: A Tribute to Guy Clark. *Photo by Brian T. Atkinson.*

I loved his lyrics and matter-of-fact voice. There was no phoniness. Ray sang like he talked, and he had Terry "Buffalo" Ware as his guitar player. Terry was Ray's right-hand man. He played just what the song needed every time and anchored things. He was a comfort blanket for Ray. It was really great working with those guys in tandem. *Crusades* was a slight departure, with Stephen Bruton on guitar. Ray brought in Terri Hendrix, Patty Griffin, and other guests. He was stretching out. "This River Runs Red" is scorching. I still hear that on KNBT [92.1 FM in New Braunfels, Texas] and [Austin's] Sun Radio 100.1 FM. Every time I hear that song come on, I think, Who is this? It sounds so different from Ray. It's riveting when he comes in. Ray's a magnetic and understated artist, but under that there's a lot of creativity boiling.

Terri Hendrix, Ray, and I went to Europe twice and had a great experience. Once was a pretty long tour. We flew into Amsterdam. They picked us up, and we probably did eight or nine days in Hol-

land, the Netherlands, Brussels, and London. When those Euro-
pean fans latch onto you, they learn almost every lyric. They knew
Ray's [songs], and all showed up with "Redneck Mother" T-shirts.
Terri and I would play for about forty minutes as a duo, and then
we'd take a small break. We'd be Ray's backing band. Terri played
mandolin and sang harmony, and I played mainly Dobro and pedal
steel. Ray's hip was bad back then. He was in some pain walking
around London. Then the Blue Highways Festival in Utrecht [the
Netherlands] brought Ray, Terri, and me back along with Terry
Allen, Guy Clark, Wayne Hancock, Hot Club of Cowtown, but that
was just a weekend thing.

I worked on the records when Ray was writing a lot more melodic,
lyrical stuff. He was really good in the Townes Van Zandt–style fingerpicking with a little Merle Travis in there. He was a very good,
simple fingerpicker. He played really cool inversions. He always
had a good Gibson or Martin guitar. We got a really good sound on
his guitar. I didn't have much history with Ray at that point besides
being in the studio. We pretty much got down to the business at
hand in the studio. It was always on a budget. The first record was
done for Deja Disc, and the others were Rounder Records. Ray
just had the stories from his past. I think he had a lot of fun in the
seventies and early eighties, but Ray had not been drinking for a
long time at that point. He remembered some of those old days.

I've seen Ray many times. I got to hear him tell the same stories every night pretty much identically, but I never tired of it. His
delivery and his stories are so compelling that I looked forward to
the same stories every night just to see if I could pick out any sub-
tle differences. I was blown away every night. Then there's Ray's
ketchup bottle story. He was probably playing a restaurant when
nobody clapped. He thought he finally heard somebody clap after
all those months, and somebody was finally reached by his lyrics.
He looked over because he heard one person clapping, but they
were beating the bottom of a ketchup bottle. Something tells me
that was probably an embellishment, but I think that's partially
true. Terri and I have used that joke on several occasions. We try
not to use it too much because we realize that most people who
have heard Ray have probably heard that. It always gets a laugh.[5]

Terri Hendrix

Ray Wylie and I were on [Rounder Records] in Europe, and Ray, Lloyd Maines, and I went on a great tour in the Netherlands and London in 1999. I played mandolin and sang harmony with Ray, and Lloyd played the pedal steel that he flew in. I also did my own set. I really wish I had my tape recorder going when we all traveled together on that tour. They told some great stories and memories, a great chunk of Texas music history between them. It was wonderful to be a part of that tour and to get to know him. Ray's fun, funny, thoughtful, easy to travel with, patient, and kind.

We recorded [Hubbard's song] "Red Dress" [from 1999's *Crusades of the Restless Knights*] after that tour. We did some gigs together after that as well. We seemed to be on the same circuit because we shared a booking agent. I got the opportunity to learn about him and his music more then. I was really into acoustic blues, and I was playing a lot of different guitar at that point. He invited me to play on his album, a really wonderful opportunity. I really enjoyed the experience playing guitar and singing on "Red Dress." I just wanted to do a good job. It was a really fun and good atmosphere with no pretense. I worked out my part in advance, but I had the luxury to get it really right on his record.

I got into the blues because of the simplicity and tones. At the point when I was working with Ray, I wasn't as into the harp as I became later on. He got me a harmonica rack that I really love. Ray's fascinating because he straddles two forms really well. I consider him a folk musician, but he's also a blues artist. He wears both hats, and they're two hard hats to wear. In the blues, there are simplistic lyrics in your face. The folk world demands greater detail and dexterity with the language. I find that there's a little bit of folk in the blues and blues in the folk, and Ray does both really well. I like blues that embraces folk elements like Leadbelly and Woody Guthrie.[6] Ray Wylie does the same, but he's not a political writer. He's very spiritual.

I think Ray's productions are a casebook study in keeping it simple. I look at "The Messenger" as the perfect song. "I am not looking for loose diamonds / Or pretty girls with crosses around their necks / I don't want for roses or water, I am not looking for

Terri Hendrix, Cheatham Street Warehouse, San Marcos, Texas, February 8, 2015. Photo by Brian T. Atkinson.

Left to right: Sterling Finlay, Terri Hendrix, and Jenni Finlay, Cheatham Street Warehouse, San Marcos, Texas, December 21, 2016. Photo by Brian T. Atkinson.

God / I am not looking for sex." His use of language and the loose rhymes that come out of nowhere, but they just fit, like *necks* and *sex*. It's poetry, and the melody is really beautiful. I always go back to a song compilation when I think about certain things I aspire to do, and that includes some of his songs.

I began working with Ray shortly after he became sober. I see his career in chapters. I think his legacy will be both chapters: the Outlaw Country movement and the blues-folk period. Actually, perhaps there are three chapters: Outlaw Country, folk, and now his blues career. His legacy will be that he wasn't a star that sparkled and faded away. He's not gonna fade away. He's written an important chapter in American music. I really believe that Townes Van Zandt, Guy Clark, Robert Earl Keen all have, and Ray Wylie Hubbard has. He's really important to the American songbook.[7]

James McMurtry

"Choctaw Bingo" happened because for a couple years the tour either started or ended on Highway 69 in southeast Oklahoma, which had a lot of weird stuff on the road. We never played Oklahoma at the time, but we were always going back and forth through there. There was a bingo parlor in Durant back then called Choctaw Bingo. You don't see that sign anymore because it's called Choctaw Casino and covers about fifty acres. It's all swank. Up the road in Tushka, there's a gun shop. They have these little signs that say *Pop's Knife and Gun* with an arrow pointing to the left. Then there was an Indian smoke shop up in Prior, which isn't actually in Cherokee Nation. It's probably in Delaware Nation, but *Cherokee* fit the meter [of the song].

There are a bunch of Indian smoke shops, but this one in particular had a sign out front that was like a cartoon Indian blowing smoke rings. The weirdest thing happened one time when I was trying to get to Kansas City. There was no Google Maps back then, but I decided to go all the way to Kansas City on Highway 69. I wound up on alternate 69 around three in the morning, and it took me through the middle of Baxter Springs. There was a lingerie store in downtown Baxter Springs that had these pink neon Rolling Stones lips for a sign. It was lit up in the middle of the night when nobody was around. I had to wake up the drummer and say, "Are you seeing that?" "Oh yeah, that's real." When we came back through during the day, it turned out it was a lingerie store right next to a biker bar across the street from a bank and a church. The lingerie store has since moved to Joplin, Missouri.

Everything I put in the song has disappeared by now. When I do a live version of that, there's an extra verse that's not recorded. I had to come up with another relative called Aunt Rita who lives over in Missouri. For a long time, there was a big billboard on I-44 with a baby that said, "Who's my daddy? DNA Testing." I thought, That's gotta go in there. Then back toward Texas there's a Red River Rehab, which fits the meter perfectly. So I had Aunt Rita going to Red River Rehab. The song started as a rhyming project because I hadn't written for a while and I thought, What the hell? I'll just put all of that into one song. That was the first song I wrote for [McMurtry's 2002 album] *Saint Mary of the Woods*.

I didn't hear about [Hubbard recording the song] until Gurf called me up and said, "Do you want to play guitar on this?" So I played on Ray's version. It's a slower groove, but he made it work.[8]

James McMurtry and Steve Earle, Sirius XM broadcast booth, Moody Theater, Austin, Texas, February 11, 2015. Photo by Brian T. Atkinson.

Gurf Morlix

I saw Ray play at Alliance Wagon Yard in Austin early on. He was great and really funny. I didn't meet him then, though. I moved to Los Angeles in 1981 and was out there for ten years. A mutual friend introduced us when I came back. I went to see him play at La Zona Rosa, and he had these songs like "Dust of the Chase" and "The Messenger," and I went, "Wow. He's really gotten good." We started talking about doing a record together. Ray came out to my house. He said, "What are you listening to?" I said, "Albums of field hollers." He said, "Weird. I'm listening to albums of chain gangs." We hit it off from that moment.

I produced *Eternal and Lowdown, Growl, Delirium Tremolos*, and *Snake Farm*. We had been working on *A: Enlightenment, B: Endarkenment (Hint: There Is No C)*, but I got too busy in the middle, and he ended up producing it. Ray was just starting to get into that grungy, bluesy, one-chord thing around *Eternal and Lowdown*. He had learned how to fingerpick and play slide. I remember digging the songs and thinking it was wide open as far as what we could

Left to right: Graham Weber, Ray Bonneville, BettySoo, Gurf Morlix, Brennen Leigh, and Noel McKay, Catfish Concerts, Austin, Texas, April 19, 2013. Photo by Brian T. Atkinson.

do. He brought songs where I could do anything. I just had to make sure I did it well. "Night Time" was such a cool song. He sings and writes so well. He's not normal and has this innate ability. He can do things that other people can't. Bob Dylan can't write those songs. No one writes like Ray does. So my only challenge was to not fuck it up. The ideas he comes up with for the songs are great. We've all driven past the snake farm down in New Braunfels a lot, but only Ray looked at it and went, "Snake farm, ewww. It just sounds nasty." Then he wrote that down. No one could think to write that song but him.

I loved *Eternal and Lowdown*. Ray said later, "Let's do another one." I said, "Sure." *Growl* was him getting more and more into his one-chord blues thing. It was the next logical step after *Eternal and Lowdown*. I thought "Screw You, We're from Texas" was really amazing. That's another one that no one but Ray could write. "Scrappy" Jud [Newcomb] played guitar and Jon Dee Graham played lap steel. They all came here with Ray to my place where I record. "Rock and Roll Is a Vicious Game" should have been a more well-known song. It's amazing, but I don't think he played it much. Ray came in with a remedial blues knowledge, but he's very astute and can do a lot of things with a small amount of knowledge that other people couldn't do with tons of knowledge.

I remember one time he stopped recording a slide part because there was a noise when his bottleneck rattled against a fret. I said, "You need to leave those noises in. That's real. There's no sense stopping for that." We cut a song one time where I had this big gym bag of tambourines and shakers. I pulled out the percussion bag, and I just dropped it on the floor. I said, "Wow, that sounds really good. Let's just use that." That was on a Slaid Cleaves record that we had Ray come in and sing on. We were just laughing like little kids. Ray thinks anything that's good is fair game. We were both trying to expand the envelope.

Ray heard "Choctaw Bingo" and said, "Those are my people. That's my family. I need to record that song." We had James McMurtry come in and play guitar on that. "The Beauty Way" is another great song, and we just had to make it a little different than Eliza's [Gilkyson] version. We had Patty Griffin come in for "Rock and Roll Gypsies," and she makes everything sound good. We had Jack

Ingram on "Dallas After Midnight," which Ray wrote. He wanted to do "Torn in Two." That wasn't my idea, but I was fine with it. "Drivin' Wheel" is one that he always did. "This Mornin' I Am Born Again" is the one with the dropped bag of percussion. Ray heard "Roll and I Tumble" and said, "Do you think we can re-create that?" I said, "Let's try." We had Cody Canada come in for "Cooler-N-Hell."

Rod Picott and I wrote "Torn in Two" in Nashville. I can't remember who had the idea, but I think Rod had "my heart's been torn in two," and I said, "That's about a tattoo." Then we were off and running. I was in Nashville and had time on my hands. Rod said, "You want to try to write something?" I said, "Sure." I'd only done that maybe three times in my life. It's only worked once. I do like that song. I forget to play it sometimes. Ray liked the song and cut it, and I was happy about that.

I fell into being the guitar or bass player in his band for years from playing on the records. I played "Snake Farm" with him a hundred times. The song's an amazing piece of work. By the second chorus, everyone in an audience that hadn't heard the song was singing along every time. That's remarkable songwriting. We recorded that record really fast at the Zone [Recording Studio] out between Wimberley and Dripping Springs. We decided to cut it as live as possible. It was one pass on a vocal with no time to decide on a part before the tape started rolling. Some of the sounds on the record maybe don't sound as good as the other ones, but it has this spark of immediacy. The rule for the whole album was "no thinking." It's an amazing album. "Live and Die Rock and Roll" is another incredible rock song.

There was a natural progression with the production on those albums. You go in and do another album and hope you've learned something in the meantime. The only thing that really changed is that Ray was getting deeper and deeper into the blues. He said, "I got down to only one chord on this record. I think I'll just moan and growl on the next record. I won't even have to sing words." He was going deep down in the mud.

We played some gigs that were pretty insane, like [Germanfest] in Muenster, Texas. We went up in Ray's van, Ray, Rick Richards, Troy Campbell, and me. We found out Germanfest and the North Texas arm wrestling championship day were both that day. There's a big stage. People are all over. They're all drinking beer and are pretty drunk by one o'clock in the afternoon. I noticed that backstage was only separated from the front by a little pink ribbon that was about a foot and a half off the ground. I thought, That's kind of odd. Anyone can step over it. We played a set, and it was great. Then they had a set of karaoke, and after that was the North Texas arm wrestling championship, with these steroid-addled country boys.

The vibe became weird and felt like something dangerous could be looming. Some guys were arm wrestling on stage and one guy broke the other guy's arm. A guy on the mic is saying, "The next two people are so-and-so and so-and-so from Oklahoma, and also can we get an ambulance to the side of the stage?" The guy's standing there holding his broken arm. Then the guy who broke his arm all of a sudden comes running across the field and just pops the guy in the back of the head. There's a giant fight immediately. There were six or eight state troopers there for security, and they all jumped on this guy who's pounding the other guy with the broken arm. Then some grandmother jumped on one of the troopers and started pounding him in the back of the head. They carried the guy off. It took all the troopers to drive him off. Then I realized: There are no troopers left, and we're behind the stage with this ribbon [for protection]. That was a pretty amazing gig. Ray always said, "Join the army to see the world. Join Ray Wylie to see the weird."[9]

Rod Picott

I had really been wanting to write with Gurf for a while. I'd seen him take a turn in his own writing, and I knew he was coming through Nashville and staying with Buddy and Julie Miller. I was stuck on the song, with just the chorus and a piece of the first verse. I told Gurf, "I have something we could work on if you want to give it a shot." So I went over to Buddy's house, and we hammered out about 90 percent of "Torn in Two" over the course of just a few hours. The song came out very easily, and we were a nice match that day. A lot of cowriting can just depend on the day and the mood you're in and what you're drawn to write about. By the end, the song was very much a fifty-fifty cowrite.

Left to right: Jenni Finlay and Rod Picott, Jenni Finlay Promotions and
Catfish Concerts' Townes Van Zandt tribute, Folk Alliance International,
Kansas City, Missouri, February 19, 2015. Photo by Brian T. Atkinson.

Gurf instinctively knew the story I was trying to write and the
character I wanted to portray. That character was a composite, like
most are for me. You're picking things that are real and vivid and
come from life, but with a song you only have four minutes. You're
trying to build a dramatic short story. As I remember, it was a lot
of fun writing that song. It was exciting because I was writing with
Gurf, and he had this great history already. Also, he understood how
I write. I remember specifically saying to him, "What's the name of
the street where you grew up where you would go to get a tattoo?"
Those specific details really bring a song to life. I was so excited
that "Torn in Two" ended up on Ray's record [*Delirium Tremolos*].

Gurf was starting to write a lot around that time. I remember
him saying, "I can't tell which of my songs are good and which are
not." I thought that was funny because he's such a great producer
and has such an ear for songs. I think it was a new chapter in his
own life. Not that he was new to writing, but I think he was being
more intentional about it. He recognized that he didn't want to be
a bandleader anymore. He wanted to make his own records. Gurf's
very quiet and laconic, but if you can be on board with that, he's

a lot of fun to be around. He's so dry and dark and likes the weird stuff. He's a really smart guy.

We wrote "Torn in Two" in the same way that Slaid and I write. We got the song to about 90 percent and then went our separate ways, so there are differences. I wrote the last verse as, "I put a thousand miles on my motor / I broke down to New Orleans." He wrote, "I put a thousand miles on my motor / I broke down in Bowling Green." New Orleans is so much more vivid to me, so much darker and desperate. Bowling Green sounds slightly comical. It just depends on how you see it. I'm always fine with that stuff if a writer sees it in a certain way. I'll fight with Slaid over that because we've known each other so long, but I was fine with Gurf's changes.

I know SiriusXM's Outlaw Country played Ray's "Torn in Two" a few times. People would send me pictures of their car radios when it was playing. I'm a huge Ray Wylie fan. That was a nice time for me. Slaid was doing really well with the cuts I was writing with him, and then I had this one with Gurf that Ray recorded. Gurf produced that record, and I think it was just utilitarian. Ray was probably shy a song or two, and Gurf pitched it to him on the spot. I don't think he had any master plan. He just said, "I have this one. What do you think?" Ray liked it. I mean, it's right in his wheelhouse.

Ray went with Gurf's line about Bowling Green, and it actually sounds great coming out of his voice. There's something darkly humorous that runs through most of his stuff. He has that odd and slightly dark sense of humor. He's fearless. I love that Ray knows what he does well. You listen to a Ray Wylie Hubbard record, and you know there will be three or four minor-key grooves that might only have one or two other chords in them. He's not thinking, How do I make a record to make more people like me? He's just thinking about making the best Ray Wylie Hubbard record. That's how I think about it, so I love that in other people.

Ray's lyric has to be so strong that it holds the entire thing up. He's not relying on this palette of musicality because he whittles down songs so much. That's incredibly difficult. He's so smart and interesting that he can do that and keep the song vivid from end to end. He writes in odd corners with little lyrical things coming in and out. It's the opposite of writing a Slaid Cleaves song, which is incredibly melodic and will have this chord turn somewhere that you don't expect. Ray's all about how deep the groove goes, the sound, and tone. He has that dark drawl that sits so beautifully on his voice and can work with one chord. His seven-minute version of McMurtry's "Choctaw Bingo" is mesmerizing.

I wrote a Facebook post last year and said, "One of my goals this year is to write a song with Ray Wylie Hubbard." Ray wrote back, "That's fine, but I just want to remind you that birds speak in my songs." He went down this list of odd things that we might encounter if we write together. He's very, very funny. We haven't written together yet this year because I haven't been very present in the world. I've been writing a book of short stories and a double record. I didn't get to some things I had in mind, but I'd love to write with him. It's been in the back of my mind because I have another ten or so that I'm working on. I'm thinking if I get stuck on one, I'll reach out to Ray.[10]

Slaid Cleaves

I was playing a Woody Guthrie tribute night at La Zona Rosa in 1993 or 1994, and there weren't that many people in the audience. I was listening to all the other people playing after I did, and this scruffy guy in a biker jacket and a red bandana came over and confided that he really liked what I did. He said, "Kid, you're onto something there," and other very encouraging words. He walked away, and somebody said, "You know who that is, don't you?" "No." "That's Ray Wylie Hubbard." I hadn't even heard of him before that, so it was a funny first meeting. *Loco Gringo's Lament* had just come out, and I went out and bought it. I became a fan.

More importantly, we were on the Rounder Records label at the same time a few years later, and they put me on a couple tours with Ray. That's when he started to be my mentor. He came along just at the right time. I came to Austin from Maine ostensibly to open for Joe Ely, but that didn't work out. I ended up opening for Ray Wylie instead. That fell into my lap. I wanted that older brother/mentor relationship where I could learn not just about musicianship but about the business, touring, performing, and writing. That was my goal when I came to Austin. It was a revelation when I ended up

Left to right: Owen Temple and Slaid Cleaves, at Strange Brew, Austin, Texas, October 19, 2014. Photo by Brian T. Atkinson.

opening shows for Ray. He was so generous in his interest in me and giving a young songwriter the confidence that I was on the right track.

I learned how to put a show together from Ray. He's not stringing random songs together every night. A show has a pace, and many of his songs were set up with an introduction, which was a set piece he'd do every night before the songs. He showed me the idea of presenting a persona on stage. I had never worked on that before. Ray's persona is so fun, charming, and unique. He has such an amazing stage presence, and that enthralled me. He encouraged me to work on my own persona. Ray was a perfect mentor off the stage as well, as far as the day-to-day travel, eating healthy, and treating staff with respect. He taught me to be humble but stick up for your principles when it mattered.

He even taught me how to fingerpick in the off time. It was a really formative experience for me. He was very generous with his attention to me and [in] wanting to see me do well. I mostly learned by observing him, but he did sit me down one time. I could tell he'd done it before because it was like a ritual. He had a speech. His shtick was basically, "You want to do this thing, but you're not sure you can. You think maybe you can't, but where's the proof that you can't? There is no proof. You need to do this and not be afraid to be ambitious." Somehow he got to the word *prosper* and the idea that aspiring to prosper is a good thing. You shouldn't feel bad about it. Go out and be successful. Do the best at what you want to do. That was a confidence-building exercise.

From *Loco Gringo* on through the other Gurf Morlix–produced albums, he sort of builds a persona over time. It's interesting to see that the songs get more elemental, going from three chords to two to one. I thought it was funny the way he devolved that way. Everything he does is so cohesive. The albums all support this persona that he's built, the gypsy wise man, ruffian character kind of thing.

I was working on "Wishbones" while I was getting ready to record the follow-up to [Cleaves's 2000 breakthrough album] *Broke Down* [2004's *Wishbones*] with Gurf Morlix. I remember I didn't even have half that song written, and I was short on songs for the album. Ray called me out of the blue and said, "Hey, why don't you come on down to Wimberley, and we'll work on songs." Again, he was there when I needed him, and we banged out the rest of that song in his kitchen. It didn't occur to me until a couple years later that Gurf must've called Ray and said, "Hey, Ray, you need to help Slaid wrap up this record." That's what I think happened, but I never got confirmation.

We only wrote that one time. I had the bare bones of the structure. He extrapolated "Wishbones," and carried it to the next level. I'm a real slow writer and work at my own pace, trading emails back and forth. So it's always hard for me to write face-to-face even with a close friend like Rod Picott. I wasn't used to writing like that, but we did it. Judy was off in the other room doing something. Lucas was at school. Ray made suggestions and provided much of the glue to make it work. I had two or three different ideas that I was trying to put together and he made them fit. I aspire to boil things down and make things as elemental as he does. I aspire to write a one-chord song someday. I haven't been able to yet. That's a real art.

I remember the first tour when we were just getting to know each other was pretty grueling with long drives. We were in Germany, the Netherlands, and the UK. Near the end, we were in Amsterdam on Ray's fiftieth birthday. I had bonded with him, and we had this little brother and big brother thing. I was trying to be like him. That was before he had his new hips, so he had a little limp. I'd catch myself faking a little limp walking behind him sometimes. I wanted to be like him so much. I was really glad to be able to open his seventieth birthday party at the Paramount [Theatre in Austin] because it resonated with the fiftieth birthday in Amsterdam. I asked to be put on the bill, and it was nice of Judy to do that. What I remember most about that night is that he was and is doing so well physically and artistically. He's even better than he was at the age of fifty, which is amazing.

He's also a healthy-living guy who takes care of himself physically and spiritually. That's something he tried to impart to me on that early tour. Take care of yourself. Eat right. He's devoted to staying on the true and healthy path. He would go to AA meetings back then. It seems obvious that's kept him so healthy, productive, and creative over the past twenty years. He's obviously written much more profound work than "Redneck Mother" in that time. He would like that work to be remembered, but I think his legacy is the resonance of his personality and support for all the young writers he's helped over the years. He's helped dozens and dozens of writers. He reached out to us. What a beautiful thing.[11]

Mary Gauthier

I met Ray at the Strawberry Music Festival in Northern California, which was the very first festival I ever played. It was around 1999, and my album *Drag Queens in Limousines* had come out. There are intense songs on that record, but I had no idea the impact they would have on people because I hadn't really [toured singing them] yet. I still had my restaurant [Dixie Kitchen in Boston, Massachusetts] and was playing open mics. I played my set and then went to the little table by the side of the stage to sell my record. There was this long line. People were in tears, and I didn't know what to do. I didn't know that's what my songs would do to people. I was overwhelmed. I couldn't sign CDs, take money, and do all the shit I'm supposed to do with all these people crying. I had to hug and comfort them.

I look up and there's Ray standing right there with two cappuc-

*Mary Gauthier, Catfish Concerts, Austin, Texas, May 18, 2017. Gauthier,
who helped country music superstar Garth Brooks reinduct longtime
Ray Wylie Hubbard fan and friend Bobby Bare into the Grand Ole Opry
on April 7, 2018, credits Hubbard with launching her career as a singer-
songwriter. Hubbard drops her name in the appropriately titled "Name
Droppin'" on his 2003 album* Growl. *Photo by Brian T. Atkinson.*

cinos in his hands. One was for me, and one was for him. It was
like him bringing comfort to me. I can't tell you how much coffee
means to people who are in sobriety. He just stood there and helped
me work the line. He was intuitively there for me. He had my back
like an older brother. Slaid Cleaves had told me about Ray, but I
had never met him before that day. When it got too heavy, I'd look
at him, and he'd go, "You got this. Just listen to their stories. Give
them a hug." He held me up. I'll never forget it.

I loved him right then, and I love him to this day. He knew I
needed him to be there for me because I didn't know what to do.
His nature's to be very aware. He keeps it in his mind who's new
and who he can be of service to, a very giving guy and one who
helps people coming up. He's awake and not sitting in a greenroom just thinking about himself. He actually models how I try to
behave. In recovery, we're taught to be of service, so maybe it was
something he learned to do. It's called walking the walk. Anyone

can talk the talk. In order to truly stay sober, you walk the walk. He learned how to do it, and he does it to this day.

Ray and I toured together when I was getting started. He was getting back on the road after his hiatus. He was ahead of me in that he had a foundation, his name had marquee value, he had that hit, and he was friends with Willie and those Texas guys. He was just getting started at being a folk singer, though. He was playing solo, and I opened for him. We were in the car together quite a while getting started, and he was very generous with me. Also, he's a pretty healthy dude and a vegetarian, which is always a tough challenge on the road, especially touring in barbecue land. We had to work around that. We connected musically but also because we were both committed to recovery from addiction. He was very helpful to me in my early recovery.

Slaid and Ray and I were having a meal one day, and they brought me over to Gurf Morlix's house. They strongly suggested that Gurf should be my guy and produce my next record. He did for the next three records, and that changed my whole life. Slaid and Ray were behind it. Gurf at the time was no longer with Lucinda Williams, but he had been a part of [1998's Grammy Award–winning] *Car Wheels* [*on a Gravel Road*], which was a huge record. He was in between working with Lucinda, producing and touring with her, and what he was gonna do next. That turned out to be working with Ray and Slaid, Robert Earl Keen, Tom Russell, and me. Gurf gave me a sound and was transformative.

I felt there was no way the great Gurf Morlix would work with me when they brought me to his house. I was just this wannabe, but they convinced me that Gurf would consider it if we went over there personally. I think that introduction did it and changed the trajectory of my life. I ended up with a record [2002's] *Filth & Fire*, which became the number one record in *The New York Times* for an independent release for that year. That led to Gurf making the next record, which was signed by Universal/Lost Highway, the best record label at the time in the country for what I do. Gurf and Ray really mentored me.[12]

Gurf broke a string one day when we were working on *Filth & Fire*. He was playing an old, old guitar. Instead of pulling out a new string and putting it on, he took the new string outside and put it in the dirt and stomped on it for a while. Then he put it on. I said, "What are you doing?" He's like, "I hate new strings." He doesn't like the tinny sound of new strings. He doesn't like anything shiny and glossy or fluorescent lights or anything with commercial sheen. He likes it real, worn, and broken in. He's amazing. He figured out that it would sound old if he stomped on that string in the dirt and messed it up. I think the recording sounded better because it sounded like all the other strings that were already old. Ray was behind us working together.[13]

Ray has an integrity that's hard to find around here in Nashville. [Mainstream country] cats want to latch onto someone with integrity because it's a model for them. Ray's fully himself, and he follows his own inner voice. Nobody's ever told him what to do or how to do it. He's never chased a commercial model. He reentered the business sober, and I think that's something those guys can feel. They may not know the language or his story, but they feel it and it's attractive to them. Plus, he's cool because he's fully himself. His songs and their integrity will hold up over time and resonate for future generations. I love and respect him. I am grateful for his sobriety, his generosity, and the hand he gave me when I really needed it. Ray's impact on my life and career is immeasurable.[14]

Eliza Gilkyson

I knew about Ray Wylie Hubbard all the way back to Three Faces West because I lived in Santa Fe and various towns in Northern New Mexico since the seventies, but I didn't meet him until 1981. That's when I came to Austin for the first time, and my big show was to open for Ray at the Austin Opera House. That was also the first time I heard him live. He doesn't remember because he doesn't remember anything from that decade, but I do. I was thinking, God, what is this cool scene, and who are these people? Ray played roadhouse music, but it had a little fairy dust around the edges. He was quirky and funny as hell even back then. There was something incredibly intimate about his show even though he was out of his gourd. He still had some sort of magic dust over what he did.

I love that Ray didn't become a victim of his own archetype. He became sober. People get famous with one sound, and they feel that they have to do that thing over and over for the rest of their lives. They don't keep growing. Ray got sober and turned his life over to a higher power, but he didn't fall into some rote religious experience. He became a redneck mystic, a Texas seeker, and that came out in his songwriting and music. He writes songs like honky-tonk Zen koans with swamp in his soul. He's authentic. Whittling songs down to one chord is him whittling himself down to what he really is, also part of rejecting the type cast about being this shit-kicker guy. That's finding yourself in your music. It doesn't mean your music will become more complex. It's often more simple and authentic.

I was psyched when Ray said he was gonna record "The Beauty Way" [on 2005's *Delirium Tremolos*]. I sang on it out at Gurf Morlix's and was just beside myself. I had had very few covers of my songs at that point. I thought, This is so cool, and I was grateful that Ray recognized something of himself in the song. Then Ray came in and sang on "Man of God" [from Gilkyson's 2005 album *Paradise Hotel*]. You can hear his voice grumbling in the background. Ray's humble and laughs at himself. He's a jewel, funny and quirky and never got above his raising. Recording at Gurf's is always like family. It's always a joy to be around those guys.

Eliza Gilkyson photo from liner notes to The Nocturne Diaries *(Red House Records, 2014). Photo by Brian T. Atkinson.*

I wrote "The Beauty Way" as an amalgam of these guitar players in my life who had a love-hate relationship with their instruments and the picker's life. It's the story of this guy who was becoming world-weary, but he didn't know how to stop. He felt his bones turning over every time he considered stopping because it was so deeply ingrained in his soul. Ray owns that song in a lot of ways that I couldn't even own it. A number of people have recorded that song, but no one ever hit it like Ray did. He slowed it down, and it was sadder, more world-weary, and had more miles on its tires. That added another level of poignancy to the lyrics.

I'm big into the mystic poets. I put that bent into my lyrics. My next record is called *Secularia*, all songs I've written over the years about the pursuit of the mystery. Ray and I share an interest in Rumi and the other mystic poets, the seekers who are driven by their love for a power greater than themselves. They never quite get to have it, which creates a sense of longing and almost madness in the endless pursuit of the thing you will never fully know or understand. Maybe you're not meant to know and understand in one lifetime. You write like that for yourself because you're not gonna make a bunch of money.

I need to dance to mindless music and enjoy that joy as well. If writing more spiritual songs is your calling, though, you have to be true to it. That's been the case with me. I think it has its booth in the marketplace. It might not be the place where a lot of coins change hands, but it's precious to me, and it's precious when others do it. I want to be moved and be encouraged to be sentient. I want to get outside of myself and serve something greater than me, but at the same time I don't want to call it god. I don't want to anthropomorphize something so mysterious. I need to hear people like Ray doing that. It helps me know I'm not alone.

Ray's a Delta mystic. His music speaks right to the heart with his truth and treads ground where not many freethinkers are gonna tread. That's a precious piece right there, and he does it with true humility and gratitude. He's able to go down trails that not everybody can go down and speak his truth. Singer-songwriters are "all about me" pretty much 24/7. You have to mine that to get to certain jewels of perspective. I think serving something greater than yourself puts yourself in a position to feel humility and gratitude. You don't take yourself so seriously. I personally think that it makes for a happier life. More loving people can come close to you because you are in a state of awareness knowing that life could be so much worse. Gratitude helps you realize that you've reached a place in your life not because of yourself, but in spite of yourself. That changes the music you write.[15]

Patty Griffin

The song I just sang with Ray [*Tell the Devil...I'm Gettin' There As Fast As I Can*'s closing track, "In Times of Cold"] put him on a whole new plane. The song came up last winter when my friend George Reiff was getting ready to pass away. He told Ray that he thought I'd make a good harmony. I was very ill at the time, but

Left to right: Tamara Saviano, Shawn Camp, and Patty Griffin, during sessions for This One's for Him: A Tribute to Guy Clark, *Cedar Creek Recording Studio, Austin, Texas, June 25, 2011. Griffin sang Clark's "The Cape" on the tribute album. Photo by Brian T. Atkinson.*

I really wanted to do it. I cranked up my energy and did. I know Ray's funny as shit and has such a wink in his eye, but when he goes to a dark place, I think he does it better than most people. He has a knowledge and wisdom. He's not afraid. He comes from a really honest place emotionally because it doesn't freak him out when it gets sad.

Ray's incredibly kind and respectful. He's walked in many different worlds, and he's gone all the way down. You need to understand darkness and sadness to really bring out light. He's evolved out of that dark place as somebody who has so much depth and wisdom because he understands the other side so instantly. He knows the stories of the underworld, visiting hell, and coming back with a lot of knowledge. Ray has a lot going on up there in his head, and he has that twinkle in his eye. He makes the medicine go down easier. If I had to wake him up, I would wake him up as the messenger.

Ray's evolved. He started with "Up Against the Wall Redneck Mother" and was a rocker, a wild person. I have great admiration for that part of his life, but now he's touching on everything that moves him, like real artists do. That's more important than ever. Sometimes I wonder what the hell I'm doing, and I'm sure Ray wonders that, too. We need to be honest and keep going there over and over again because we will reach somebody someday. It will help somebody who needs to hear that and to get through a time. That's what we're doing as musicians. I have an admiration for the amount of work Ray's done. It takes so much strength to evolve as a musician the way he has.[16]

Chris Knight

I was a teenager when the Texas Outlaw movement was going on, and I listened to Waylon, Willie, and Tompall Glaser, but I was more into singer-songwriters like John Prine, Jackson Browne, and JJ Cale. I wasn't really familiar with the Outlaw movement, but Ray being there when the whole thing went down is pretty cool. I heard "Redneck Mother" a long time ago. I started hearing his music when I got into the music business and started going to Texas. I think he made a comeback around that same time, and I started doing some shows with him. We probably did four or five

Chris Knight.
Courtesy Michael
J. Media.

co-bills, and I've opened for him. I heard him on KHYI [95.3 The Range in North Texas] because we have several mutual friends in the radio business.

The crowd loved him. He's a funny guy with a lot of stories, and that helps on acoustic shows. The crowd wants to hear you tell stories. Also, he has good lyrics. "Screw You, We're from Texas" and "Snake Farm" are funny and cool songs. Ray's real easygoing, with a great personality. I've never seen him get pissed off or even act uncomfortable when fans were around. He always seemed very laid-back and gracious. He's a cool dude. Ray's a big influence on a lot of people. You can hear that when you listen to the younger generation of singer-songwriters in Texas music. Everybody thinks a lot of him. Ray's legacy is gonna live on. I don't see how it couldn't.

If anybody writes a book about Texas music, I know Ray's gonna be in it.[17]

Kevin Russell

The first time I heard Ray Wylie's name was on Jerry Jeff Walker's double album *A Man Must Carry On* with the live version of "Redneck Mother." Jerry Jeff calls out: "Ray Wylie Hubbard." That's such a colorful and musical name, and I always remembered it. So like most people, my introduction was realizing he's the guy who wrote "Redneck Mother." I didn't even know that he was a guy with a whole other musical career. It didn't dawn on me as a kid. I was never a big fan because I didn't come from that singer-songwriter thing. I came more from classic country and punk rock when I was younger, but I became more aware of his music after moving to Austin years later.

The Gourds were playing a show in downtown Austin one day, and Ray was on it. I asked him to sing "Redneck Mother" with us, but he didn't seem too thrilled. I know it's an albatross to a certain extent, and it's like, "Oh god." I get that. He did the song with us,

Kevin Russell, Tin Roof, Nashville, Tennessee, launching Eight 30 Records' Cold and Bitter Tears: The Songs of Ted Hawkins, *October 14, 2014. Photo by Brian T. Atkinson.*

though. He did it his way, and we had our own way. It was a bit of a train wreck, but it was funny. That's how I got to know him. Also, the Gourds had a poster with "kicking hippies' asses and raising hell" as a tag. He liked the poster and wanted to get an autographed copy. I don't know if I ever got him one.

You have to learn to love the song if you write "Redneck Mother" or [cover Snoop Dogg's] "Gin and Juice," like the Gourds did. We struggled with that. The Gourds stopped playing "Gin and Juice" for a time. We said, "No, we're not playing it," but that didn't work. People got mad at us. You can't tell the fans what they want or don't want. The fans know what they want. That's why they're at the shows. Ray's discovered that you don't have to play it every night. You have to play it *almost* every night. You know which shows you can get away without playing it and which you really need to play it. You can feel it. You become a greater judge of what audiences want from the show. Always give the people what they want. I'm a big believer in that, but it's a challenge when you have a song like that.

A great, genius song like "Redneck Mother" will always stand as an accomplishment and be a significant part of his legacy, but "Conversation with the Devil" is ten times smarter. Ray has such great economy in his wit and his songs. He's a great writer and never says too much. People around here will remember him for the collective work. That's the way you have to look at him. "Redneck Mother" is a milestone, a great novelty song that captured the spirit of the moment. That's what a poet does, but we judge all true artists by their entire body of work. He's a true artist, and I don't see him departing from that philosophy any time soon.

I got to know Ray better when I started working with George Reiff. I sang and did some mandolin on a couple songs on *A: Enlightenment, B: Endarkenment (Hint: There Is No C)*. I think it was like a barter: "I sang on your record. Now you'll sing on mine, and we'll call it even." That sounded good to me. I had had Ray do the bridge on "East TX Rust" [from Shinyribs's 2010 album *Well After Awhile*]. I was looking for another voice for that bridge, and it sounded like Ray Wylie Hubbard. He was a little intimidated by that. He was like, "No one's ever asked me to sing on their record before. I don't know if I can do that. I just sing the stuff that I know. I don't really sing what other people write." I don't know if he was joking, but it turned out fine. He did a good job, but he's never repeated the performance.

Ray was great at George Reiff's memorial concert [on December 17, 2017, at Emo's in Austin, Texas]. I thought we might could get "East TX Rust" together for that, but I had other plans. The memorial was a sublime evening. The reason for it was sad, but enough time has passed by now that people are in the later stages of their grieving. We aren't quite as in shock about his passing as we were this summer, but still people can't quite accept that he's gone. That was a common conversation. The impulse to communicate with George is still there. They still go to text or call him. The thought that he's gone hasn't quite sunk in. It was a somber evening at times, but it was a beautiful gathering of people who loved George.[18]

There was no ego or attitude at all with all the great creators who were at the memorial. It was beautiful. Nobody got mad. Feelings did not get hurt. It was like working with George, working with an old friend, very personal and intimate, creative, inspirational. George knew how to inspire people. He always knew how to get the best from people and himself, too. He was always striving for greatness. That rubbed off on me. Yeah, you're capable of good things, but you might as well try to be better than can be. It seems trite and cliché, but when you see somebody live by that philosophy in life and work that way, you get it a little better. Monkey see, monkey do.

My most memorable Ray Wylie story is when the Gourds agreed to play the Grit 'n Groove Festival [in 2011]. We said we would, but then we got a deal [from Vanguard Records] and were recording at Levon's [Helm] barn in Woodstock with Larry Campbell. I told Judy, "Hey, I don't think we're gonna make the Grit 'n Groove because our recording sessions are going through that weekend." She guilted me into it. She's like, "That's fine, but that's not the Gourds I know." So we cut our recording short to make the festival, and let's just say it was subpar, not a real successful festival. I was a little put out that we agreed to do this. We were playing an all-star jam at the end, and Ray leans over and goes, "Hey, you wanna buy a festival?" He let me know, "I know what you're thinking and feeling." It made everything all right. He said thank you and made me laugh.[19]

Walt Wilkins

We were at [MusicFest in] Steamboat [Springs, Colorado] one year, and I was in the lobby walking to my room. Kids were everywhere. Ray was coming the other way toward me, and we stopped to talk. We said some greetings and tucked ourselves into the hallway to catch up, and after a few minutes this drunk twenty-two-year-old kid comes up, like in a movie. He was like, "Oh my god, Ray Wylie Hubbard." Ray goes, "Yep, and this is Walt Wilkins. What do you need, buddy?" "I just can't believe that I can just talk to you." Ray says, "Why is this such a big deal?" The kid goes, "Because you're so famous." Ray looked at me and goes, "Walt, if this is fame, I want power." I always thought that was great. He wasn't telling a joke. It was straight out of life. Ray's very quick.

I was on his radio show *Roots & Branches* several times. He was always fun and funny. He had just written that movie script for [2010's *The Last Rites of Ransom Pride*], and I got in and was

Left to right: Walt Wilkins and Verlon Thompson, Catfish Concerts, Austin, Texas, January 25, 2018. Photo by Brian T. Atkinson.

really tired. We were having a hug before the show, and I had my back to the audience because I didn't want anyone to hear what I was saying. People were just six feet away. I said to Ray, "Have you ever been just so tired? Man, I need a moment, a month to rest and write again. Have you ever felt that way?" He put his hands on my shoulders and switched positions with me, maneuvered me so his back was to the audience. He said, "Walt, if this movie becomes a hit, these people will never see me again." I laughed. He said, "No, Walt. Never again."

When Ray Wylie was our guest at the first and second Red River Songwriters' festivals, we walked into the Motherlode Saloon, which is where "Redneck Mother" started. Ray said, "You know, I haven't been here in forty years." I thought, Damn. That's cool. He said, "It has not changed a bit." I'm sure it hasn't. He wrote "Redneck Mother" on a whim, which he didn't even remember. That's how clever and fast he is. All the work he's done since then totally outweighs what he did as a young guy, though. His is an enviable catalog of quality work. He's written great songs that revisit the same themes, but he comes from different angles. I go out and buy his records because of that. He's been a great role model for me in how to be a professional and a meaningful figure in this state, a real important cornerstone for this generation. Also, I like him. I smile when I see him.

He talks about things I find interesting in his songs. He's great at balancing earthly and transcendental. I love that he sings about what does life mean and why are we here? That's what gets me. He's very encouraging. Those songs are good mantras. I love "A. Enlightenment, B. Endarkenment (Hint: There Is No C)" because I believe it. You gotta get up, stay at it, and be positive. That guy should know. He's been through some real dark times, so I take him at his word. Also, I love his guitar playing and how he switched from old folkie country guy to really being serious about this Zen blues. I dig that whole sound.

I played this show in Corpus Christi one time with Ray, Cory Morrow, Hayes Carll, and me. The four of us played two nights. Ray played us [2003's *Growl*] that has "Screw You, We're from Texas" on it. That was when he was getting into not changing chords, just playing these one-chord songs. I said, "God, Ray, what are you

gonna be doing on the next record, be a stick on a log and chant?"
I thought it would get a laugh, but he didn't. He was like, "I don't
know." He's got a persona, but it's grown out of what he is. It's not
a put-on. He's organic. He's the guy who likes to read and make
you laugh, and he's a great storyteller. He'll tell the same story for
years onstage, but it'll still be funny. That's a gift.

It was a pretty significant time when he went from country-
folk to country-blues. I think it was symbolic at the time and grew
out of him being sober. It was him saying, "I'm not the cute, funny,
goofball guy." He's a great songwriter, and it may have been a way
for him to tell the world and himself that this is different. It was
a real change inside that felt authentic growing out of him. Also,
he's a really good guitar player with a good style. That's the heart.
He's a bulletproof player. I'll say one other thing. You know how
he's called the Wylie Lama? I'm pretty sure I invented that phrase
when I was on Pat Green's bus for a year. I called him that. I just
wanted to tell someone before I'm gone. Ray's always treated me
with great respect, and I think he's a real tenderhearted guy. I completely dig how he's changed his whole deal. He's always a pleasure to be around.

Gratitude resonates with me because I'm fifty-six, and that's
the only way it works for me to do quality work and show up as a
half-decent human. Stay gracious. Stay in that mindset. Of course, I
don't sometimes, and I'm sure Ray would say the same about himself. It's hard to do all the time, but that sure makes for a better life
and a better path. One thing I love about Ray and Judy is watching
Lucas grow up. He's a great kid and always has been. He's been
great every time he's been around my son Luke. That's work and
not some pie-in-the-sky deal. Ray really found authentic gratitude,
and it worked. That's the way to live and probably had a lot to do
with becoming sober, too. Personally, real gratitude helps me stay
not too dark. It's not the same as people who walk around saying,
"Everything's a blessing." Well, bullshit, but if you can really look
deep into your life and feel gratitude, it sure helps you have a better day.

Rodney Crowell, Telluride Bluegrass Festival, Telluride, Colorado, June 20, 2004. Photo by Brian T. Atkinson.

Rodney Crowell

Guy Clark mentioned Ray Wylie Hubbard to me in the early eighties. I paid attention. I wasn't around Ray a lot over the years, but I've gotten to know him better in the past couple. I'd call him a friend. We've done shows together in Santa Fe with Hayes Carll, in Augusta, Georgia, the Outlaw Country cruise, and in and around Austin. His songs are poetry. Ray Wylie's also a really, really great guitar player and a very seductive performer. He respects the intelligence of his audience, so he doesn't couch it in any bullshit. He brings it like it is and with really smart writing. Lucinda Williams would argue that there are poets and there are songwriters, and neither are the same. I'm gonna beg to differ with Ray Wylie.

Lightnin' Hopkins scared the shit out of me. He scared me away from seeing if I could get that country-blues across. I could get the Hank Williams version across naturally, but Lightnin' was a deeper thing. As I've gotten older and have more gravity in my voice and my approach, I started really getting back into Lightnin' and Howlin'Wolf, Muddy Waters, Big Bill Broonzy, Big Joe Williams, all those blues guys. I haven't asked Ray if it's the same for him, but I noticed when I started playing this Gibson 000, the guitar asked me to be a better guitar player. What I landed on was that I know how to strum this thing, but I need to learn how to *play* it.

I remember Ray saying he was really into Lightnin', and I'd put him at the top of the heap for sure. Listening to Big Joe and Lightnin' and watching videos of Big Bill, I started figuring out that the blues is a grown man's approach to music. I've become a better guitar player for my money. Finding the right guitar is incredibly important. I was a rhythm player for a lot of years and I had a really fine Collings C10. I've had other great guitars, but I landed on this mahogany, twelve-fret, lightly braced 000 and suddenly my relationship was [different]. I really need to play this guitar and become a better guitarist. In my own narrow way, I've become a more confident guitarist. I've noticed the thumb-pick style that Ray uses, and he's really adept at getting that minimal blues thing in there. That's a conversation we should have. Blues and that guitar picking became a way for me to enrich what I do. I should say that blues is a grown woman's approach, too, and not be misogynistic. Listen to Jessie Mae Hemphill. She's just as important as R. L. Burnside.

When you whittle down a song like Ray, you better have your language together. You can't hang paper on that thing. Your couplets have to be really succinct, and you can't have soft rhymes when it's down to one-chord blues. I talk about the poetry of Ray Wylie because his language has developed over the years to where he can bring it with that gravity. He has this tune ("God Looked Around" from *Tell the Devil...I'm Gettin' There As Fast As I Can*) that basically rewrites the story of Adam and Eve. It's perfect, with not a word out of place. He somehow makes colloquial language span three thousand years. How do you do that?

Maybe at some point in your life you look around and think, How do I become better? How do I understand more about doing this? You discover that Ray Wylie Hubbard's a pretty good place to look. Eric Church always seemed like a pretty game guy who was looking around for stuff to find, and I would speak well of him, knowing [he's a fan of Hubbard]. If you're a country singer, there's no reason you shouldn't be looking toward Tom Waits, Elvis Costello—someone like Ray with a different sensibility but who's bringing really solid language.

The blues has been wrung out of modern country music. Maybe my generation came along and fused the Beatles with country music. Maybe we suggested we stay away from the blues, but Johnny Cash sang "Folsom Prison Blues." The blues was in Hank Williams, Merle Haggard, even Hank Snow. Let's cut to the chase: Ray Wylie Hubbard's a blues man. Also, longevity [depends on] remaining interested in yourself. I don't mean that in the egotistical way. I mean, your songs from 1978 and 1982 can become a parody, wallpaper. You have to reconnect with the material if you want to play gigs until you die and relate yourself as relevant. As a casual observer, I'd say it was really smart of Ray to distill his live show down to his son [Lucas on guitar] and [Kyle Snyder] on that kick drum and sell themselves as people who know what the fuck's going on.[20]

Radney Foster

Ray opened for Willie Nelson during my senior year in high school in 1977 at the San Angelo city auditorium. I was there for a tennis tournament with couple guys staying in my camper van. We went to see the show, and I was like, "That guy's cool. It's not that he just wrote the 'Redneck Mother' song." Quite frankly, I didn't pay much attention until I was forty and started seeing his later records like *Growl* with "Screw You, We're from Texas." There were songs about mescaline and Buddha. Wow. I was like, "Man, this guy is bringing it, and he's crazy good. Now I'm a fan."

Music's a young man's game. I take my cues from Ray. He's a role model as you get older as far as how to do it with grace and dignity and honor the craft. He's never rested on his laurels. He's always trying to write another song that really challenges you, like any great songwriter. I've seen guys whose spark comes when we're young and then goes out, but I was reminded of those who keep going at the show last night watching Jack Ingram play "Biloxi." Jack wrote that at nineteen. I didn't write anything worth a shit when I was nineteen that anybody wanted to hear again. Jack is

Left to right: Radney Foster and Bill Lloyd, Waterloo Records,
Austin, Texas, June 25, 2011. Photo by Brian T. Atkinson.

still taking that gift that you're given and trying to rework, hone,
and sand it down to make it smoother. He's forever trying to make
it perfect. You can get that from Ray: Never stop.

  You look at so many others, who will remain nameless, and
they just stopped. They had that moment in time when they made
art happen, and then they either give it up to do something else
or they go on and keep playing those same songs and doing the
same thing over and over in order to make a living. There's nothing wrong with that. Those are the majority, but people like Ray,
Guy Clark, and Rodney Crowell, who I count as heroes, never say

die. They're always trying to figure out another way to be creative. That's inspiring. I hope I'm still writing songs in my seventies that are worth a damn and that people want to hear and think about.

"Snake Farm" is funny, but it's also brilliant. How do you put *ew* on the lyric page? How do you spell that out without an editor's note that says you shake your head and lick your lips at the same time? Brilliant and screenplay-worthy. You get through "snake farm just sounds nasty" and "pretty much is" down to "snake farm, ewwww." It's physical and awesome. Ray's always had a sense of humor and irony. I told him recently, "You're the master of irony. That's really hard to do." He turned to me and said, "Yeah, but the problem is that not everybody understands irony."

You can find songs anywhere you look, but you can't always find good ones. If you told me, "Radney, you've got an hour and you have to have a song." I might say, "Okay, there's an empty cup of coffee in front of me because I'm fixing to go to breakfast." I'm gonna write a song about that cup, but whether it's worth a damn is the question. Ray could write a song about an empty cup of coffee that could make you laugh and cry within the same song. He brings that. It's funny, writing my book of short fiction [2017's *For*

Left to right: Lucas Hubbard and Ray Wylie Hubbard, Waterloo Records, Austin, Texas, August 17, 2017. Photo by Brian T. Atkinson.

You to See the Stars], I've understood the laughter-to-tears arc, but I don't know that I've accomplished it in a song like Ray can. It took me 3,500 words to make that happen in a short story, and I consider myself a pretty good songwriter.

We did a show together about four years ago. Everything he did was just devastatingly great. There was nothing in his set that didn't move me. A couple songs were the hits for the sake of the audience, but I realized just how brilliant and remarkable they were. He'll always get down to the nitty-gritty somewhere. I tend to be a guy who says, "This is either a happy or sad or funny song." Ray has the ability to weave everything together. How do you write a song about the man and a woman with mescaline in it ["Drunken Poet's Dream"]? That's not the norm. That's not where people tend to think a song through.

I think people are finally going through his huge body of work and finding inspiration. Part is seeing guys like Hayes play his songs. They go, "I like that Hayes Carll song." Someone else says, "Hayes is a great writer, but that's a Ray Wylie Hubbard song." "Oh." Once people discover Ray's body of work, they're off to the races, and now I'm in Austin for when they induct him into the Texas Heritage Songwriters' [Association] Hall of Fame tonight. You know, if you told me when I was nineteen years old and singing "Up Against the Wall Redneck Mother" in a band in college that I was gonna get to know him on a first-name basis or be there for the induction ceremony, I'd have told you you lost your mind. I consider that such a privilege. Ray was one of the guys who made me go, "I want to write songs and sing them. I want to write songs that are so good that somebody else wants to do them." Ray Wylie Hubbard gave me that amazing gift.[21]

Verse Three
Dead Thumb King

Ray Wylie Hubbard at his home, Wimberley, Texas, November 14, 2017. Photo by Brian T. Atkinson.

I'm not conscious of mentoring. There are certain guys that I like and have the opportunity to hang around with and maybe show them something. I got to show Hayes Carll and Slaid Cleaves fingerpicking patterns. It's just, "Hey, I want to show you this chord." It's stuff I didn't learn until after I was forty, but I wished I learned it earlier. There are a bunch of goobers with guitars, but Slaid and Hayes, Aaron Lee Tasjan—cats like that are good hangs and don't have big egos.

They're into this as songwriters and songwriting as a lifestyle as opposed to getting cuts. It's a livelihood in Nashville. You have four or five songwriters in a room trying to write a song some big-shot country guy will record. The lifestyle is you write these songs, get in a van, and go play them in funky little clubs. People ask me who I listen to and I say, "Friends of mine," like James McMurtry, Hayes Carll, Slaid Cleaves, Gurf Morlix, Jamie Lin Wilson, Kelley Mickwee—people who have a good vibe around them.[1]

—RAY WYLIE HUBBARD

Hayes Carll

I met Ray Wylie at the Old Quarter Acoustic Café when I was tending bar there and doing open night mics. [Club owner] Rex ["Wrecks"] Bell introduced us. I watched Ray do soundcheck, which was one of the coolest things I'd seen up to that point in my life. He came in with an old Gibson and had it in open tuning, which I had not discovered yet. He got up there and started fingerpicking these wicked grooves. It was fascinating. Rex introduced us after the show. All I knew about Ray was from mythology of the Texas songwriters. I had a book that had photos of Willie Nelson, Jerry Jeff Walker, Steve Fromholz, Townes Van Zandt, and Ray in there. I only knew he was this legendary character.

I watched a lot of shows working at the Old Quarter, and Ray's was the most engaging, funny, interesting, moving performance that I'd seen at that point. He won the audience over from the get-go and put them at ease. He combined all these things I was drawn to. He had a sense of humor and the cool factor, with songs that

Left to right: Author, Jenni Finlay, and Hayes Carll doing a video interview during sessions for Eight 30 Records' Highway Prayer: A Tribute to Adam Carroll, *Cheatham Street Woodshed, San Marcos, Texas, March 4, 2016. Carll recorded Carroll's "Girl with the Dirty Hair." Photo by Russell Tanner.*

had depth, substance, and a real cool style with the groove. I hadn't seen anyone put it all together like he did. The next time he came through, Ray had agreed to let me open the show. If I remember correctly, Ray went to a funeral a couple weeks before the show and ran into somebody who asked if they could open. Ray obligingly said, "Sure." So I got demoted to being the opener for the opener. I did the show and met Judy that night. I think Lucas was sleeping in the merch box at the side of the stage. Then they asked if I wanted to go on the road. It was like Christmas to me. "Absolutely." They took me out on gigs, and we did quite a few in Dallas. Ray was really big up there. We had captive audiences.

I left [Crystal Beach, Texas] and moved to Austin after the first time we met because Wrecks had told Ray some of my plans. Ray said to Wrecks, "He gets it." I didn't have any gigs and couldn't find any work when I moved to Austin. I didn't even have a press kit. I called Ray and said, "You probably don't remember me, but I'm the guy who was tending bar at the Old Quarter. You said these three words to me. Can I use them for a press kit?" Ray very generously said, "Absolutely. Do you need a place to stay?" He offered his home. That always stuck with me. I'd never met anybody who was as kind and open and supportive. I did a show with Jeff Plankenhorn the other night. He was living in Ray's house when I met him. Ray and Judy just opened their home to him. I can think of fifteen guys who had been over to the house to write or get a guitar lesson.

I learned that he did that with everybody as I got to know Ray more and he took me on the road. He'd teach people how to fingerpick or write songs or just give you life advice. That was really important for me because I didn't have that kind of teacher. There wasn't a school for that. I had Wrecks Bell, who had some questionable life advice, so it was good for me to have Ray mentor me like that professionally and personally. It was really important to me. His advice was stuff like how to stay out of the ditches on the road, but I took away more from observing him and how he handled himself, how he treated people, and how he approached his craft and life. He always seemed to be grateful that he had this second chance.

He spent a lot of years in a fog and came out with a mission to learn how to play guitar. It took a lot of humility at forty years old to take guitar lessons when he had a name in the business. Ray let that go and tried something new because he wasn't satisfied with where he was. I was inspired by the way he approached the craft of music, writing songs, and the way he was paying it forward by putting some good in the world. Those were lessons that I got from him. I have not always applied them to my own life, but to this day I say Ray's quote at least once a month: "The days my gratitude is above my expectations, I have really good days." That's resonated with me in a deep way for a long time.

Ray's human, and I'm sure he gets pissed off about some things and wishes he had more acclaim, but he's put his head down, made good music, lived his life the way he's wanted to live it, and lived by his own rules. He's been a good soul along the way. It was really important to watch somebody live like that. On a more day-to-day level, his joke is that he's always the guy who gets Willie Nelson's [annual Fourth of July] Picnic back on schedule. Whenever somebody would come back and say, "Hey, Ray, we're gonna bump the show up fifteen minutes and start a little later," he'd say, "Doesn't matter to me. I'm still ending at the same time." He's always had that humor and wit and wisdom, and he handled things with grace. That's not easy to do when you're grinding it out on the road. He dialed into what was important for him, which was making the music he had to make and worked at it every day.

I called Ray up one day and asked if he wanted to write a song. He said, "Sure, come on over to the house." I went out there and said, "What have you been writing about lately?" He said, "Farm animals." He had songs about roosters, rabbits, and horses. I'd never really done much cowriting, and I think it was my second or third time. I didn't really know what to do. I didn't get writing about farm animals. He started this little lick on the guitar and started spouting out this mystic hillbilly wisdom and observations: "I got chickens in my front yard / What they do is scratch and pick / One of these days I'll go out there / Find me one and wring its neck." I said, "Okay, this isn't what I normally write about, but sounds good to me."

I'm not sure how much I had to do with that song. I hung out and remember what a cool experience it was to hear him come up with all this stuff. "If it rains today / The backyard will turn to mud / If it don't, it won't / Either way, won't rile my blood." It was a lesson for me. The crew I was running around with wasn't dropping that stuff in their songs. What he initially did was similar to what I do now with my knowledge of an E scale, but when we wrote the song, it was in that ballpark. I've always loved Ray's guitar playing. It's an underrated element of what he does—funky, gritty, and real. He's got the groove, which can take a song to the next level or another world. I have my poor man's version, but he's way more committed to learning all the tricks of the style.

I had this line that felt like the Band for "Drunken Poet's Dream." I had been sitting it on for a long time and couldn't figure out what to do: "I've got a woman, she's wild as Rome." I was stuck there, so I called up Ray. He came over to my apartment, and I played him that line. He looked at me and said, "She likes to lay naked and be gazed upon." We were off. We spent an hour going from there and got a chorus and a verse, and he had to run. We were both excited about it. He went home and finished it up on his end, and I stayed home and finished it up on my end. One of us called the other the next day and said, "I got it." The other said, "I do, too." We ended up with two different songs with some similarities. He says I'm showing off because I added a bridge. I had no idea that the song would connect with people in the way it did and become one of the more popular songs for both of us. Something about the song that resonates with people even though they're different versions.

I knew Ray had never been asked to play *Austin City Limits*. So when I got the call to play it the first time, I was thrilled, but it felt unjust. I wouldn't have been in the position I was without Ray. I'd opened all the shows over the years, and he had been so kind to me. There were times when I would open and we'd have a good crowd. Ray and Judy would throw me significant bonus money, which no one had ever done and was completely unnecessary. When the time came, and I got the call from *Austin City Limits,* I called Ray and asked if he would come sing with me. I don't know if he'd pissed off someone at *ACL*, but there were petitions going around to get him on the show. He had never been invited after thirty-five years. It was really special to me to pay him back in some small way.[2]

Jeff Plankenhorn

"Hey," a friend said, "I want you to come to Folk Alliance. I want you to meet this guy named Ray Wylie Hubbard." Then he played me some songs off *Dangerous Spirits*. So I went to Folk Alliance. As Ray Wylie was walking up the street with a different writer friend one day, my friend said, "Hey, this is Jeff Plankenhorn. He plays Dobro." Ray said, "Do you want to play a gig tonight?" "Sure." He said, "All right, I'll come to your gig, and if I dig what you play, you come up to my room and learn a couple tunes." He saw me play, and we went up to his room and played "When She Sang Amazing Grace," "Without Love," and "Last Train to Amsterdam." Ray said, "I'll see you at eight tonight."

I'd been living in Nashville, and about a year later Ray said, "You should move to Texas." I drove to Texas with a hundred dollars and some guitars in a Geo Prizm, and I lived with Ray and Judy for about three months in the beginning of 2000. We played together pretty heavily for a few years, and we still do sometimes. Everyone I've played with since then pretty much has been one degree of separation from Ray: Ruthie Foster, Willis Alan Ramsey, Bob

Jeff Plankenhorn, Catfish Concerts' fifth annual Townes Van Zandt tribute, March 18, 2018. Plankenhorn sang Van Zandt's "Don't You Take It Too Bad." Photo by Brian T. Atkinson.

Schneider. I met every one of them through Ray. I really wouldn't
be here or know anybody without him. I've had a pretty good solo
career the past few years and have been sticking with that, but I
played a whole bunch on Ray's last record and that was a home-
coming.

We cowrote a song called "Tooth and Nail" on my new record
Sleeping Dogs, which turned into a duet in the studio. I said I wanted
to write a song called "Tooth and Nail," and he said, "I'm in." He
loved the title. I told him it was about the difficulties of the songwriting craft and torture a musician feels being on the road. *Tooth
and Nail* pretty much describes what we do. I had some images like
seeing Hayes Carll tending bar on a Saturday night, the hungover
choir in the Baptist Church, and other writers. Then he started
putting in his images, and we went back and forth. Then we sat
down one day and turned it into a song. He came in when we had
most of the song done, but he played a little guitar. I said, "Man,
why don't you sing the second verse?"

We don't think in the studio. He taught me so much about being
in the studio and how to not get in your own way with that. Ray
has really great instincts as to what he wants. He was one of the
first major artists whose record I played on. Literally, that's the lesson: Do not get in your own way and do not overthink things. We
would lay something down and go, "Yeah, that's great." That happened on the *Tell the Devil* record, too. I laid down the lap steel
with my "Plank" guitar on "Tell the Devil...I'm Gettin' There As Fast
As I Can" and was cutting heads [on guitar] with Lucas Hubbard,
and we were done. I was like, "Okay. Good." That's it. Ray's really
good at not overthinking in the studio. That taught me a lot when
I went in to produce records for other people.

Ray taught me all the etiquette as both a front man and sideman. I learned everything from him from how to treat your band
to how to treat your audience. Ray used to say, "If you're an opener
and your set goes until 9:30, you get offstage at 9:29. Never play
over." There were so many things about how to treat the staff. He
would teach me, and then I would teach my band. I've seen it go
on down the line. I think that was a key for me getting gigs with
other people, whether Ray introduced me or they were just connected somehow. They knew that if I could play with Ray I was good

and I knew the deal. I knew whose name was on the marquee and could be a good sideman. Then when I became a front man myself I knew how to treat people. Ray is fantastic about that.

You have these fears about being a songwriter. Who's gonna listen, and why am I doing this? If you get through to the other side of that, there's something really beautiful there. Ray literally talks about that in his lyrics in songs like "The Messenger": "Our fears are like dragons guarding our most precious treasures." The opening lines to "Tooth and Nail" talk about the craft and being a musician day in and day out: "It's joy and misery every time, it seems you have to prove it / Like an old cat having kittens, you just crawl under the porch and do it." Only Ray would come up with that second line. There's no way I would ever come up with that. Another thing Ray likes to say is that we're the glory and the shame of the universe at the same time. You know, Ray teaches you whether you like it or not. You're gonna get it just being around him.

Ray gave me one of my first trials by fire when I first got to Texas, and it's so representative of our relationship. We were playing Gruene Hall for the first time, and it was a sold-out house. We had an incredible band with George Reiff, [drummer] Rick Richards, and me. Lucas was still a kid and wasn't playing yet. Ray was going around at the end of the show giving everyone their pay. He looks at me and goes, "Thanks for sitting in, Jeff." I was so green and felt like it was an honor just to play with Ray, so I was like, "Oh, okay." He grabs me and says, "Just kidding, man." Then he gave me the money. He'll mess with me and get me pretty good, but he'll teach me a lesson and show me how much he appreciates me at the same time.[3]

Aaron Lee Tasjan

Ray and I were at a Red Horse Ranch party on the Sunday after South by Southwest in 2012. He gave me a copy of *The Grifter's Hymnal*, which was about to come out. I flew back home to New York and put that record on out of curiosity, and it was all I listened to for the next year. I kept hearing all these lines in those songs and was thinking, Man, that's exactly how I feel, but I would never be able to say it like that. Ray's tapped into the underlying consciousness of humanity, and there was an immediate connection

Aaron Lee Tasjan, Continental Club, Austin, Texas, October 17, 2017. Photo by Brian T. Atkinson.

with the music and lyrics. Then the more I got into his music, the more I was interested in what he was doing with the guitar, how he puts a band together, and the way he plays his shows. He's one of my absolute favorites.

Ray seems to love everybody from Robert Johnson to Elmore James to Otis Rush. He's developed his own guitar style that's based on the lexicon of American blues and roots music. You get guys who can play really fast with fancy licks they've either copped off a record or a video they saw on YouTube, but Ray's beautiful simplicity in his playing makes it universal. He doesn't really use a pick. He fingerpicks with his fingernails and sometimes uses open chords. In fact, he has a song called "Open G," which is a whole song of him telling you how to tune a guitar to open G. I thought that was absolutely genius and completely Ray Wylie Hubbard.

Open tunings create a situation where chords are more like piano voicing. You can get chord qualities and tonalities from the instrument that you can't normally get just because of the way it's tuned. You can play things with open strings in certain keys and get those clustered chord qualities where you're gonna have close second harmonic pitches, cool suspensions, and things that are gonna give the music more teeth. When Ray does that, usually it's with a slide on the acoustic guitar. Open tunings really open up a deeper harmonic structure that's outside of what you usually hear on a standard tuning guitar.

His guitar playing is very rhythmic and understated, a perfect vehicle that creates this beautiful bed for him to lay his voice and lyrics on. The heart of his band when he plays live is his rhythm guitar playing. That's what ties it all together, and his drummer Kyle [Snyder] is so great at accenting his rhythms throughout the song. He's a guitar hero for guys like me, but he doesn't play the things you'd normally think a guitar hero would play. He's not flashy. He plays the truth.

I love that he plays his acoustic through an amp. He has it rigged up in a really specific Ray Wylie Hubbard way. He has a regular acoustic guitar under the saddle pickup, but he also has installed a gold foil electric guitar pickup between the bridge and sound hole of his acoustic that he runs a separate line out of into an amplifier as well. It sounds like a couple guys are playing at once when he plays guitar because the sound is coming from these two very distinctive and very different pickups in the same instrument, which is very cool.

I opened a show for him at 3rd and Lindsley here in Nashville. After the show, he told my manager that he wanted to offer me the opening slot on every show he was playing the rest of the year. I toured for about a year and a half almost constantly opening for Ray, which was really the first major break I had as a touring artist. Ray inviting me up to play onstage during his set was a very special thing. When that happens, it's like the artist is putting his arm around you, saying to the audience, "Hey, man, I really think this guy's all right." That's the most important endorsement you can get from an artist, and it really established an audience for me, especially in Texas, because what I do isn't always right down the pike. There are a lot of fringe parts, and Ray Wylie strikes me as an artist who's similar. He doesn't do the obvious thing, which makes it special. I thank the rock and roll gods every night when I say my prayers before going to sleep for being able to get that endorsement.

We in East Nashville admire the fact that he made the music he wanted to make and when and how he wanted to make it. For me, the last decade or so has really crystallized the idea that if you want to make music on your own terms for a long time, it's possible in a way that exceeds even our own expectations. We want that same career path. Ray's making the best albums he's made in his life, and the dude is seventy. Pretty impressive. We revere Ray Wylie Hubbard. His mentality fits right in with the East Nashville singer-songwriter mentality. "Hey, man, I'm not trying to be on the cover of *People* magazine and win country music awards." There's so much campaigning that goes into getting into that circle. It seems exhausting. What about just making something from the heart that you believe in and doing it for the right reasons every day when you get up in the morning? What about going out and giving that to people? Ray Wylie is evidence to us that it does work.

He's really developed his own language both in lyrics and music. It's like that Guy Clark song "Stuff That Works." He's really honed in on this place within him that just works. You never want to stop discovering things as an artist, but you do want to stay true to the parts of yourself that translate to an audience. He's quite adept at that. I learn the lesson over and over again when I see him sing a new song live. I see the way people react to it, how he stayed true to that thread that runs from his heart to everyone in the audience listening, and how he can pluck that thread. I've taken that to heart while trying to figure my own thing out.

"Redneck Mother" is such a storied part of that musical movement that still has a purpose in modern day. I mean, that Sturgill Simpson record *Metamodern Sounds [in Country Music]* seems like a page straight out of that time in music. Obviously, it really resonated with people in a significant way. Ray's always gonna be a major part of that story, but I think how the song is remembered is less important than the fact that it *will* be remembered. So many times when people have a big hit, that song becomes the lasting legacy. Once you do something that influences people outside your own generation, that story and those works are what get carried on and the next generations. I think like bands like Big Star or the New York Dolls, the influence Ray has had on other artists will truly be the legacy.[4]

Tim Easton

Ray Wylie Hubbard's my guru. He was playing with Amanda Shires at the Bristol Rhythm & Roots festival two nights ago, and his guitar strap fell off. He said, "Oh, that's my casual professionalism." His stage persona and comfort level really appeal to me. When some mistake happens at my gig and you can see behind the curtain, I always say, "Do you have any questions about my professionalism?" You have to acknowledge it. Ray can acknowledge everything that's going on with the feel and vibe of a venue on any given night. I want what he wants when it comes to being relaxed onstage singing the country blues.

Left to right: Will Sexton, Tim Easton, and J. T. Van Zandt, Catfish Concerts' first annual Townes Van Zandt tribute, Austin, Texas, March 18, 2014. Easton performed Van Zandt's Lightnin' Hopkins–inspired twelve-bar blues song "Brand New Companion." Photo by Brian T. Atkinson.

I don't pretend to be a country musician from Texas who fully understands where he came from, but as a performer I can certainly appreciate the vibe that he delivers onstage. He seems at home and so comfortable that you feel like you're at a house concert even if it's a big club. I'd like to make people feel the same way. Also, we like similar music. I'm a huge fan of Mississippi John Hurt, Doc Watson, Sonny Terry, and Brownie McGhee and that casual, happy, lighthearted blues style that they deliver, but they do it with serious stories, ones of experience. Only a musician that's been on the road as long as Ray Wylie can really deliver a show like he does.

Sobriety doesn't make songwriting easier, but it might make it more focused. Songwriting's a constant learning process and basically opening up a bag of magic tricks that's really difficult to explain whether you're high on drugs or sober. No one can explain it; otherwise everybody would be a songwriter. I'm relatively new to this sobriety gig, but I can say that it has caused a lot of introspection for me personally. In Ray's case, it appears that he just gravitated toward what's comfortable and what inspires him, which is telling stories with a country-blues backbeat. Ray's a lover of life and stories, and that's contagious. He appeals to the East Nashville bohemian mentality and people who do this because they love it. We're lifers who will do it forever no matter what. Ray's music is not for people who are on some false fast track to fame. His storytelling and the nature of his songwriting [are] for the students and troubadours of life.[5]

Elizabeth Cook

We love Ray Wylie Hubbard in [SiriusXM's] Outlaw Country. I discovered him through a girlfriend burning me a disc, and I heard the song that lured me in right away. I'd go on to discover a rich stockpile of all manner of songs, but "Screw You, We're from Texas" was it. You know the joke about the young bull and the old bull sitting on the hill staring down at all the cows they wanna go make love to? Ray is the cooler, older bull. He doesn't put a boot up anyone's ass while yelling over overwrought guitars, unless that accidentally happened on his way to the bar on his way to some gypsy-laden back room. He draws me to the dark side in a spiritual, sometimes

*Elizabeth Cook,
Cheatham Street
Warehouse, San
Marcos, Texas,
2015. Photo by Jenni
Finlay.*

*Ray Wylie Hubbard, the
Long Center, Austin,
Texas, September 19,
2010. Photo by Brian T.
Atkinson.*

comical way. I think it's his ear for detail. Also, he can make mon-
ster grooves and tones with next to no instrumentation.

I think he has yet to see his full influence surface in Nashville,
but it's coming. He follows his muse at all costs. I try to follow
my muse at all costs, but it takes practice, at least for me, being a
blonde in Nashville who back in the day had unartistic trappings.
Ray Wylie tried to teach me a fingerpicking pattern once on Enron
notebook paper. I'm still working on it, and I should get my nails
done. His lessons in how to write a line worth a million words is
something I try to keep in mind. I think Ray captures a vibe on
every level of his music-making that's gonna continue to be discovered and appreciated. It all jibes lyrically and musically into
this really unique thing that nobody but Ray does.[6]

Jaren Johnston (The Cadillac Three)

We signed with a management company down in Austin when we
started our band and played Texas shows a lot. We'd drive down
and play three shows and then drive back to Nashville. We were
hanging out with Josh Abbott, Kevin Fowler, and Cross Canadian
Ragweed. Those Texas storytellers would rave about this dude Ray
Wylie Hubbard. Then we played this writers-in-the-round benefit
in Austin at Midnight Rodeo with Josh Abbott, Jack Ingram, Kevin
Fowler, and Ray Wylie. He blew my mind with songs like "Snake
Farm." I was like, "This is the shit." We would listen to him on the
bus for the longest time. That was also our pump-up music before
the show and our walk-off music. As a songwriter, I've always been
into storytelling. We talked and became fast friends that night, and
we've been close ever since.

I'm a huge fan of cool syncopation and telling a story your own
way. Ray doesn't really care if something rhymes. He's not worried
about that as much as telling the story. I think that's really cool.
People write to rhyme, and they can lose their story because they
want their hook. Ray gets all that without even thinking about it.
It seems really natural. I'm a huge fan of Dylan where he's just
talking over a beat and a guitar riff. Some of my favorite people
like Shawn Mullins do that. Ray does that better than pretty much
anyone. I take a lot from that as far as what we do. Now other guys
like Eric Church have stumbled upon him, too.

My favorite Ray song right now is "Open G" on *Tell the Devil...I'm Gettin' There As Fast As I Can*. We had him open some shows on the last tour, and I couldn't stop talking about that line: "Take a glass or brass slide that's just the right weight / You take that slide, and shake the Jell-O on the plate." I'm like, "Who says shit like that?" It's brilliant and so conversational like that [James McMurtry song "Choctaw Bingo"] he does, "with a great big ol' hard-on like a bois d'arc fence post." He's amazing and has a way of saying things. He's one of those guys that songwriters want to rip off.

His songs seem really elementary, but they're harder than you would think. Songs like ["Mother Blues"] are intricate stories. He's doing them live, and nailing them word for word. I can tell you from firsthand experience that's not an easy thing to do. I forget lyrics all the time. He's doing more lyrics with more depth than I am, and I've never seen him slip up. I'm singing a verse and a chorus, going, "Oh god. What's next?" This guy's on a different level. The fact that he can sing about things so elemental like a snake farm and still grip you in is awesome.

Tour poster for the Cadillac Three's Legacy *(Big Machine Records, 2017). Left to right: Neil Mason, Jaren Johnston, Kelby Ray. Ray Wylie Hubbard opened the Cadillac Three's sold-out album release show for* Legacy *at the Ryman Auditorium in Nashville, Tennessee, on August 31, 2017. Photo of poster by Brian T. Atkinson.*

JAREN JOHNSTON (THE CADILLAC THREE)

I was born and raised in Nashville, and I was into country music in the 1990s like Garth Brooks and his songs like "Papa Loved Mama," but I was also into Rage Against the Machine and Beastie Boys. I naturally gravitate toward that musical style with heavy backbeat with me spitting the lyric over it in a very natural southern way. Ray does that, but in a more cool, old school Texas approach. When we were going down to Austin every weekend, we'd come home and write, and I'd be like, "That sounds like Ray Wylie." There was so much cool music coming out of there. I'd never heard that Texas thing before. I guess that stompy-talky thing is what ties us and Ray together. Also, he stumbles upon hooks in a way that I like to as well.

My songs like "Soundtrack to a Six-Pack" and "Peace Love & Dixie" were inspired by Ray. We were on the bus in Oklahoma when we wrote that last one. I had had the title "Peace Love & Dixie" for a while. It's basically the story behind that party scene at the moon tower in *Dazed and Confused*. That was pretty much us in high school: "Party at the moon tower? Hell, yeah." It's a real southern hippie thing, with kegs in the back of the truck. At the same time, we were listening to a lot of Ray Wylie. There have been a lot of songs as an outside songwriter in Nashville that I've had a lot of luck with, like that Jake Owen song "Beachin'" [cowritten by Johnston, Jon Nite, and Jimmy Robbins]. It was a big old hit, and it's because I'm into that vibe and way of telling a story. I get a lot of that from Ray.

We did a tour last year where we had five or six openers like Brent Cobb, Aubrie Sellers, and Ray. He did about five or six shows. I'd been friends with Ray before that, but then we got to travel together and hang. So much fun. I watched his show every night. I think there's just a mutual respect between our own bands. We both do our own thing, and we're not trying to be a part of any club. He's the same way. He does it his way. We got to talking at the end of that tour, and I was like, "Man, I'd love to do this again." We talked about getting together and writing some songs, but we haven't yet. So when we knew we were gonna headline the Ryman when the new record came out, I was like, "The coolest route to go for support would be to get Ray Wylie and the boys up here." Sure enough, he said, "Hell yeah."

Having one of my favorite songwriters open for us at a sold-out night at the Ryman [in late August 2017] was the perfect top-off on a bucket-list night. There was a tornado that night in Nashville, and I had my new child. I was on our bus with my wife and child and unfortunately didn't get to see his set. That's the only time I didn't get to see him, but my dad watched and said it was amazing. My dad went to a lot of those shows Ray did with us. He'd be the first one in there to see Ray because he loved his jokes. I love that bit when he says, "If I were a girl, I'd be a big old slut."

Ray's real. The older fans are there going, "Hell yeah, this guy's still out here doing it with passion at his age and still rocking." The young kids appreciate the coolness of the songwriting if they have any taste in music. Ray works for everybody. I think "Snake Farm" will be a song that lives on forever because it's so different and groovy and tells such an interesting story. I think Ray will be remembered as one of the most underrated songwriters, but I would love for him to get bigger than Dallas. Of course, the other half of me hopes he stays right where he is so he can be my little secret. We support him because we love his work. I think we're gonna take him back out on the road again and maybe take him to Europe, too, because I think they would freak out over him.

All three of us were born and raised in Nashville, and we've been pretty much shouting his name for the last five, six years here. Eric Church is a big fan now.[7] Sometimes it only takes a little spark with an artist who's already super cool and talented with their own vibe. People [catch on] here, and it spreads like wildfire. I remember talking to our drummer's uncle in Seattle, and he said, "Oh yeah, I used to listen to him in the seventies." Ray's still out doing it, and he's the coolest one in the room. He doesn't think that, but we all do. I'm always sitting around trying to get his autograph and get my picture made with him. He's the dude songwriters want to be.[8]

Eric Church

I started writing with Nashville songwriters in 2000. Those guys are craftsmen, the best in the world, but there's freedom and wildness in what Ray Wylie's doing. Ray's so damn creative. He taps into my soul with his songwriting and the way he plays, sings, and crafts a story. You think the characters he develops come from his imagination, but then you look at places he's been and things he's done. These people are characters he's met through his time playing. I love what the freedom in his music makes me feel like. Ray Wylie's a damn national treasure, a poet and absolutely one of the best we've ever had. He sets a scene better than anyone. You're already in when he sings, "I've got a woman who's wild as Rome / She likes being naked and gazed upon" [from "Drunken Poet's Dream"].

I had the title "Desperate Man" and knew where I wanted to go with the song. Ray Wylie and I sat down, and the first thing he said was, "I've been there. I once went to a fortune-teller to get my [future] read. She told me I didn't have one. That's pretty desperate." We fell into the song and finished it in a few hours. Ray has always been good about the visual element of lyrics. You close your eyes and listen to him sing these words, and you can absolutely visualize, feel, and see [the story]. His words aren't just filling a space. Ray's meticulous and places every word well. He painted colors on the canvas for "Desperate Man" and made the images come to life.

I told Ray we were going into the studio the next day and cut "Desperate Man." He sent me a text one day and said, "How did 'Desperate Man' turn out?" I said, "Well, I cut it, and it's gonna be the first single [and title track to Church's 2018 album]." All he sent back was "Damn." I said, "We're gonna do a video, and I'd love for you to be in it." We got him to come up. We had him play a middleman, but instead of drugs, we were dealing vinyl. He said, "This is not too foreign for me. You know, back in the seventies, this is pretty much what I did." I told him he played the part so well. He said, "Yeah, this is reality."

Ray's a funny, interesting guy. You can't take your eyes off him. We had fun spending all day with him when we were shooting the video. We hung out and talked about music, all the years he's played, and where he's played, a pretty special day for me. He's been a troubadour for forty years, and success hasn't mattered. He's just played. I have such a respect for his love of music. We need more of his uniqueness. He can do something in a way that no one else can. He's the dead thumb king. I think he deserves to be in [Nashville's] Songwriters Hall of Fame. More younger artists listening to Ray Wylie Hubbard would be better for the health of country music.

I was meticulous in choosing who I name-dropped in [the

Eric Church promotional photo. Courtesy Essential Broadcast Media;
photo by John Peets.

title track to Church's 2015 Academy of Country Music Album of
the Year–nominated record] "Mr. Misunderstood." I chose Elvis
Costello, Jeff Tweedy, and Ray Wylie Hubbard because they influenced me and are people who I think are badasses. I don't know
how many people in country music would immediately recognize all
three names. Some might know one or two. Name-checking them
was about respect, but also I was putting something out there that
people might not listen to all the time.

   Ray Wylie contacted me after "Mr. Misunderstood" came out,
and we chatted. He said, "Thank you. I love the song." I was on the
tour not too much later and knew we were gonna be in his neck
of the woods. The only show we had on that leg in Texas was in
Dallas. I reached out to Mother [his wife, Judy] Hubbard and said,
"Hey, does Ray wanna come out and play?" He said he'd love to
and asked what song I wanted to do. I said, "Screw You, We're from
Texas," which was the first song I knew from back in 2003. I said,
"It's gonna bring the house down." He said, "Let's do it." He drove
himself to Dallas in a van. We got calls that there's this guy at the
gate in a van, and he says he's Ray Wylie Hubbard. We said, "Well,
shit. It probably is. Let him in."

Ray made soundcheck around three o'clock. We didn't play that song in the show until probably ten-thirty, so we set Ray and Judy up with a room there. We hung out and had a really cool day. We knocked around onstage and jammed. I know it was a cool day for me, but I think it was for both of us. There's no reason that Ray Wylie Hubbard shouldn't be playing [the American Airlines Center] himself. Music's weird. There probably were twenty thousand people there that night. It was really, really cool to be able to bring him out. He brought the house down just like I thought he would. People will still come up to me now and say, "I was at that show where Ray Wylie Hubbard came up."[9]

Ronnie Dunn (Brooks & Dunn)

I received a voicemail maybe five, six years ago. This guy says, "Hey, man, this is Ray Wylie Hubbard. Tony Joe White told me to call you about us maybe getting together to try to write a song or two." I was touring pretty heavy with Brooks & Dunn back then and, truth be known, [even] after having over fifty Top Ten and twenty-six num-

Left to right: Lucas Hubbard, Ray Wylie Hubbard, and Ronnie Dunn. Background: Kyle Snyder. Texas Heritage Songwriters Hall of Fame induction ceremony, Paramount Theater, Austin, Texas, February 24, 2018. Courtesy Texas Heritage Songwriters Association; photo by Ted Parker Jr.

ber one radio hits, I was a little intimidated. I didn't return the call for a few weeks. Mojo flows through his veins like fine aged wine.

I went to school in Abilene, Texas, which is way north of cool by Austin standards. My buddies and I grew up on the Outlaw Country movement. In fact, it was the catalyst that nudged me into developing a real interest in country music. Willie, Waylon, Jerry Jeff Walker, and Ray Wylie, to name a few, weren't Nashville country. They brought a broader sensibility to the table. They turned their backs on boxed-in commercialism. They wore their defiant rock demeanors like gunfighters wore six-shooters. They were dope-smoking, whiskey-drinking, hard-living hippie cowboys. They checked out, turned their "give a shitters" off when they walked onto the scene. They took pride in flipping off redneck kickers and play-by-the-rules, all-for-money commercial country music, and the world went crazy over them.

Ray's a wise philosopher-poet these days with a restless force down in him. He has something to say, and that twisted-hungry, cut-to-the-quick humor that drove him as a young man to write "Redneck Mother" drives him in true troubadour fashion to continue to pursue the craft of songwriting even more so today. He's driven by a force that lures him through a maze of bars, beer joints, and honky-tonks that have a way of chewing men up and spitting them out torn and tattered. By the grace of God and rehab, he's victoriously survived the pitfalls of this journey we call music. He's come out the other side as a wise and meticulously distilled force. I'm proud to know and call him a friend.[10]

Chris Robinson (Black Crowes)

I would put Ray in the same tradition as Townes Van Zandt. These are people who have surrendered all rationale for the muse. He's on a different trajectory, but he's in there as far as what a troubadour really is. He's in the tradition of great American songwriters, whether that's John Prine, Townes, or Tom Rush. Ultimately, I see Ray more as a folk character. He's someone who's done what he's done outside the mainstream and defies the genre-specific confines that the business needs to keep all the numbers in order. I think true expression flows through a real writer's fingers like

Left to right: Ed Jurdi (Band of Heathens) and Chris Robinson, Grit 'n Groove Festival, Luckenbach, Texas, 2010. Photo by Robbyn Dodd (www.robbyndodd photography.com).

water to mean something else to the listener and to someone who covers his songs. Ultimately, Ray has in his pocket the magic bag of poetry. Either you have that bag or you don't.

I tried to get out of the Black Crowes in the early 2000s. I called my good friend Charlie Sexton. I said, "Do you know any bass players?" Charlie said, "I know a great bass player, and he's also gonna turn out to be your best friend." I was like, "All right." It was George Reiff, and we were very close. We did lots of tours and made lots of recordings and did sessions together. So my friendship with Ray Wylie was born through George. He was an outstanding musician and an outstanding person, one of the best out of all of us who live out there on the golden road.

My friends in Austin lost a great friend when George passed.

George played in Ray's band, engineered and mixed Ray's records, and produced him. I know Ray loved him. He was a great friend and confidant. Ray's not just a good-time person. He's also very sincere and caring. He's been really helpful with checking in with me and being really compassionate since we lost our friend. I surrendered myself to the muse many years ago, too, and I think those kind of relationships are [valuable]. I respect Ray. He inspires me.

I first heard about Ray through ¡Viva Terlingua! and the early records I collected, but I didn't know him in the same way I would from George, who got me thinking about Ray and into his orbit. Ray had me on some of his shows out there in Texas, and in the past eight or nine years we've kept up with correspondence and friendship. I had Ray come open a show for the Black Crowes last time we attempted that no-win situation. Of course, the crowd in New York [dug him]. He's naturally charming, and there's something interesting about Ray that makes people gravitate toward him. He has an appeal to people that's really unique.

I always like people who blend the inspirations of roots music and make them their own. He's not a blues artist. He's not a country artist. He's both those things, but I see Ray as a quintessential rock and roll character. He's blessed with the storyteller vibe, and the devil's in the details, with the poetic construct in a traditional way. I like when a songwriter is closer to a poet and really lives outside the music business, so I like the independent streak in Ray. Of course that translates to the songs he's writing, whether they're heartfelt or humorous.

He has the Texas charms and colloquialisms. That language comes from another time and era, like musician language through country music and the blues through folk music. Even though the world around us changes, the energy and the language don't. We use the same imagery that represents the human condition—good, bad, and indifferent. That's where Ray's lyrical prowess reigns supreme. He can make it alive, which is the real test.

I played a couple of Ray's Grit 'n Groove festivals, which are super laid-back and funky in the coolest way. I met a lot of people and had a great time the first year. The second year I played [in 2011], it was a little bigger, so there was a cool collection of people there like Tony Joe White and Joe Walsh. Ray's eclectic ways pulled

Left to right: Tony Joe White, Ray Wylie Hubbard, and Chris Robinson, Grit 'n Groove Festival, Whitewater Amphitheater, 2011. Courtesy Judy Hubbard; photo by Matt Mendenhall.

Ray Wylie Hubbard, Grit 'n Groove Festival, Whitewater Amphitheater, New Braunfels, Texas, April 2, 2011. Photo by Jenni Finlay.

all these people together from different elements, but it still had a cohesive afternoon and evening of music, not a show-biz trip like, "Hey, Cleveland, how are you doing?" Ray has a wit and charm and connection that people find compelling. He has cool style, being an old Texas character, the coolest-looking old guy I know. I hope I look that cool when I get old, but I don't think it's gonna happen.

As you would imagine, Ray Wylie's one of my favorite people whenever I get the opportunity to hang out with him or be on the phone. Any interaction with Ray is always a big smile, and I think most people you talk to would do anything for the guy. He's a sweetheart and as charming as can be, with a beautiful family. I think the world would be a much radder place if we had a couple hundred thousand more Ray Wylie Hubbards walking around.[11]

Paul Thorn

I heard Ray Wylie Hubbard name-checked me on *Tell the Devil...I'm Gettin' There As Fast As I Can* [on "Lucifer and the Fallen Angels"], which is pretty cool. I met Ray when an early booking agent got me a gig to open up for him for one hundred fifty dollars. It was in Texas, and the actor Bill Paxton was there. I remember that I went cuckoo over Ray's music when I saw what he did. He became one of my favorite writers and an influence on me as a writer. I learned a lot of my writing style from him. I like that Ray Wylie has a killer groove, and there are lots of biblical references in his songs. They're not gospel at all, but he references the Bible a lot. I relate to that, growing up a preacher's kid, and that's in my music a lot.

Spirituality is everything in my songwriting. That's what made me the way I am because of my history in the Bible Belt and Deep South vernacular. I'm from Tupelo, Mississippi, and literally grew up going to the churches that Elvis Presley attended. We had the black churches and the white ones, and most people only went to the church of their color. My family enjoyed services with both folks. They used to sing what I call country-western gospel in the white churches, with the quartets and all that. They played a more rhythm and blues gospel in the black churches. I cut my teeth in those environments just like Elvis. Early gospel music is definitely the biggest contributor to what I do.[12]

Paul Thorn promotional photograph. Photo by Lee Harrelson.

I wrote "I Backslide on Friday" [from Thorn's 2014 album *Too Blessed to Be Stressed*] as a tongue-in-cheek song about the human condition. The term *backslide* is something they say in church. They say you backslid if you get right with God and then you sin. You know, sometimes I tell myself I'm only gonna eat ice cream on Sundays. Then you eat it every day because you're weak as a human being. So I just wrote this song about "I backslide on Friday to make everybody else comfortable." They know they're not alone in their struggle to do right. I've been singing it at shows and people connect. They all relate to weaknesses causing them to backslide.[13]

Everything Ray does inspires me. He can get you interested in the most mundane things, like "Snake Farm," such a cool story about two people having a love affair in a snake farm. He has this song "Wasp's Nest" [from *A: Enlightenment, B: Endarkenment (Hint: There Is No C)*] that's about having a wasp nest on his porch and how he was gonna deal with it. That's such a simple thing, but he made it interesting. He makes the listener want to kill those wasps because they're stinging everybody. The wasp is a metaphor in life. It could be an actual wasp or a person, your next-door neighbor who you can't get along with.[14]

David Lowery (Cracker)

There was a radio station called KFAT [94.5 FM, from 1975–1983] in Santa Cruz, California, an alternative hippie beach town with surfers and skateboarders back in the eighties before Silicon Valley came across the Santa Cruz Mountains. That station, [which became influential Americana station KPIG], as near as I can figure, was the first alternative country station ever. They would play really eclectic music like the Grateful Dead and the more roots-leaning stuff like the Blasters, Willie Nelson, Outlaw Country, and Texas music. I first knew of Ray Wylie Hubbard when I heard Jerry Jeff Walker's version of "Up Against the Wall Redneck Mother" on that station.

There was this place there called O. T. Price's [Music Hall], which was a disco, but they always had these underground Outlaw Country nights that KFAT would present. All my friends and the Camper Van Beethoven members knew that this was an isolated thing for California. Nowhere else would anybody else really know about this music. It was an early outpost for Americana, alt-country, and Texas music in California at the beach along Monterey Bay. In a lot of ways, that's where the country influence gets injected into Camper Van Beethoven's otherwise indie folk-rock music. The music had many elements of what you like at twenty-one, music that seems real and authentic.

The music was saying things that mainstream music doesn't say. We were into punk rock and the post-new-wave underground music, and this music had a similarity. There's a mystique with songwriters like Ray Wylie Hubbard and Terry Allen. Terry was popular in Santa Cruz back then. We'd go see his shows, and that was part of this rather obscure underground [movement] in California culture that got to us. Ray Wylie Hubbard was right up there for us. He and Terry Allen were an alternative voice in country music. X, the Blasters, and the Los Angeles punk bands were dabbling with country elements in their music, and we looked to people like Ray Wylie Hubbard as founding intellects and writers of this movement.

Cracker's *Countrysides* album came together between 2002 and 2004. At that point, a serious Americana and alt-country movement had come along. In our mind, a lot of that referenced the more polished, sweet, less honky-tonk edges of country music. *Countrysides* was us leaning toward something edgier, harder, more shitkicker honky-tonk music. This isn't a dis on the Old 97's or Ryan Adams or anyone, but we felt like the shitkicker stuff wasn't more represented. *Countrysides* is us diving right into that. I've always loved [the album's third track] "Redneck Mother" and had dabbled with it over the years.

I feel like I heard that song again in the UK on one of the eclectic BBC Radio channels around that time. That's the thing about

Left to right: Cracker's David Lowery and Johnny Hickman, South by Southwest, Austin, Texas, March 2005. Photo by Brian T. Atkinson.

someone like Ray Wylie Hubbard. I feel like I could be in a small town in Germany, and at least some people would know who he is or would be very familiar with other Texas writers. I said, "You know, we ought to pull that into our repertoire." We covered that song because it represented a missing chapter in the history of non-Nashville country in California. I like covering songs like that, where the writers and performers haven't gotten their due from the general public.

We had put "Redneck Mother" into our repertoire, and we ended up on some shows that were a mix of southern rock and country. We were either in Little Rock or Shreveport playing with four bands one time. We were the first band on the bill, and Lynyrd Skynyrd was the headliner in this coliseum. We had about thirty minutes to play, and "Up Against the Wall Redneck Mother" was the second-to-last song in our set list. When we started playing that song, the whole crowd stood up and started singing along with the chorus. So we got to the end of song and I said, "Thank you. Goodnight." The other guys were confused, but that's where you want to end the show. You're not gonna follow that with one of your own songs. I think we had one of our hits like "Get Off This" or "Teen Angst" last, but we didn't even play it. The response to "Redneck Mother" was overwhelming.[15]

Cody Canada

My older musician friends from Stillwater, Oklahoma, went down to Jerry Jeff Walker's Labor Day party in Luckenbach one time. They came back ranting and raving about Ray's song "Wanna Rock and Roll." They were singing it at [Stillwater's] the Wormy Dog. That's when I really got turned on to him. I was eighteen or nineteen. I was fortunate that we met not long after. He said he wanted to write songs together, and I told him that I was really nervous to be around him. He said, "Well, you're gonna have to get over that." I never forget that. I use that with folks these days when they say things like that to me. "You're gonna have to get over being nervous if we're gonna get any work done."

Ray brought the idea for "Cooler-N-Hell" to me when we were doing his *Roots & Branches* show at KNBT radio in New Braunfels.

I was driving this candy apple red Camaro, and we were inside getting ready to do the show. He was talking about writing a song about a car. I said, "I got a Camaro," and took him out back to show him. He said, "There it is, man. Candy apple red." That song really just rolled off the tongue from there. It really started flowing once he had that line written: "A '68 Camaro, candy apple red / Four-speed transmission, chrome heads / Rev her up and she casts a spell / Some things here under heaven are just cooler 'n' hell."

Poster for Cody Canada and Stoney LaRue song swap at Cheatham Street Warehouse. Courtesy Jenni Finlay archives.

Ray's a really good cowriter. He cheerleads. You know he has the lines himself, but he wants to write with you. So he'll give you the "You're almost there. Keep going. Just a couple more twists and turns, and you'll get it." I'm sure he could just nail the song and walk away, but he really enjoys writing with other people. I'd give him a line on "Cooler-N-Hell," and he'd say, "There you go. I knew you had it." He's so good about encouraging and helping you weigh options. "Maybe try a couple lines and see which is your best one."

Going into Gurf Morlix's studio to record "Cooler-N-Hell" for *Delirium Tremolos* really brought me back to reality. Cross Canadian Ragweed went from recording in Denton to Cedar Creek [in Austin] and then to California to some bigger studios that the label paid for. Gurf's showed that you don't really need a giant all-wood studio with acoustics everywhere. You can do this without spending all this money. I remember walking into Gurf's with my guitar in a case, and he said, "You can bring one or the other in: the guitar or the case." There wasn't enough room for both in there.

Ray warned me long ago about volume onstage. He said, "You don't need to be the loudest band on the scene. Eventually your ears are gonna pay for it." He was right. I listened. As far as playing with him, even now I look next to me and think, Wow, that's Ray Wylie Hubbard playing with me. I can't believe I'm onstage playing or that he invited me. There's a lot of trust between us, and we were very straightforward with each other in the beginning. That's what you get onstage with him: trust and confidence. That's something a lot of us lack sometimes. There's good days and bad days, but he showed me gratitude. You know, you could be digging a ditch. Get up there and strut your stuff.

I started playing "Wanna Rock and Roll" live with my friend Mike McClure from the Great Divide, and every time we were in the studio, that song always came back up. We had enough original songs on Ragweed's *Soul Gravy* [2004], but I always like to throw something in to show people my influences and where I come from. We did the song in one take because we'd already played it so much. You know, we were extremely busy at that point. We'd pop into the studio for a day get tones, record two songs, break down, then do it again. "Wanna Rock and Roll" was the last song recorded for the record, and it really was a labor of love. I called Ray, got his blessing to record the song, and whipped it out.

Ray taught me don't take yourself so seriously. When I started out, there was no safety net, and I regret some of those songs. That was before I met Ray. I would belt it out, record, and move on. I'd listen to it later on my radio or in my car and go, "Man, I wished I would have tweaked it a bit." Then I got carried away with being too picky. Ray told me one time, "Do it if it feels good. We were born with instincts." I've carried that with me a long time. Ray really took me under his wing when I moved down to Texas and helped me shape what I'm doing nowadays and I do give him credit, but I don't think I've given him enough. Now that I'm getting older, I think in terms of when you're a kid and your dad tells you something. You're like, "Eh. The hell's he know?" Then you get older and realize he knows what he's talking about. That's where I've been with Ray over the last few years.

We talk about getting together for a cup of coffee every time we see each other, but we still don't do it. He's like, "Man, when I'm home, I'm home." That's how I am, too, but it's nice to know that he's there. Also, he hooked my kids up with meeting Joe Walsh a couple years ago in Houston. I got to do a pretty good-sized show with Joe in Las Vegas from that meeting. Ray's the friend that keeps on giving for me.

We talk about a lot of music. We always go back to old blues, the music that formed us as musicians and made us do what we do. We also talk about cars, guitars, and kids. Now his kid's a grown man, but Ray was good to me when I first had kids. I always had questions for him: "How long is too long to be gone away from your kids? What's too long at home when the family gets tired of you?" I hope I have the fans that he has when I'm seventy years old. We went on a whole month run last month from Washington to Wisconsin, and there wasn't one night that we didn't play "Wanna Rock and Roll." There wasn't one night when there wasn't someone with a Ray story to tell and the nice things he said about my wife, me, and our kids.

As much as Ray hated it before and then came to terms with it, "Redneck Mother" is gonna be his legacy. There's so much more to his music when you dive headlong into it, but that song hooks people in. There are so many songs that are so much better than "Redneck Mother." I'm not dogging the song. Everybody wants to have a tune that makes people laugh and makes the bar rowdy and fun. Hopefully, he won't kill me for saying it, but his legacy will be "Redneck Mother," and he should be very, very proud to wave that flag.[16]

William Clark Green

You know, Roger Creager has "The Everclear Song" that says, "I'm bigger and badder than John Wayne / And cooler than Steve Earle." In my head, Steve Earle might have been their cool guys, but for my generation they're Jack Ingram and Ray Wylie Hubbard. Ray Wylie Hubbard and Jack Ingram are so fucking cool. Jack walks in, and he's the coolest guy in the room. I still get nervous talking with him. I don't know why he's cool, but he is. Ray's the same way. Ray can play an E and an A chord for thirty minutes, and you're glued to him. He doesn't give a fuck. He has such aura and confidence. Everything they say has purpose and substance. They listen twice as much as they talk, and I think that translates in the songwriting.

I saw Ray for the first time at the Cactus Theater in Lubbock with my dad. I was a freshman or sophomore in college. Ray was playing with Chris Knight, and my dad and I are both big Chris Knight fans. I guess my dad heard Chris Knight on the radio. He drove from College Station to Hastings in Conroe to pick up a tape of his first record. He liked it a lot. Chris Knight was something we could agree on, and there's not much at that stage in life that a father and son can agree on. When we found out he was playing in Lubbock, it was a chance for my dad and me to hang out. He opened for Ray Wylie. I don't think my dad's a very big fan of Ray Wylie, though, which probably made me like him even more. My dad's big on music, but he never got into the hippie cowboy stuff like Jerry Jeff Walker and Ray Wylie.

I loved Ray's banter. He was hilarious. I was writing songs back then, but I wasn't taking my professional life seriously because I didn't think it was possible. I remember how entertaining the show was outside of him being a super talented writer and guitar player. It was very creative and funny, a lot like Jack Ingram's *Acoustic Motel* [2005]. I love those records so much because of the stories you get to hear. They show you the humility of the artist and open up a whole new world as opposed to just me thinking that you

Left to right: William Clark Green and Kent Finlay, Texas Music Theater, San Marcos, April 27, 2014. Photo by Brian T. Atkinson.

could only impress people onstage by singing with an opera voice or play guitar like Jimi Hendrix. Banter was a whole new thing, and Ray's the king.

I love the obvious Ray Wylie songs, but also "Cooler-N-Hell." Everybody heard "Redneck Mother" and "Snake Farm" that night in Lubbock, but when he played "Cooler-N-Hell," it was a strange transformation. He transformed into this biker-type coolness. He got this Jack Ingram thing where he's just badass. Ray and Hayes [Carll] wrote that song "Drunken Poet's Dream," and I don't really have a version that I like more than the other. Ray was always a mentor to the songwriters I looked up to like Hayes. I never got a chance to talk with Ray much outside of being on *Roots & Branches*. I never got a chance to go to his house to write with him, but that's probably more my fault than anything, since I don't live in the Austin area. Ray's just a legend.

There's such a huge debate on when the Red Dirt scene started, but for me it was with Guy Clark, Lyle Lovett, Townes Van Zandt, Ray Wylie, Jerry Jeff, and Rusty Wier. That's when there were more poets than anything in the Texas songwriter scene. They're the forefathers. Ray's a songwriter's songwriter in that legendary category. The cool thing about him is that he can play a college festival like Larry Joe Taylor's, and everybody in the freaking crowd will sing along to his songs. He can play a sit-down show with a dinner-and-wine atmosphere, and everybody would have a good time, too.

He's a classic and timeless songwriter. Also, he doesn't give a fuck the older he gets. I know he thinks he's the "Redneck Mother" guy, but my generation thinks he's the "Snake Farm" guy. I don't know if he likes that or not. "Redneck Mother" got him out there, but my generation knows "Snake Farm" pretty well. It's such a creative song. Seeing something out of the box and being creative with it is how [Green's 2015 album] *Ringling Road* came about. I'd rather do that than write songs that are just good for radio. Songwriters could learn a lot from the way he writes. You can flirt with this and that in your writing. Ray's like Guy Clark. They write the greatest songs we love.

I think the best part about Ray as a songwriter is that he can write a tongue-in-cheek song like "Screw You, We're from Texas." It's really hard to sing something without sounding offensive these days. I can see the artistic value in it and the sarcasm. He's saying people in Texas have this amazing pride in being from there, and it's a jab at that, but I can also sing that song in my head and go, "Screw you, we're from Texas." I love the duality. He can get the rednecks and the super thinkers both singing along to it. It's impossible to do that. Ray should run for president.[17]

Roger Creager

I discovered Ray when I came of age as a music lover and music maker in the 1990s. I had known about him growing up, but that's the age when you begin to explore songwriting. You hear a song and say, "I hear what they did there." Sometimes you say, "I see what they were *trying* to do there." There's never that moment with him. He always nails it. I think of Ray Wylie as blues, rock, and folk more than country. I mostly do country, but when you mention Texas music, there's a pretty wide spectrum. Stevie Ray Vaughan, Jerry Jeff Walker, Willie Nelson, Waylon Jennings. There are four very different styles right there. Ray Wylie has his own unique style and has found a niche, and it's awesome.

I think his songs are beautiful and timeless, and they will stand on their own. I've always been drawn to his lack of BS. His songs aren't flowers and perfumes. They're teeth and hair. "Snake Farm" is hilarious. "Conversation with the Devil" is, too. Being funny in songwriting is extremely difficult, but Ray does that. He's one of the best. Comedy doesn't usually lend itself to music unless you're a comedian like Rodney Carrington, and he's never been accused of being a great songwriter. Ray Wylie Hubbard captures comedy without losing the song's integrity.

I've met Ray multiple times at shows, and I've seen him be a ringleader. I used to do a songwriting tour throughout Texas around Christmas. I brought down these songwriters from Nashville who

Roger Creager, Larry Joe Taylor's Rhymes and Vines Music Festival, Stephenville, Texas, September 2011. Photo by Dave Hensley.

were all CMA songwriters of the year, big hit makers with multiple Grammys. I'd see him ringlead the whole operation like, "Hey, guys, let's move it." He was not intimidated by them. He became friends with them, but he certainly was not enamored by their success or anything else. He's very comfortable with who he is and how he does it. I think that puts everyone around him at ease.[18]

Cory Morrow

Ray was at the forefront of [today's Texas country] movement way before we all got involved. I remember him telling me stories about running around with the [Fabulous] Freebirds. I was a Von Erich fan, and the Freebirds were the bad guys in professional wrestling. I watched Friday-night wrestling when I'd visit my dad in San Antonio as a kid. Ray was there at all those San Antonio matches, and he'd tell me stories from them. The background on Ray's life is surreal. We have a really unique relationship. We don't see each other very often, but when we do, we pick up right where we left off and the love is as strong as the day we last parted ways. My heart wishes I could spend more time with Ray and Judy, but our paths cross as they should and I'm grateful to know him.

I like sobriety better simply because I can remember more. There was a time when I was doing a lot of drugs, and I didn't think I could write a good song unless I was messed up. Ray and I had a conversation about that. You learn that you can write whenever you want once you learn to write sober. Sobriety is very important. It's easy to get off track and think maybe taking this or that would help, but the truth is, you have the opportunity to get to a peaceful place with sobriety. Your natural energy can come out and you can tap in and write something that comes from deep down. You can tap in with drugs, but then you're tapped out for a day.

Honestly, sobriety's not the change I point to in my life. God and Jesus have been the change and the point of focus for me. Sobriety came as a result of realizing that nothing I do after taking a drink is a good thing. I decided to remove the hindrances in my life, and that started with alcohol and drugs. I was in a better place to receive God's word after I did. I can really focus on studying what that's all about and what my life means. As far as writing goes, being sober is just a side effect of my focus on trying to write truth and being truthful about the words that I write down. I don't want them just to be poetic and pretty. I want them to be truthful as well.

Ray and I have talked about spirituality, but we haven't dug into the faith in Christ. We do both agree that there is a God and a power higher than ourselves, and we seek to know more about that. I think Ray would agree that we're all constantly evolving and that evolution is what keeps the spark going as far as being a songwriter and performer. If you're not constantly growing and challenging yourself in your life and writing and spirit, you can get run down into a rut. I think my getting sober and finding God after twenty years of being a drunken idiot is a similar path to Ray's. We both found something greater and realized where our faults and weaknesses are. We realized that we're not gonna have much of a life as singer-songwriters if we're killing ourselves with drugs and alcohol.

Cory Morrow,
Luckenbach,
Texas, February
2017. Photo by
Robbyn Dodd
(www.robbyndodd
photography.com).

Ray's the godfather for all the younger singer-songwriters as far as approaching the craft. His gravel and realness really draw me in. He's a poet who writes gutsy songs that aren't pretty and perfect like "Conversation with the Devil," "Screw You, We're from Texas," and "Drunken Poet's Dream." "Snake Farm" cracks me up. He has a way with words and letting the truth come out. I think his legacy will be one that's held with high reverence. We all stand humbly before Ray, and yet he humbles himself before us as well. Everybody wants to go write with Ray. Everybody wants to be his friend. What's amazing is that all you have to do is knock on the door, and you're automatically accepted. He loves each and every one of us with equality. He sees something beautiful and meaningful in us, and I think that speaks to his spiritual depth.[19]

Randy Rogers

I was from North Texas, so I heard a lot of George Strait on the radio. I started listening to people like Jerry Jeff Walker, Robert Earl Keen, and Ray Wylie Hubbard when I got to college in San Marcos around 1995. Honestly, Ray's completely different from anything I would have listened to growing up. His songwriting was completely new and fresh to me, even though Ray had been around a long time. The bluesy thing was something I could dive into and listen. *Dangerous Spirits* and *Loco Gringo's Lament* were the first two records I was privy to when I got to college. Obviously, "Wanna Rock and Roll" stood out to me and the friends I was running around with at the time. That opened the Pandora's box to Ray.

I grew up dreaming about playing Gruene Hall, and I got to play there for the first time because of Ray. I was working for a publicity company called Propaganda Group as an intern in my junior year of college. I got to know Judy and Ray through that agency. I had sent my CD to Gruene Hall. They told me that I wasn't country or Americana. I needed to have an edge that I didn't, so they wouldn't book me there. It was frustrating to say the least, because that was my dream. I was working at a pool company at the time, and I was out in Wimberley cleaning up this pool that had been flooded. My phone rang, and it was Judy.

She said, "What are you doing?" I said, "I'm cleaning up this

Left to right: Kent Finlay and Randy Rogers, Cheatham Street Warehouse, June 14, 2014. Photo by Brian T. Atkinson.

flooded pool." There was literally a flooded toilet in the pool. It was a disgusting job. She said, "What do you have tonight?" "Nothing." "Get your ass to Gruene Hall. You're gonna open up for Ray." I quit my pool-cleaning job on the spot and got my guitar player. We hauled ass to Gruene. We set up some stools on the stage, and we were gonna open acoustic for Ray. We were soundchecking, and Judy walks over and says, "You need to get rid of those stools. When you open for Ray, you stand up, and you don't play thirty-one minutes. You play thirty minutes, and you get your ass off the stage." We became friends after that, and we opened for Ray with a full band a couple times at different places and festivals.

We always talked about routing [a tour together], but we never did. [Eric Church and Patty Griffin producer] Jay Joyce and I started talking about Ray and the song "Fuzzy" [on Rogers's 2013 album *Trouble*, which Joyce produced]. The idea we had for that song fit his style and guitar playing and everything he can bring to the table. Jay and Ray had been friends through Eric Church, so I called Ray up, and he was kind enough to come in to do the song with us. It was a lot of fun. Ray's so laid-back and easy to work with. He's kind and thoughtful. He really dug into the track with us. We got everything we wanted. His raspy voice screaming "Fuzzy" was just cool as shit to me.

People like Ray have endorsed [younger bands] like us, and now we have a good gig because they did. He and Judy were people for me who said, "Hey, kid. You got this. You just gotta focus and write songs and be serious about the music business, not just the music. You have to put yourself in the right situations and make the right choices." I'll forever be thankful. I didn't know him when he was young and partying, but he would have been the alpha male in any situation. He has such a vibe, a cool factor that very few people have. People look at Ray and say, "I wish I looked that cool" or "I wish I was that cool." There's no way to learn that, man. He has a swag to him. Ray's just the coolest fucking guy in any room.[20]

Nino Cooper (Dirty River Boys)

We cowrote "Down by the River" with Ray Wylie Hubbard about drug violence in Juárez, Mexico, which borders our hometown, El Paso. Where we grew up is its own musical bubble. It's so separated from the rest of Texas. When we grew up and were forming the Dirty River Boys, we weren't even familiar with the Texas scene, but living on the border, you're definitely having some Latin influences and that desert feel in the songs that you're writing. I grew up learning old Mexican songs from my dad and sitting in with a band he called Los Paisanos that did Mexican and American folk songs. I don't know if you can consider El Paso part of the Texas music scene, but that might've helped us develop a more unique sound than a lot of Texas bands.

"Down by the River" was a personal song for us. Drug violence has been part of the El Paso culture for years. You go over to Juárez to restaurants and bars and enjoy the day life and the nightlife, and there's a bar there called the Kentucky Club that's been there since my father was in high school in the fifties. They'd cross the border and go to the bar, and when I was in high school we did, too. A lot of that changed because of the drug violence. People were not going over because there are massive amounts of drugs and murder. People were shot and places were getting burned down, but I think it's getting better now.

Dirty River Boys tour poster, Maria's Closet, El Paso, Texas. Photo of poster by Brian T. Atkinson.

I had this groove that I thought would be great for Ray Wylie to cowrite with us. Sure enough, he agreed. He came over to Austin, and [bandmate] Marco [Gutierrez] and I wrote with him. We showed him the idea and we talked about the story behind the song and what we wanted the song to be. I had a verse and we tweaked that, and then he had an idea for the chorus. We knew we wanted it to be a chant piece, an all-vocal chorus. Ray Wylie had the great idea: "Undertaker looks like crows / Red eyes dressed in black." It's that classic Ray Wylie image-provoking lyric. We're all Ray Wylie fans, so it was an honor to write with him.[21]

Outlaw Folk is the name we gave our genre of music. I think when people say *folk*, they get this notion that it's a guy sitting on a stool singing songs. I love that and it's great, but it didn't encompass what we're doing. It's about the songwriting and lyrically building the song, but when it comes to arranging and putting a show together it was so much more than that. It almost ends up being a punk rock show with us. It's very high energy, so we didn't think that folk really encompassed what we're doing. I mean, there's Outlaw Country. It's an edgier and different outlet of country, and we're just shooting to do that with folk music. He does add that special touch.[22]

Jonathan Tyler

Ray swings in this groove, a pocket, a traditional thing that's timeless, the space between the two and four beats. On top of that, his lyrical messages resonate with me on a deeper level. I think he's a brilliant, poetic writer and lyricist who's creating art at its highest point. Ray really cares about writing poetry. He finds the soul and spirit and conviction, and he plays with themes that all the greatest writers do—good and evil and gambling with the devil. He has a way with words that speaks to deeper things. His lyrics are not to be taken lightly. Having the lyrics and the groove is as good as it gets.

We'd been hanging out a lot, and were talking about writing a song together. I went over to his house after I played Antone's in Austin one night, and he showed me some fingerpicking techniques. He showed me this blues thing I'd never heard before, and I had this other riff, one I'd had in my pocket for years and never used. It reminded me of Ray Wylie, so I played it, and he dug it. We just started riffing on words for "Hey Mama, My Time Ain't Long." We came up with that first verse in about thirty minutes together. We were talking about how there are spiritual people in places where you wouldn't expect to find them.

I left his house, and we weren't even close to having a full song. We just had that first verse. Then Ray sent me an email a week later with all the lyrics. They were so good. I was like, "I'm not gonna try to change any of these." Cowriting with different people is like playing sports. You have a dynamic, and everybody's different. You just play off each other. Certain people bring out different things in you. Ray brings out a greasy side, a darker, edgier side of another songwriter. We went into that headspace, and that was

Left to right: Jonathan Tyler and Ray Wylie Hubbard, Austin, Texas, March 2015. Photo by Lindsay Lohden.

it. That song was just going back and forth between emails, which isn't that glamorous. The original inspiration is what was fun with Ray.

We have different writing styles. I definitely think of Ray when I'm writing and what he'd do in a moment, but I always just try to follow my muse as well. I don't think I consciously try to do what he does, but it does creep in from always paying attention to what he's doing when we play onstage together. I watch and show respect and try to fit into whatever world Ray's trying to create. He's the elder. You could definitely call the songwriting process spiritual. My grandmother plays organ in a Pentecostal church, and coming from a church background, I grew up singing old, old gospel songs. That really has an influence over what I do. Blues and gospel music just feel like home to me. It's so ingrained in who I am. It's almost second nature.

I think Ray carries a torch from this part of the country where gospel music and religion and church is so ingrained in us as people. It's hard to explain if you didn't grow up in the South and the church and singing gospel songs. It's a mix between gospel, blues, and rock and roll, a melting pot southern black and white music. You have to grow up around it and have people show you what it is. It's a tradition, like reading *The Grapes of Wrath*, a torch that was passed to Ray. The behind-the-scenes wisdom that you get from hanging around a guy like that is really important. His legacy is being a brilliant songwriter and also being a good human being.[23]

Scott H. Biram

I was already a fan of the snake farm, but his song jumped out at me. The snake farm is a roadside attraction much like the Thing in [Dragoon], Arizona. You drive by and say, "What is it?" The snake farm has different kinds of snakes in there, and you can go through and say, "Those would be cool boots." It always had this seedy legend that there were trailers out back at one point. You ask for change for a fifty, and they send you to the prostitutes out back. I don't know if that's true. I do a little spoken part in my song about the snake farm called "Truck Driver," which actually came out before

Scott H. Biram, C-Boy's Heart & Soul, Austin, Texas, August 16, 2018. Photo by Brian T. Atkinson.

Ray Wylie Hubbard's song. In the live version I say, "If you ever go down to New Braunfels, Texas, ask for change for a fifty, and they'll send you to the pretty girls out back. Don't let those monkeys throw any caca at you."

Ray and I definitely have Lightnin' Hopkins and Mance Lipscomb in common as influences. I grew up listening to Lightnin'. I remember my dad buying this Lightnin' album the first time I went to the record store when I was about three years old. Lightnin' has always been my favorite blues guy. He sticks with me. I dreamed one time that I was his handler and he was so drunk that he couldn't stand up. I was carrying him around in my dream. It was cool. Felt like I met him. I really got into Mance when I was starting to play the blues as my main thing. I liked him because he was a fairly obscure guy not many people heard about. It was the Texas version of the Delta blues. Mance was a songster, too, so he doesn't just play the blues.

Ray's down-to-earth. He takes the bare bones of the blues and the raspy voice, and he turns it into a real feeler. He always puts a weird touch to it or gets all crazy transcendental on you, which makes it very interesting. He'll be talking about what kind of amp or guitar he's using in a very straightforward story, and then he'll say something wacko right after that. He keeps you on your toes, but his songs are not highly orchestrated. I guess you have to find the fine line between checking yourself and letting yourself do whatever. If you check yourself too much, you'll give up on every song. You just have to stick to the small circle around the heart and spell things out clearly and efficiently. I've always been impressed by Ray's songs and how down-to-earth he is. He'll make statements about plain things like something that's on the table, but he makes them interesting.[24]

William Elliott Whitmore

I was on tour in Europe around 2007 and did a show in Glasgow, Scotland, opening up for Ray Wylie Hubbard. It was a big thrill. I got to meet him, and what a cool guy. He's very sincere, down-home, down-to-earth, humble, interesting. I played my set, and he was very complimentary, which was like praise from Caesar. Then

*William Elliott
Whitmore, poster for
Australian tour, March
2013. Photo of poster
by Brian T. Atkinson.*

he called me up onstage during his set, which was a total shock.
"Hey, come do some songs with us." I didn't know what songs it
was gonna be or what chords, but I accompanied him on banjo. I
was nervous. He said, "This one's in the key of C." It was one of the
coolest things in my life, a real shining moment.

I had heard the name growing up, but I started really paying
attention after we met. He was in my songwriter hall of fame with
Townes Van Zandt, Billy Joe Shaver, and all those Texas guys. My
parents were big fans of country music, and Ray Wylie Hubbard's
name was right among them. He has such a catalog of material
and tells the greatest stories. That's another thing that struck me,
the stories in between the songs. What a true storyteller. I started
getting into guys like Guy Clark because of him. There's a certain
thing that happens down in Texas that really had me paying attention.

Ray mixes styles from country to blues in a way that I think is
interesting, and I love his lyrics. "Dust of the Chase," the first song

on *Loco Gringo's Lament* has that line, "Patience is a virtue that I don't possess / And I can't deny that heaven lies beneath a cotton dress." Oh my god, that's just so good. Songwriters look up to guys like him, and I'm just so grateful that Ray Wylie Hubbard exists. We're all standing on the shoulders of giants, and I'm trying to steal from the greatest like him. Anybody that does singer-songwriter music looks up to the people who come before us. Ray is one who makes it okay to have different songs and not be afraid to be amorphous and shift from one style to another.[25]

Chris Fullerton

"Black Dog" was the first Ray Wylie Hubbard song I [ever] heard. I was blown away. The band's really tight, and the mix is really good. I wanted to be that right away. I was gaining my own voice at that point, and I was really starting to be influenced by Steve Earle's *I Feel Alright*, different Townes Van Zandt records, Dale Watson's "Whiskey or God," and Bob Wills. The band I had at the time sounded like a culmination of all those put together. Then I found Ray Wylie Hubbard, and my writing started to sound darker.

Chris Fullerton at his home, Austin, Texas, August 17, 2017. Photo by Brian T. Atkinson.

It makes sense. I grew up Catholic and have been wavering on that my whole life. I've always been interested in the darker sides of the Bible.

He catches me in his writing that's infused with religion. That's where he gains his footing and where the strongest parts of his writing are for me. He does it just to a point so you can draw your own conclusions. A song could be about redemption or complete hopelessness. I try to be like he is. The way that he writes narrative into a poetic verse is extremely important and hard to do. That's true especially when you're not writing a pop song, but instead you're writing about the darkest things. He does that so well. A song's empty if you're just saying shit and stringing words together. There's no end goal. There's no beginning and end if there's no narrative.

I've had an obsession since I was a kid about demonic possession. My mom made the mistake of renting *The Exorcist* when I was younger because my brother really wanted to see it. I watched some of it, and I got so scared that I had to stop watching. I called one of my friends as a safety blanket about three-quarters through. I was so scared for years, and I would stay up at night, frightened that I would be possessed by the devil. I would have my mom come into my room and read Bible verses to me. The impact that something like that can have on a child is immense. I still feel like it has some sort of odd traction in my brain. These religious fever dreams are Ray Wylie Hubbard songs. They're sometimes what I was frightened of as a child. Those are the songs where he must be sitting in a room going, "Fuck yeah, I'm writing some good shit here."

Ray Wylie Hubbard, Bruce Springsteen, and Hank Williams have had the most impact on me as a songwriter. I wrote my song "Bad Winds" before I heard of Ray Wylie, but I think it matches up. I had a vision of what I wanted my songwriting to be, and when I heard Ray, I was like, "Fuck. He got to it first." Now it's an exciting rush when I listen to Ray's songs, the ones that are about what frightened me as a child. I wish I could still feel that way. I would have the safety of religion if I could believe in God. I would still be afraid of those things, but I would be able to inhabit that place where I'm safe from everything going wrong in the world because my God is taking care of me.[26]

Carson McHone

I actually wrote one of my first songs because of Ray Wylie Hubbard. He wanted to score the movie from his screenplay [2010's *The Last Rites of Ransom Pride*] with young up-and-coming songwriters doing the music, and I saw this call on his website to young singer-songwriters: "Here's the feel of the movie, a Western thing out in the desert." He gave a loose plot and asked people to write something along those lines and submit it and it might make its way into the film. I was in high school at the time, and I had been gifted a guitar for my birthday. I learned how to drop my guitar down into double drop D, and I wrote this murder ballad called "The Desert Song." I wrote the lyrics about this woman protagonist out in the desert. I never turned it in to Ray, but I still play it all the time today.

I met George Reiff years later, and we became fast friends. He said to Ray, "Man, I want to get this girl in the studio. I think she can do something on this song." It was a sweet, almost gospel-like song called "Too Young Ripe, Too Young Rotten" [from *The Ruffian's Misfortune*]. I did this really delicate vocal even though I'd never sung harmonies on anybody's record. It was just George and me

Carson McHone, San Marcos, Texas, 2014. Photo by Laura Hajar.

messing around at his home studio and him walking me through it. I liked the song and had always been a fan of Ray's, so I was just happy to have the opportunity to work on it.

A few weeks later, George called and said, "Hey, I have this other idea I want to try out just for kicks." I went in and wailed on "Chick Singer Badass Rockin'." That was also totally new for me. I don't use my voice like that when I sing my songs. It was fun to try out and let loose. They ended up not even keeping my part on "Too Young Ripe, Too Young Rotten." They only used the vocal on "Chick Singer Badass Rockin'." Ray really liked it. Then he was like, "It'd be really cool to get her in on the video." He had a bunch of other footage of cool rocking references for the video, flashes of these badass rockers. I thought it was cool that he wanted to include me.

I was actually on my way to a gig that day, but we hung out for an hour and a half and took a bunch of photos. We had fun behind the scenes. He felt like an uncle I'd always known, even though I don't even know him that well now. I've had these cool and strange interactions with him that are pretty sweet. He's a hoot to hang out with. He was all excited about this app he was using to make the video. We sat around trying to use our phones, and I'm not very phone savvy. We were just like, "Shit, how do we get this? Go back, go back." It was like we'd known each other for a million years. He was really laid-back and funny. We had a lot of fun. Of course George facilitated the whole thing. I wouldn't have met Ray otherwise.

I've run into Ray and Judy at other shows, and they're really kind folks. I think that's the cool thing about musicians in and around the Austin area. The older cats are really happy to put a hand down and reach out to help and talk and tell you about stuff. That's a big deal for younger people who are trying to find their feet. He's a great role model, and he's supportive of everyone. Ray's totally rootsy, which makes people comfortable. He's got an older crowd because of his down-home feel, but he's so Austin that he's not afraid to call you out or bring stuff up.

He's not blatantly political. I think he's more poetic, but he's definitely not afraid to speak his mind or ask questions. Austin has always been a place where it's safe for people to do that. He's a total perfect weirdo. Also, his music is familiar. Older folks can relate to it, but so can the younger folks who are more edgy and rocking. I think that's a great representation of Austin. He has a little bit of everything. I was a kid when I started listening to him. My folks were into him. We always had similar interests in music, which was lucky [for me] as a kid and young teenager. My folks were into the same rootsy and folky stuff that I was. I grew up listening to Ray.

I've always appreciated his lyrics. I dig how they can be spooky, dusty, and gritty. He's a growler, so eccentric and wily. I hope that he inspires people to be themselves. He's such an honest songwriter. I was inspired by him to write songs when I was a junior in high school. You can go out to his shows and see little kids to teenagers to young songwriters to the old Austin crew study his songwriting. He's fun and thoughtful and that's represented in his songs. I guess I should play him "The Desert Song" sometime.[27]

Jack O'Brien (Bright Light Social Hour)

I met Ray Wylie through Troy Campbell four years ago. Troy does a music licensing supervisor thing, and we were meeting. He was planning to meet with Ray Wylie right after. Ray came in and sat down, and Troy said, "Hey, this is Ray Wylie Hubbard." I just freaked. My stepdad grew up in Corsicana, Texas, and he was very into him. He'd seen him since the seventies. "Oh my god, are you serious?" Ray was super sweet and said, "I'll get out of your way and let you do your meeting." He was really interested in hearing about the Bright Light Social Hour. We were looking for a record label and licensing help, and he was really eager to put me in touch with the people he knew. We ended up emailing and hit it off as quick friends.

I really dove into his stuff at that point. I've always had a lot of respect for his unique voice and the style of music he does. I wouldn't necessarily think of his stuff as psychedelic music, which is what we were playing at the time, but it has a lot of drony, hypnotic aspects, and I found it incredibly psychedelic. I think music that puts you in a trance can be mind-expanding. It encourages you to be wondrous. Also the lyrics. He gave me a copy of *The Grifter's Hymnal*, and there's that line: "The truth of the matter is I really can't sing / But I can quote Martin Luther King / His words are

Jack O'Brien (Bright Light Social Hour), Sunset Sound Records, Los Angeles, November 18, 2017. Courtesy Bright Light Social Hour; photo by Yvonne Osorio.

stronger than angel dust is / 'The arc of the moral universe is long / But it bends toward justice'" [from "New Year's Eve at the Gates of Hell"]. He speaks some really great truths.

Ray Wylie has never been afraid of speaking truths or saying something controversial. I think it's really especially brave for someone in the country scene. I mean, you're not really that brave if you're in a punk band shouting out stuff that's a little controversial, but I think Ray is doing what Willie Nelson does: He's bringing rednecks, hippies, and Eastern thought together. "Screw You, We're from Texas" is great and defiant. We've written a lot of songs in that style, but they're not as clear and concise as that. When we brought him out to play that at our record release show at Stubb's in Austin two years ago, I felt that represented something we could all easily jump up together and shout.

My favorite thing was his face. He came out onstage and was giddy and said, "Man, thanks for making an old cat feel young again." So cool. I think it was really special to everyone because there were a lot of people like me who grew up with his music around but weren't really familiar. Our version of "Screw You" was like this psychedelic krautrock take on the song, and the music hitting so powerfully was cool, but being the backing band for this amazing legend was a unique, incredible experience. We'd never done anything like that before.

I've taken from his songwriting a real earnestness and being real honest about yourself in the lyrics. Ray inserts himself into the narrative in a way that's very self-aware. Sometimes you feel self-conscious and needy singing about yourself, but Ray does it in a way that's more "Hey, this is me and what I'm going through, and I'm letting it all hang out."

We just recorded this song with him called "The Rebellious Sons" on his new record *Tell the Devil...I'm Gettin' There As Fast As I Can*. He brought a bunch of verses, a drony guitar lick that he had, and we tried doing it a whole bunch of different ways. We've always started songs with the music first with just a jam, and then we'll add vocals and lyrics. Going through that process with him, we almost totally reversed our songwriting process. I'll often write a poem or a story that's the message, and then we experiment with different ways to get the music to support that. I think it ends up being a much more powerful story that way.

The bass line was the first thing that came on "The Rebellious Sons." Muddy Waters's *Electric Mud* popped into my head. It's an album that he put out in 1968 when Jimi Hendrix was blowing up and Chess Records said, "We need to reissue a record with all your hits but with this acid-drenched psychedelic band." Critics hated it at the time, and it was an unpopular record, but if you go back and listen to it, it's incredible. It was a really interesting presentation for a lot of his classics. So I immediately thought of those real deep bass grooves, and I fiddled with that and the drummer came in and that's when I could see Ray Wylie getting really excited.

It felt like that bass line was a real backbone for the song. He came over to our studio, and we just jammed it. We got our arrangement, and recorded it on the iPhone. We did that in about an hour and a half. Then he invited us to the Zone [Recording Studio] in Dripping Springs, Texas, where he was working on the record. We left, and I never heard it until it actually came out. I was like,

Singer-songwriter Jaimee Harris's T-shirt, Austin, Texas, August 28, 2017. Photo by Brian T. Atkinson.

"Damn, he left that bass line front and center. Nice." Now I'm brainstorming a project like the Gorillaz where it's a bunch of different people collaborating. I daydream about that a lot and would love to do more collaboration with him in that way.

As an aside, when we were in the studio, we found all these old musician terms he'd throw out really entertaining. We didn't know what he was talking about all the time. For example, he would tell [Bright Light Social Club guitarist] Curtis [Roush] to lay down a solo, and he said, "Curtis, why don't you squirt some weird on it?" Curtis did not know what that meant. "You mean you want me to put some effects or delay on it?" "No, no, just press record and squirt some weird down." Then listening back, he'd say, "Are there any clams on that one?" Apparently, a clam is a mistake. We also learned that "take it for a ride" is another way to say solo. We thought our communication breakdowns were hilarious.

Anyway, I think there's a lot of watering down, a lot of very safe music to appeal to a wider audience in these country and blues and older formats. There's a fear of breaking the rules. Ray Wylie reminds us that you're always gonna cut deeper being your true, honest, deepest self. You're gonna get some blowback, but he's showed us how to be all right with that. Also, I think it's really important—especially in our country right now, as the political climate gets more divided—to find points of connection. His music preaches acceptance, open-mindedness, and compassion.[28]

Ben Kweller

Ray Wylie and I eventually met when I moved to Austin through our mutual friend Jenni Finlay, and we've been friends ever since. I'd known about Ray Wylie since I was a kid. My buddy's dad had a music room with some acoustic guitars and CDs on the coffee table, and there was *Dangerous Spirits* with this dude on the cover wearing purple sunglasses on the cover. His name was Ray Wylie Hubbard. I was like, "Huh. That dude looks cool." This was the one CD my buddy's dad had with a name I'd never heard. Everything else was like James Taylor, Neil Young, and all these big, famous artists. The name Ray Wylie Hubbard and his look stood out. I must've been nine years old. I started hearing more and more about him as I got older.

Ben Kweller, Jenni Finlay Promotions'"office party" at Enoteca Vespaio, Austin, Texas, December 8, 2011. Photo by Jenni Finlay.

Anyway, I moved back to Texas in the mid-2000s and got deeper into the roots of Texas music from Jerry Jeff to Ray Wylie to Willis Alan Ramsey. I even went through a Stevie Ray Vaughan phase. Growing up in Texas, you always hear about Stevie Ray. It was never really my cup of tea, but when I moved to Austin I found out that I lived on the same street that he had lived on. I was like, "Well, shit, I need to listen to Stevie Ray Vaughan for sure." I bought up all these Stevie Ray records. I would go through different artists each month, and Ray Wylie was definitely in there. I didn't know that there was a connection between [Ray's sobriety] and Stevie Ray.

I like music where I feel like I'm hanging out with the person when I'm listening. I write that way myself. I like when songs have this plain straight-up, on-the-nose, no-beating-around-the-bush in-your-faceness. Ray Wylie knows how to do that. He's one of the best in the world. I love that he feels free to sing about turning up the tone knob on his old amp and the way his guitar strings feel. "Coricidin Bottle" [the opening track from *The Grifter's Hymnal*] really appeals to me. Some of the terms are insider musician-based stuff, but he does it in a real loving way. He's legit. He feels it in his soul. It's probably even cooler for people who don't play music because it's like an in for them. Everyone can relate to it 100 percent.

The Grifter's Hymnal was a really special album, but I love fucking *Snake Farm*. I know Ray will hate this, but going back to the *Cowboy Twinkies* album, there's something so cool about "Belly of Texas." I've actually been looking for that album on vinyl. I can put aside all the production stuff. I've been in those shoes where you're working with a producer who totally changes your shit or the A&R guy at a major label who changes how your album should be. Certainly most of us who have put out music, there are some we're not fond of down the road. Putting that aside, to me that album sounds like a cool Texas record from the seventies. I love the sound and the references to Interstate 35. "Belly of Texas" takes me to a place when Austin was a little town. Austin was a ten-minute town when I moved here. I could say, "Dude, I'll be there in ten minutes." I imagine Austin was a five-minute town when he put out that first album. Now it's like a forty-five-minute town.

Drummer John David Kent and I had a band called Radish back in the nineties. We were best friends growing up in Greenville,

Left to right: Ben Kweller, Kinky Friedman, BettySoo, and Gurf Morlix, Austin, Texas, March 2013. Photo by Brian T. Atkinson.

Texas, and we got our first record deal together. He's been doing the Texas country thing since Radish broke up, and he's opened a lot for Ray. He has this one classic story that embodies Ray and his humility. They were backstage at some shitty club in Lubbock, and one of the guys in the band said something like "This shitty dressing room..." Ray was sitting there and said, "Well, I'm just grateful to have a gig tonight." That's the shit. We should all remember that it's a gift and an honor and a privilege to play your music on any stage. It all starts sitting on your bed as a kid singing to no one. Even if you're just singing to one person and they're singing your lyrics back to you, it's an honor. Holy shit. That's the dream. You have to always remember where you came from. Ray always does. I really appreciate that humbleness.

I will always think of him as one of the authentic, real artists who represent what Central Texas is all about. Ray was doing his thing way before *Keep Austin Weird* was even a fucking slogan. He

Left to right: Ray Wylie Hubbard, Jenni Finlay, and Kyle Snyder (background), first annual Rebels & Renegades showcase, Threadgill's World Headquarters, Austin, Texas, March 19, 2016. Photo by Brian T. Atkinson.

marched to the beat of his own drummer and always has. I really relate with that. So I feel like we're kindred spirits despite our generation gap. I think he feels that, too. We're on the same plane, and our friendship is really cool in that way. I think it's a good example of how art transcends time, place, age, color, race, belief systems — all of that bullshit.[29]

Bridge
Name-Dropping
(The Songwriters
behind the Songs)

Jessie Mae Hemphill, from cover of Jessie Mae
Hemphill & Friends: Dare You to Do It Again
*DVD, 219 Records, 2004. Photo by Brian T.
Atkinson.*

*I was getting ready to do the harmonica ride on "Drunken
Poet's Dream" at this festival near San Francisco, and I
looked over to the side of the stage. There's Charlie Musselwhite, one of the greatest harmonica players ever. My
lips locked. I didn't play a very good harmonica ride, but
I got to meet Charlie after. He was so gracious, kind, and
cool. He told me all these old blues stories about his life,*

*and it just fell into place that I was gonna write "Mr. Mus-
selwhite's Blues" about him.*

   *Spider, Snaker, and Little Sun were heroes of mine grow-
ing up in the folk craze who made me realize folk music
didn't have to be that sweet and pure like Kingston Trio
and Peter, Paul, and Mary. It means a deal when people come up and say, "Hey, man, I never heard of Spider,
Snaker, and Little Sun, but I heard your song and checked
them out and I love them." It's gratifying to spread knowledge of cool things to the world with songs like "Mr. Musselwhite's Blues," "Spider, Snaker, and Little Son," and
"Jessie Mae" [about legendary blues guitarist Jessie Mae
Hemphill].*

   *Oh god, Jessie Mae, I just adore her. Hopefully some
young person will hear that song, find her, and just fall in
love like I did. I enjoy not thinking, Well, is somebody on
the radio gonna get this? I doubt if "Spider, Snaker, and
Little Sun" has been played on any radio ever, but it doesn't
matter. I heard that John Koerner heard the song, and he
really liked it. That makes it worthwhile.*[1]

                         —RAY WYLIE HUBBARD

Charlie Musselwhite

Bill Bowker [a deejay on KRSH 95.9 FM in Santa Rosa, California] turned me on to Ray Wylie Hubbard. "Snake Farm" is a classic American folk song. Hundreds of years from now folks will be singing that song and "Screw You, We're from Texas." Anybody can take that song and make it their own. I could say, "Screw You, I'm from Mississippi." If you go to Europe, you can say, "Screw You, I'm from America." It's useful. I like his groove and humor. He paints pictures. You go to the movies when he's singing and see it all as he describes it. Ray has a beatnik cowboy attitude. I know he's a loner, a seeker, a lifelong learner, and I like to think we have these things in common. Blues makes sense. Blues tells a story and you go, "Yep. That nails it." Ray Wylie Hubbard has real talent and nails it with great stories in his songs.

I just liked blues in the beginning. I didn't have any dreams about being onstage or getting famous or having a recording. I liked all kinds of music from hillbilly and gospel to jazz and world music, but blues sounded like I felt. It made me feel better and was my comforter. I really gravitated toward blues, and then I got to thinking that if it makes me feel good, I bet playing it would make me feel even better. I had harmonicas and thought, I have harmonicas,

Charlie Musselwhite promotional photo. Ray Wylie Hubbard has been inspired by legendary harmonica player Musselwhite and recorded "Mr. Musselwhite's Blues" on The Ruffian's Misfortune *(2015). Photo by Thom Gilbert; courtesy Henri Musselwhite.*

and I like how it sounds on those records. I went out in the woods and started teaching myself how to play. Before I went to Chicago, I made it a point to meet a lot of the old-time blues singers who were in Memphis.

I hung out with them and had fun, but I was going to school and didn't even know it. I would've paid much more attention if I knew I was preparing for a career. I went to all these blues clubs in Chicago, and I wasn't even telling anybody that I play. John Lee Hooker lived in Detroit, but he would play in Chicago regularly. We were instant friends the first time we met. It was like we'd always known each other, and we stayed friends until he died. He was the best man at my wedding. So I'd be at the show and would request songs, and guys like Muddy Waters would say, "How do you know that tune?" "Well, I got the record." This waitress told Muddy one night, "You ought to get Charlie to play harmonica." That changed everything. He insisted I sit in, and other musicians who were hanging out there that night started offering me gigs. That was real good and turned the corner for me right there. It was my ticket out of the factory.

I remember discussing harmonica technique with Little Walter, but that's as close as he came to showing me anything. Talking about technique is about all you can do anyhow. The harmonica is the only instrument that you can't watch somebody play. You can't even see what you're doing yourself. I soaked it up by osmosis when I listened to the music. Things just emerged when I started playing. Something would get my attention, and I'd try to play it. I guess anybody can learn to play the harmonica. It's tuned to an open chord, so anyone can pick one up, blow on it, and get a nice sound. I just felt so strongly attracted to the blues. It felt like the blues picked me as much as I picked it. I had to have it. I had to play it. I just had to. The music made me feel more alive and still does.

The harmonica sure was my ticket to a better life. I've gone all the way around the world with the harmonica, and I have a better life and endless adventures because of it. What an honor for Ray Wylie Hubbard to write a song about me ["Mr. Musselwhite's Blues" on *The Ruffian's Misfortune*] and mention me in another song ["Dead Thumb King" on *Tell the Devil...*]. I'm so flattered that he would do that. I can't tell you how much that knocks me out. I'm real proud. I think it's one of the best songs ever written in history. I really think the world of Ray Wylie Hubbard and consider him a friend and kindred soul. I look forward to seeing him soon. I hope we can sit down to write a tune.[2]

"Spider" John Koerner (Koerner, Ray & Glover)

I listened to [Hubbard's "Spider, Snaker, and Little Sun" from *Tell the Devil...*] a few weeks ago—certainly an interesting song and not exactly expected. He's talking about the old, old days. I'm flattered. Coffeehouses were spreading all over the country back then. There was one here in Minneapolis where I was playing open mics, and it was in a neighborhood where Dave Ray lived. He was very interested in Leadbelly at the time. I went to see Dave in New York City later on when he lived there, and I met Tony Glover. It turned out that we all had an interest in the old country blues, old black blues guys recording in the 1920s and '30s.

Country blues was something that I never knew existed before I met Dave. There was a certain interesting sensuousness which

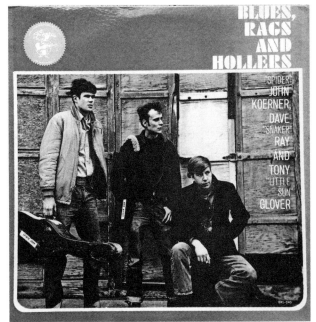

Cover of "Spider" John Koerner, Dave "Snaker" Ray, and Tony "Little Sun" Glover's landmark debut album Blues, Rags and Hollers, *Elektra Records, 1963. Album cover photo by Brian T. Atkinson.*

ended up resonating with people. Those songs had interesting poetry and turns of phrase. We got it mostly from records until we went to the Newport Folk Festival. A lot of those blues guys had been refound and brought in by white folklore people. You could see the ones we'd only heard about.

The Newport Folk Festival [when Bob Dylan went electric] was pretty interesting. I knew what he was gonna do because I heard him practicing, and I knew a couple guys in his band. Dylan got up and went electric, and I was backstage at the time. Backstage was separated from the audience with a chain link fence with a tarp over it so you couldn't see the audience and they couldn't see you. He played ["Maggie's Farm" and "Like a Rolling Stone"], and I heard a sound I did not understand. I pulled up over the fence, looked, and heard people booing. It was a traumatic event and quite interesting. There was a rumor that Pete Seeger was looking for an ax so he could cut the electricity. Some people were crying. It didn't take that many months before people were on board with that approach, though.

Left to right: Ron Hoddinott and "Spider" John Koerner. Courtesy James Higgins.

I get accused of [being an influence on Dylan], but I deny it. I knew him before he went to New York City and became famous. There was an area here in Minneapolis called Dinkytown where a coffeehouse was. We got together sometimes, worked on songs, and played some jobs together at different places. It would be an exaggeration to say that I influenced him. In a way, we all influenced each other. Dinkytown is different now. University and money people have moved in there, and it's more upscale. It was a funky area back then with a coffeehouse called the Ten O'Clock Scholar, a focal point for the music. There were people playing chess and writing poetry and different kinds of artists around. There used to be apartments above the place, and there was a place called the Dirty Grocery where we could get beer and go up and party. It was an all-around scene and gathering place for people who liked to drink a bit and play music.

We had been playing some songs together, and we had enough material to make a record. They talked this guy in Milwaukee into recording us, though he wasn't real interested in us. We did it anyway. So we made *Blues, Rags and Hollers* [Audiophile, 1963]. Jac Holzman at Elektra Records was interested, and he signed us up and that record was re-released. We went out to New York to make a second album [1964's *Lots More Blues, Rags and Hollers*], and by Jac's influence we got in on the Philadelphia Folk Festival. We were a little drunk, and we got up and did our thing with complete abandon. It was quite interesting. I don't think any of those people had seen three white boys play that kind of music. We got signed up to go to Club 47 in Boston, a major hub of that kind of thing. That put us on the national scene.

I decided to quit music forever in 1972. I was married to a Danish woman, and we moved to Denmark. Quitting music forever lasted about a year. We had a [Alan] Lomax folk collection in the house, and I started learning those songs. Some were really choice pieces of work. That's why they lasted. I had a little band in Denmark with harmonica and washboard players. I decided my job at that point was to play traditional American folk songs and lay over them my approach to the blues. We were playing in bars, which isn't like playing in a coffeehouse. We put in a lot of heavy rhythm. It was a bit of a shock to people back in the States, but they got used to it. I've been presenting traditional American folk music to people who didn't even know what it was since then. I'm glad to be able to do that.[3]

Olga Wilhelmine Munding (Jessie Mae Hemphill Foundation president)

Ray Wylie seems like a cool dude. I listened to [Hubbard's "Jessie Mae" from *The Ruffian's Misfortune*], and I know that Jessie Mae would have gotten a kick out of it. I knew her well. As I was listening, I started laughing out loud at certain parts and could hear her laughing with me. She had a great laugh. She would have been thrilled that somebody wrote a song about her. Jessie Mae's own music was very interesting to me even though I wasn't very familiar with the North Mississippi–style blues when I discovered her. I originally came across her going through records and discovering new artists for my radio show in Colorado. Hill country blues is nestled up in the hills in Mississippi, and it stayed truer to its origins longer than the music that made its way up to Chicago and went through a metamorphosis. You can really hear the West African influence in hill country blues.

It's very unusual to find a woman guitarist in the blues, and I thought Jessie Mae's music sounded old but also really modern. I played her on my radio shows, and then I found out through my friends [brothers Cody and Luther Dickinson] in North Mississippi Allstars that she was actually alive. I got her mailing address and wrote her a letter when I moved to New Orleans. She wrote me back by dictation because she wasn't able to write anymore. She had had a stroke, and her right side was paralyzed. She wasn't able to perform. She asked me to call her in the note. I did, and she answered the phone. She had a really young voice that sounded immediately familiar to me. She kept asking if I was sure that we hadn't met before because there was something about me that sounded familiar, too. We discovered that we had the same birthday during that conversation.

She was like, "You have to come up for our birthday." So I drove up to Mississippi and was pleasantly surprised. People had helped her get a new trailer because her old one was literally falling down. I was very happy to see that she was not totally destitute. I knocked,

Olga Wilhelmine Munding (Jessie Mae Hemphill Foundation), still shot from Jessie Mae Hemphill & Friends: Dare You to Do It Again. *Photo by Brian T. Atkinson.*

and she opened the door and said, "Oh my lord, I believe that Jesus sent you to me. You better get in here, girl." I visited her on a regular basis and stayed with her for periods of time. She'd stay up late at night, get into these lucid headspaces, and talk about her life, her grandfather and mother. She'd even get a little prophetic about things I'd do with my life. It was a pretty intense experience and relationship with her. For whatever reason, we had a spiritual connection that was unusual considering her background and mine. That connection remains now even though she passed away in 2006.

Jessie Mae was really strong and had a really strong personality. She was really proud that she was able to accomplish what she did in music, which was unheard of for a woman. She went to Norway, Sweden, and France, and she did really great overseas in her heyday. She won a couple W. C. Handy Awards [blues music's equivalent of a Grammy, now called Blues Music Awards]. She talked about jobs that she had while she was playing gigs. She worked in a restaurant in Memphis washing dishes for a while. She worked for a wealthy white man for a while, taking care of his kids and house. She had a couple high-profile love affairs with B. B. King and Robert Nighthawk. Jessie used to say if a relationship wasn't going on well that she would put the man on wheels and roll him right out of there. She said, "You better do that, too."

She wasn't really able to play anymore when I knew her, but she did have cassettes. She had a song called "Shotgun" that was never recorded that she wanted me to learn. I haven't played it in a long time, but there are cassette recordings of us doing it somewhere. She said it was okay to tape it if I wanted. My whole experience in Mississippi was a yin and yang thing. There was a lot of pain. The last couple years I've really tried to live in joy because life is short. I don't believe that in order to be a blues musician you really need to live the blues. There are experiences that you need to have to tap into blues, but you can live a joyful life.

Jessie spent a lot of time with her grandfather and aunt Rosa Lee [Hill], who was also an unheard-of songwriter and guitarist. There are only a handful of Alan Lomax recordings of her, but Jessie refers to Rosa Lee in some of her songs. Rosa Lee also felt like her music was robbed from her. Knowing Jessie Mae really defined my life in many ways. She had five miscarriages, but she didn't have any children. She wasn't able to carry a baby to term, but she felt like I was one of her babies in my way. She called me "her Hemphill," and I was honored. One of these days I'm gonna write a book about my time with her, but I'm not ready to spill the beans and stir up a hornet's nest quite yet.[4]

Verse Four
Without Love

Left to right: Judy Hubbard, Lucas Hubbard, and Ray Wylie Hubbard.
Photo by Geoffrey Himes; courtesy Judy Hubbard.

My guitar teacher Sam Swank showed me these patterns, which opened the door for these new songs to come through. I wouldn't have gotten "Without Love" if I hadn't learned fingerpicking.

—RAY WYLIE HUBBARD

Judy Hubbard

I was smitten with Ray long before I met him. He used to play at Mother Blues [in Dallas] when I worked there, and I'm sure we talked because I introduced him to [Jimmy] Buffett one night when Buffett was playing Mother Blues. He wanted to meet Ray. So I took him to Fannie Anne's and introduced them. We weren't friends, though. I went to see him at Poor David's Pub in Dallas with friends when I was thirty, and I specifically remember him playing "Portales." I was blown away. He was so funny. I said, "I'm gonna marry that guy." I went over and stood by the backroom doorway, and he came out. I was looking nonchalant like I wasn't there to meet him. I guess he'd seen me at the AA meetings, too, and he asked me if I wanted to go to a show at the White Elephant in Fort Worth the next day. I did, and we've been together ever since.

Mother Blues was a blues club where Muddy Waters and Lightnin' Hopkins played, but you would also see Willis Alan Ramsey, Jimmy Buffett, and Ray there. It was an old two-story house, and the upstairs was the office and greenroom. They had poker games after hours. I'd stay after hours, work the door, and serve drinks

Judy Hubbard. Photo by GypsySun; courtesy Judy Hubbard.

at poker games with Freddie King, Steven Fromholz, and Buffett. Gertie's was a club next door, and it was specifically geared toward rock bands. Gertie's was open until four in the morning, so any time arena bands like Alice Cooper and Robert Plant would come through, they'd party there after hours or they'd come next door to Mother Blues and snort coke with us upstairs. I think the owner eventually went to prison for dealing coke, and they ended up shutting down. I worked there in 1973 and 1974.

I loved the Texas music scene at that time. I had a really rough childhood, and my escape before I found drugs was music. Then when I found drugs, my escape was drugs and music. There was a lot of chaos going on in my house. I started going to Mother Blues because I could get a fake ID, and that's where I could see music. I needed a job, and when their door girl quit, they asked me if I wanted [the job]. I did. Bars always felt at home to me because that's where music was. So I wasn't looking to get into the music business, but it was a natural fit because I spent my time at clubs and festivals.

I'd lost touch with the girl I used to run away from home with and go to shows, but she got my number from my dad later and called me and said, "Who did you marry?" I told her. She said, "You did not." "Why?" She goes, "You don't remember what you used to say?" I said, "What are you talking about?" She said, "Every single time we'd go to a festival or a show when Ray was playing, he'd get onstage and you'd say, 'One of these days, I'm gonna marry that Ray Wylie Hubbard.'" She said, "It got to the point that we'd say it with you because we knew what you were gonna say." I was fifteen, sixteen, seventeen years old, and there were a lot of drugs between those times, so I didn't remember. That explains the deep, soul-level connection I felt at Poor David's.

We got married at a Methodist church even though neither one of us was a churchgoer. The minister at the time bought cars from the dealership I was working at and was a friend of my dad's. We had the reception at the country club in North Dallas with all of Ray's friends and all of my friends, and whatever musicians were there got up and played. It was fun and more formal than we were, but I did it that way for my dad. My father paid for it.

Becoming Ray's manager was a natural progression. I was in the car business. My father was general manager of the whole conglomerate of dealerships that this man owned. He was real well known by mobsters, athletes, and politicians. All the well-known people who would buy Lincolns would buy them from W. O. Bankston. My dad was his right-hand man, and I was used to waiting on well-known people. I was self-taught, but I learned different aspects of the business and was able to pick it up really quick. When I married Ray, his ex-father-in-law, who was a criminal attorney, was his manager. He basically made sure Ray was represented legally.

Nobody was really doing anything for him. He was calling to get his own gigs. Honestly, I had no idea what I was getting into financially. I was making really good money at Bankston, enough to afford not having two incomes at the time. I didn't need his income to afford his house. I was living in a house I bought off Inwood and Lovers Lane in Dallas. I obviously didn't marry Ray to get wealthy in the music business. I knew he was playing clubs in Poor David's, but I didn't know what that meant, and it didn't matter at the time. I have such a strong belief in his songwriting and his stage presence that I couldn't believe that he wasn't doing better than he was.

I couldn't sit by and watch. I'd pick up little pieces like helping him get contracts signed and back to the club. I started calling the clubs. Of course, we're talking about days before computers and mobile phones. Everything we did, we had to do on a dial-up phone or pay phone if we were on the road. I would go get the newspapers and *Buddy* magazine and see what clubs other people who were like Ray were playing. I asked him, "If you could have any audience, who would you want?" "I want to sing in front of Guy Clark, Townes Van Zandt, and Billy Joe Shaver's audience." I would make a spreadsheet with a pencil and paper and write down all the clubs they played.

It was difficult. Ray had burned bridges with the clubs. He'd either be drunk or he wouldn't show up or he wasn't drawing because he didn't put out many records in the eighties, and the ones he did weren't notable by any means. He got sober in '87, but he did coke during most of the eighties. I'd call [Gruene Hall owner] Pat Molak, and he'd say, "We're not booking him here." I couldn't believe the reception I was getting. I'd call back and say, "Why?"

"Why don't you ask Ray? The last time he played here he didn't show up." I'd tell Ray and he'd go, "Oh, no, that was probably Gary P. Nunn or Jerry Jeff Walker. They get us three-name guys mixed up all the time." I'd call back and say, "Ray says maybe you got him mixed up with another three-name guy." Pat would say, "Why don't you ask his band? They showed up." Click.

Ray had been sober about five years by the time we put out *Lost Train of Thought* in 1991. We started getting a bit of airplay around Dallas and some in Austin, and people saw that sobriety wasn't gonna be an on-and-off-the-wagon thing, [so things] started to pick up a little. I toured with him for the first eight years because it was only weekends unless he went to Europe. I was tour manager, booking agent, publicist, and manager and would sell merchandise while I was working sixty hours a week in the car dealership. I was fortunate that the dealership was lenient with me. They weren't gonna fire me if they walked into my office and I was booking a gig on the phone. They believed in Ray, and all the owners liked him.

I quit working full time when we moved to Wimberley, Texas, about twenty years ago and I decided to do this full time, which was really scary. He still wasn't making as much money as I was making on my own in Dallas. We couldn't get a record deal. I reached out to all the majors. We had our honeymoon in Nashville in the middle of winter in an ice storm, thinking that while I had a weekend off work, I would go get him a deal. I was so naive about the business. I thought that's how it worked. I was so driven and passionate by the fact that I was blown away by his songs. Then I got to Nashville on our honeymoon and everybody passed. Ray still wasn't the guitarist and musician that he is today. His songs were basic.

He [had] already had the run with Warner Bros. He hated the Cowboy Twinkies record and said, "Fuck you, I'm not gonna work it." That word gets around. Also, he was past the age where people were getting signed. Willie Nelson told him years ago, "You're too country for rock and too rock for country. You're about ten or fifteen years ahead of your time." He was still too edgy for country and too country for rock. I sent letters and promo packs out, and we couldn't get anything. So we started our own label and knocked on doors at record stores to drop off CDs. We went all over Dallas and everywhere we could get.

I think the first change was with *Loco Gringo's Lament*. The writing, production, and guitar playing were all at such a higher level than *Lost Train of Thought*. That's when people started giving us airplay who wouldn't before. Journalists who wouldn't before started writing about him. Another big uptick happened after *Snake Farm*. Once you do well for more than one or two records, people start to take notice that you're not just a one-trick pony. Also, when SiriusXM Radio started playing him as much as they do, that opened up a nationwide audience that we might not have gotten. Being on *Late Night with David Letterman* and the Conan O'Brien and Jimmy Fallon shows made a huge difference, too.

Ray would always write after I went to bed back before computers and when I had a full-time job. I commuted an hour and a half each way the last couple years in Dallas, so I would have to go to bed at nine o'clock. He stays up late. He would do a lot of his writing when I was gone. Once we had Lucas, he would take care of him a couple days, and we would put him in day care other days so he could write when I was at work. Now that we've been here for twenty years, I can tell when he's in the writing zone by looking over his shoulders. If I walk in from my office, I can see that he's on MasterWriter on his computer. I know not to interrupt him unless it's a time-sensitive thing. Otherwise, I just save everything until later in the day when he takes a break.

I'm an introvert in a lot of ways, so it works. I like to putz around and do my own thing when I'm home. I'm fine not being entertained or entertaining him all the time, but he still stays up and writes a lot at night after I go to bed. If he's really in the zone and I have people in the house like the tour manager or I'm just making noise, he'll go up to the guest bedroom, close the door, and finish writing. Honestly, he sits on the couch with his computer and guitar in his lap from the minute he gets up to the minute he goes to bed. He never stops. He might not be writing a song, but he's always either rereading something that gave him ideas before and he wants to explore more or he'll just need inspiration and he'll read a biography. He always has something percolating in his mind, and he's always in his spot in the den with MasterWriter open if something strikes him. I've looked at his MasterWriter, and he has a lot more songs in there than ones he's finished.

The melody and lyrics of "Stone Blind Horses" brought me to tears when I heard it and for the first month he was working on it. I don't usually like to listen until they're finished because I don't want to find myself critiquing or asking questions that would throw off his mojo. I want it to be his song until he's ready for it to be our song, but "Stone Blind Horses" stopped me in my tracks, like the day I saw him play "Portales." I said, "God, talk to me about this." He said, "I've had this melody for thirty years and have never written a song that did the melody justice until just now." Who can keep a melody on hold for thirty years?

Ray has a son, Cory, from his first marriage, who will be forty in April. He was nine years old when Ray and I first got married, and he would stay at our house on Wednesdays and every other weekend. Ray was always very hands-on and a great daddy. When Cory got older in high school and was interested in girls and friends, we didn't see him as much. Then he went to Texas A&M University on a tennis scholarship and got jobs out of state. He lives in New York now.

Ray was very, very hands-on when Lucas was born. Lucas was premature, so his feeding schedule was every hour and a half. Ray wrote the whole *Loco Gringo's Lament* [during] overnights with Lucas. He took the midnight to five a.m. feeding schedule, and he would sit by Lucas's crib and rock him to sleep and write songs. I think "The Last Younger Son" about an outlaw named Cole Younger was written about him. Lucas's middle name is Cole. Ray got inspired a lot by the midnight hours with Lucas.

I always had dreams of Lucas going to law school because I couldn't. We took him on tour everywhere because we didn't want anyone babysitting him. I was too scared someone would hurt him. Lucas was used to being on the road. We'd be on tour in Boston, and I would take him to the steps of Harvard and have him sit down and close his eyes and visualize going to school there one day. Somewhere in high school when Lucas realized his strengths were math and science and he had absolutely no desire for history and English and political science, he told me one day when he started looking at schools, "Look, Mama, it just ain't gonna happen. I'll probably go get a science or math degree, but I don't want to be a lawyer."

He had no desire to wear a suit or go into an office. The main thing is to be happy. He loves playing with Ray, and they share the same dry, sarcastic humor. There's always been more to him. He wants to invent something or create a business and be self-employed. We still see [Lucas playing in Hubbard's band] as a stepping-stone to whatever he'll be far from now. He has a great gig because he's Ray's son, but that doesn't mean it's gonna be forever. He's well aware that not everybody has a great gig. I think that working at Gibson has let him see the business side that he really likes. The big advantage is that he gets to spend every working day with his dad and his dad gets to spend every working day with his son. It's a good way for me to keep an eye on the kid and they have quality time with each other while Ray's still alive. When your dad's in his seventies, you want to spend as much time with him as you can.[1]

Lucas Hubbard

I started messing around with the mandolin around nine or ten years old. I was always fascinated with guitars and instruments, growing up with them all around. The mandolin was smaller and less intimidating, and I picked that up pretty quickly. I would play songs with my dad, sitting around on the couch. He went to a guitar show when I was twelve and bought this three-quarter scale Super 0 1960s guitar. He says he and my mom have a thing: He gets a new guitar, she gets a new quilting machine or whatever. It was her turn to get something, and he shows up with this guitar. She's like, "What is that? You just got a guitar." He's like, "It's for Lucas. Come here, I'll teach you how to play." He taught me the pentatonic blues scale. I grew up on all those old blues guys like Lightnin' Hopkins, Muddy Waters, Freddie King, Bill Withers. I like the whole no-rules aspect of their playing because I didn't want to learn to read music. I knew the blues scale and could play whatever I wanted.

There are football dads where the dad plays in college and then pushes his kids to do it. Ray's the complete opposite of that. He

Left to right: Lucas Hubbard and Ray Wylie Hubbard. Photo by Judy Hubbard.

was definitely there to teach me all the time and enjoyed teaching me new things, but I could basically do whatever I wanted to do as long as I wasn't a Republican. We played, and he would teach me at least an hour a day. He wasn't pushing it on me or to the other extreme, like "Don't get into this music business." He definitely had to earn his way. There were hard times, but I don't think he was ever afraid that I was gonna go down that path in the music business.

I always aspired to play like Gurf [Morlix] once I got to the age and skill level where I could really learn new things and I understood them as far as his tone and his unique way of playing. My friends were copying Stevie Ray Vaughan and the Jimi Hendrix style and fretting, but I was always fascinated by how different Gurf was. [While I was] growing up, Seth James was probably the one who sat down with me the most and taught me different licks and showed me a lot. I always had a guitar with me, and anytime we were around guitar players they'd show me new licks. I wouldn't say that I had a guitar teacher when I was growing up, but I definitely learned a lot from his friends like Gurf, Kevin Welch, Buddy Miller, whose playing was a really big influence on me.

The actual Goldtop Les Paul that he grew up playing didn't make it through time and get passed down to me. I do have a Goldtop that he got me, though. That was one of my first nice, expensive guitars. I took it in and distressed it to age and relic it, and I made it look like a '58 Goldtop. I had pictures of his to base it on. Unfortunately, there's not a crazy story of Ray having it through the years and passing it on. The Goldtop guitar [in "Mother Blues"] is a metaphor, but I've always played Gibson guitars. They gave me my first and it was a blue Les Paul. I was probably fourteen.

I love old, vintage Gibson acoustics and especially 335s. I've been into the semi-hollow body guitars recently like the 275s. A different tone is required playing with Ray, and I think that's why Gurf was such a killer guitar player on the records. It's not really pedals and the typical lead tone. There's a natural tone and grit with small old amps that you just really crank up. You can really hear the tubes. I think I have two pedals besides the tuner. There's something about the Goldtop that has that gritty, gnarly tone that I've always liked. I make it really bass-y because we don't travel with a bass player. It's important to do that as opposed to a Telecaster or a Fender that's more treble and cuts through for the lead stuff. I started working for Gibson about a year ago, and I get to try out a lot of different guitars. I wouldn't say that I have had a guitar for the past ten years that I always like to play. I like to try out different things and experiment with new guitars and amps.

The Gibson showroom in Austin isn't open to the public, but it's an amazing million-dollar room with a stage. We have four hundred guitars, and we do a lot of events, sponsorships, and finding new artists to loan or place guitars with. I do the tech work and day-to-day stuff. They were the ones who gave me my first Gibson when I was thirteen at Willie's [Fourth of July] Picnic. I asked to play one onstage, and I came off. They were like, "How do you like your new guitar?" I was like, "What do you mean?" "It's yours." Of course, I freaked out. Fast-forward to ten years later and I moved back to Austin and needed a job. I knew they were hiring a guitar tech. They asked me, "Have you done guitar tech stuff?" I lied my way into the job. "Yeah, yeah, I can do that." I learned as I went. I really love it. I have learned so much about guitars and the tech side from working there.

Playing "Mother Blues" on *Late Night with David Letterman* was intense. I've been around the music business and have been thrown into big situations really young, like Willie's [Fourth of July] Picnic and *Late Night with Jimmy Fallon*. I almost never get nervous or anxious, but there's something about Letterman. It was one of those surreal moments when you're inside your head. I mean, this is David fucking Letterman. We got there and there are the lights and makeup and he keeps his studio at forty-eight degrees. Everything's freezing cold and fast-paced. It was a little overwhelming, but it was so exciting. That song means so much to my dad and is almost his memoir in a song. We were all really proud of him and proud to be there.

We went in to rehearse the Wednesday before. The Letterman show was maybe on a Saturday. We were playing the song, and I felt comfortable with my lead, but I felt like it needed something different. I asked my dad, "Hey, what if I played this in open E?" That can add a different dynamic. He was like, "Have you ever played in open E before?" "No, not really." That describes the whole experience, all new stuff. Never playing in that key added another level of nervousness, but it was exciting and surreal to say the least. We cut out a verse and maybe the lead guitar part. I think we had three minutes and thirty-six seconds to play it, and the record cut was maybe four minutes and twenty seconds. Ray doesn't like rehearsing, but that's what we did for the show. He likes the more natural, original aspect, but we sped it up quite a bit in rehearsal. We took some of the air, the pauses, out of it. I think we got it right on the dot with the required time.

Ray sticks to 50 percent of the same live show with "Snake Farm," "Drunken Poet's [Dream]," "Redneck," "Mother Blues," but he does each show depending on the crowd. We don't do set lists or go over it before hand. He goes with whatever he's feeling and how the crowd's responding. That justifies if we're gonna be more rocking, or if we're playing at a church or a theater, we might be more folk or blues. We very rarely rehearse even when he comes out with a new song. We just run over it at soundcheck or he'll pull it out in the middle of the set and we'll wing it. We're fortunate that our drummer Kyle Snyder is amazingly diverse and super creative. That helps us play on the fly.

I take guitar playing one day at a time. I don't have any expectations of myself where I need to follow in my dad's footsteps. I've always really wanted to create my own name instead of just being Ray Wylie's son. I love playing, and it's obviously my dream to continue playing guitar and make a living out of it, but I've been so spoiled growing up with such musicians and gigs that I will never want to start playing just to play where it's not fun anymore. As long as I'm still having fun performing, then I'd definitely love to keep doing it. Who knows? I like the business side, too, like the copyright [laws], and I get that from my mom. We'll have to see.[2]

Seth James

Ray and I met playing the same venues and then I opened some shows, and he invited me to play on a couple gigs. We love the same kind of music like Lightnin' Hopkins, Mance Lipscomb, old school blues. He was one of the few people I could have conversations about that music in the Texas music world. We enjoyed that common thread. We'd swap licks and obscure turnarounds. Lightnin' was simplistic, but he had a real unique way of doing things. Soundchecks with Ray aren't really soundchecks. You play a Lightnin' riff and I'll play a Lightnin' lick. Of course, when you travel with somebody the most fun part's sharing music. We'd listen to old, obscure stuff.

I got turned onto blues early in life in a place where that doesn't happen. I grew up in Northwest Texas on a ranch, and they played complete cowboy country. All the music you got was what was commercially successful on the radio. I was lucky to have an older brother who lived in the big city, and he would filter me music. I

Left to right: Seth James, Jenni Finlay, and Ray Wylie Hubbard, at the third anniversary party of Jenni Finlay Promotions, Cheatham Street Warehouse, August 13, 2009. Photo by Clay McNeill.

was listening to Robert Johnson, Howlin' Wolf, and Muddy Waters as a freshman in high school. We didn't have the power of the Internet or Pandora back then, so I had to work real hard to find that music. It was very genuine music, and it stirred me up. That was my go-to music.

Lucas probably has learned the same way I have, which is listening to the right people. I don't think there were lots of actual guitar lessons for him or me. I had my first guitar lesson two weeks ago, and I've been playing for twenty years. He probably learned from me just by us being around each other. You get it by osmosis. He was a young man when I was playing with his dad and he was excited and hungry. If we traveled on a bus, he'd usually come along, and we would sit and pick back and forth. I know that's a big deal with me when I have someone I look up to. If I have the opportunity to sit down with that person, I still get real excited to learn a few things from them.

Lucas's greatest strength would be similar to his dad's. There are all kinds of paths you can take as a guitarist. There's the guitar slinger path, where you're really bombastic, have a lengthy vocabulary, and know all the licks and notes, and you play them all. That's not what I'm drawn to. I was drawn to Ray because of his simplicity. I like people nodding and honoring people who came before them. It's one thing to copy someone, but it's another to honor their bluesy playing. It's not the way that usually gets you the jobs or sells all the records versus someone like Joe Bonamassa, who's a guitar slinger. He's big and loud.

I'm sure Lucas knows about playing to serve the song, since he grew up with a songwriter dad. The idea's not to step up and have your moment as a guitar player. You do that, but he does that to support his dad's music and fill in gaps. He knows what his dad loves and listens to because he grew up doing the same thing. There's really no need for Ray to ever hire another guitar player again, since he's basically duplicated himself in a way with his son. Ray wouldn't want a guitar player showing up with a 50-watt Marshall [amplifier] and a starship pedalboard and nine guitars. You need to know Lightnin' Hopkins as his guitarist and make one E chord really funky. You're in the right place if you can do that. As simple as that sounds, it's not that simple to do.[3]

Jamie Lin Wilson

I flew with Ray to Key West, Florida, recently. He stood up when we landed, and I wondered if all these people on the plane were wondering who the hell he is. He looks like a rock star and carries himself like he's on top of the world all the time. Ray and Jack Ingram walk around like they know people are looking at them. Ray's wearing a jacket, and he has all his scarves, his hair, pointed boots, guitars, and fingernails. I have a feeling Ray's been charming his whole life. I never saw his shows in the eighties and don't know what they were like, but when you're that charming, you can make anybody do anything. I do know a lot of people who learned a lot about stage presence from Ray, that's for damn sure. They go, "I wonder if I could tell stories like that." He has taught many people whether he knows it or not.

"The Lovers in Your Dreams" from *Crusades of the Restless Knights* was the first song I heard when I was in the [Sidehill] Gougers, and it's one of my favorites. "Do the lovers in your dreams wake up, too?" God, I love that song so much. I remember thinking Ray was untouchable for a long time like any of our other heroes. I learned he's actually very approachable and really nice when the

Left to right: Jamie Lin Wilson and Chris Fullerton (with Blaze Foley photograph courtesy Chuck Lamb), during a session recording Foley's "Clay Pigeons," Cheatham Street Warehouse, San Marcos, Texas, February 19, 2018. Photo by Brian T. Atkinson.

Trishas were beginning. I was so surprised, but I don't know why. You always think that your heroes are in a different category, and they know that. I do think that he does understand his role as a father figure to so many, and he takes it so seriously.

Ray's always willing to help. I had been a guest with Ray before on his *Roots & Branches* show on KNBT with the Gougers and then solo, but [Trishas bandmate] Liz Foster was living with Ray and Judy when the Trishas started, and that got us close to them. It's one thing to sit on a stage and sing songs and have him interview you, but to become his friend is something else all together. I know he would do anything if I asked him for help. Any time I have a business question or wonder if something has happened to them, too, and don't know what to do, Ray and Judy are the ones I call. I think I'm one of many who do that. He gives harmonica and guitar lessons to anyone who needs them. He just wants everyone to be better, and we're lucky to have them.

I started crying watching [Cody Canada's son] Dierks Canada playing guitar with Ray on a video from Gruene Hall recently. I was like, "Judy, do you realize what you just did for that kid?" She said, "Well, Cody was the first person to ever ask Lucas to play guitar with him onstage who wasn't Ray. All we could do was return the favor to help his kid." They have such big hearts, and that's the thing we need everywhere. I did *Roots & Branches* for the first time by myself seven or eight years ago, and I played a song near the end. Ray said, "Man, you're one of those real songwriters, huh?" I just looked at him and was like, "I don't know what that means, but thank you." I try to be. I'll never forget the look of enjoyment on his face. He really likes my songs.

Ray doesn't bullshit. He doesn't compliment people just to say nice things. He's really encouraging like [late songwriter and Cheatham Street Warehouse owner] Kent Finlay was, and if he loves a song, he'll let you know. If he doesn't really, really love it, he'll let you know that, too. He doesn't sugarcoat things to make you feel good, but everything he says is right. If he doesn't like something, you go, "Oh, yeah, I probably need to work on that. It's not very good. I should rethink this." I think he's doing us all a service by being real like that and by being willing to help all the time. I hope that he knows we appreciate it so much. I think he does.

I love Ray's conversational writing so much and have taken that from him. I listen to Ray's songs and go, "Man, he nailed it. He didn't think too hard." I'm sure that he actually does, but it appears that he doesn't. He conveys an idea with such great imagery, but the songs are so simple, it seems like he's just telling you a stream-of-consciousness story straight out of his mouth. Sometimes he probably is. I've thought about that a lot for this last record I just finished. I tried to be real and conversational like I was telling a story to a friend and put a melody to it. I learned that from Ray.

They let us sit high above the stage at that festival in Key West. I watched the crowd as Ray was playing all night, and they never stopped moving. He has a groove right there in the middle with nothing too fast and nothing too slow. He's all Zen and had this meditative groove going. Everybody kept their eyes on him, and he was completely mesmerizing the whole night. The crowd had a pulse. You could see everybody's head's moving throughout the whole time like a magic show. I was like, "These people just sat here for forty-five minutes completely mesmerized by him." He's leading everybody else on a ride with him to the circus.[4]

Liz Foster

I had been writing songs for other people, but I had never written them for myself. I finally recorded an EP with three or four songs I had written, and a buddy and I were at a show Ray and Chris Knight were playing at Love and War in Grapevine, Texas. My buddy was running sound, and he told Ray that he wanted him to meet me. My buddy gave Ray my EP and said, "You should listen to it." I was at work as a project manager for a credit union a few weeks later when I got a call on my cell phone. The voice on the other end said, "Is this Liz?" "Yeah." "This is Ray Wylie Hubbard." I was like, "Yeah. Who is this?" "No, it really is Ray Wylie Hubbard." I thought I was gonna pass out.

He and Judy had listened to the EP, and Ray said he'd be interested in helping me. The Trishas all became close with Ray and Judy. We're like a family, and we all call Ray "Snake Daddy." He's very protective of us. When the Trishas first got together, Ray would always have us come up at shows and sing songs like "Papa Was a Rolling

Liz Foster and Ray Wylie Hubbard, Hubbard's 71st birthday celebration, Paramount Theater, Austin, Texas, November 17, 2017. Photo by Jim Chapin; courtesy Liz Foster.

Stone." I think we sang "Whoop and Hollar" [from *A: Enlightenment, B: Endarkenment (Hint: There Is No C)*] at Luckenbach with him and a few other times. When it came time to record it, he called us and said, "Hey, will y'all come in and do this? Y'all just go for it." There was intentionally not much structure in that recording. It was a ton of fun. Ray's so intelligent, but he's also one of the funniest people I've ever met.

I lived with Ray and Judy in Wimberley for two months when I first moved to Austin. Those were some of the most special moments in my life, being able to be mentored by one of your favorite writers and just observe his writing habits. We'd be hanging out in the evenings after dinner and play with songs or talk about ideas, and then Ray brought "Train Yard" [from *The Grifter's Hymnal*] to me. We might've been on a bus to Luckenbach when he brought it up. That was months before we actually sat down and worked on it. We ended up writing it over one or two evenings. The song was super slow and sultry when we first wrote it, but I loved what he did with it on the record. He had me come in when he was cutting it so I could hear.

Most people hold back and have a filter on what they say, but what Ray says onstage about us writing "Train Yard" is true. He's a really honest writer, and some of the lyrics he threw out were great, but I was like, "I don't think." We were originally writing that song for me to sing on a record my ex-husband and I were recording and Ray was producing. He kept throwing out certain phrases like, "Let's take that cross off the wall and do da-da-da." I was like, "I cannot sing that." Then it became a joke. He plays on it a lot, but that is a true story. I started telling Judy that all he needs is some red heels and some fishnets.

I've taken away so much from Ray as a lyricist. I mean, half the time I say, "This isn't good enough." The way that he delivers the truth in his lyrics [is inspiring]. He's a mystic [Rainer Maria] Rilke and a gnarly old blues cat combined into one mind. I don't think that anybody writes like him. He writes insanely beautiful or thought-provoking or funny lyrics, and then he puts them to these gnarly grooves. I don't know anyone else who does what he does when he pairs the music together with the thought of the song. I remember watching him read every day when I was living with them. He and Judy are extremely educated, intelligent people. Ray constantly reads everything from poetry to books on Mexican drug cartel songs. He's not sitting down to write just thinking, "Oh, this is a cool title." He puts a lot of thought into his songs. I've learned that from him.

I have a real soft spot for "The Messenger." That song makes me cry every time. Songs like that make you really think about what you're writing. I have been a huge fan of Ray's writing since I was a teenager, and I've always appreciated the truth in his extremely poetic lyrics with all the different grooves. I learned to have truth in my lyrics and not to be scared to have more truth than I think should be in there. There's a lot to learn from him, and his writing reflects who he is as an individual. As a person and a writer, he really sets an example for how to carry yourself and deliver material. I think he deserves so much more recognition than he has gotten.[5]

Kelley Mickwee

I've gotten to know Ray and Judy pretty well over the years. I've traveled with them, opened for him, and worked for Judy in the office. I've learned from Ray both how to be a good human and about having patience as a performer, especially after a show. For example, he'll come out and sign autographs nine times out of ten

*Left to right: Kelley Mickwee
and Chris Fullerton, El Pres
Recording Studio, Austin,
Texas, February 13, 2018,
during Mickwee's session
for Eight 30 Records'*
Floater: A Tribute to the
Tributes to Gary Floater.
Photo by Brian T. Atkinson

until the last person is gone. He's like Willie Nelson. He's been doing
this a long time, but he has a lot of patience. He gives everybody
a minute to give a hug and sign an autograph and take a picture
with him. He's like Buddha, a kind, gracious person who always
has something calming to say in a situation where I might be over-
reacting. He'll say, "Go with your second thought. Don't overreact."
Of course he always keeps his gratitude high and all the things he
learned in AA and applies to his daily life. He's so grateful to still
be playing music and be successful.

We've written a few songs together over the years, but obviously
neither of us liked them enough because we haven't recorded
them. We wrote one with Liz Foster called "Hell or High Water."
[Coincidentally, Hubbard's song "Dust of the Chase" was included
on the soundtrack to the 2016 movie *Hell or High Water* starring
Jeff Bridges and directed by David Mackenzie.] It wasn't an ideal
setup for me to write with Ray. The Trishas were having different
songwriters come by to write with us when we were working on
our record, and we met him in a conference room at a hotel out on
Lake Austin, which was not the kind of place where you're gonna
get a soulful song.

Ray and Liz have written many times out at his house. He likes
to be home when he's writing songs. Ray's patient with songwriting and will let you throw out all your ideas. He's always told me
when I'm asking for songwriting advice that there's inspiration on
every corner. He always uses "Snake Farm" as an example because
it's not about love and heartache, like most things we write about
are. His two biggest songs are about a redneck mother and a snake
farm. He gives this rap where he says, "Never second-guess your
inspiration. Write it all down. Get it all down. It's okay to rewrite,
but when inspiration hits, don't edit at that time. Have it be a flow.
You write and edit later." Songs are always being edited right up
until the moment they're being recorded.

I've generally written "woe is me" songs about being sad because
that's the easiest thing for me to get out, but that rule can be applied
to most of us. We look at these songs that Ray has recorded and
look at his career. He's as relevant as Willie. Willie came here to
Texas to play music for people who weren't gonna judge him. He
played whatever the fuck he wanted to play. He was fifty or so. Ray
was the same. He didn't really make good money and have success
until way later in life. He's still relevant, playing, and touring.

You can't look at Los Angeles and Nashville, where it's all about
the look and how young you are, and get inspired by that if you're
an aging woman nearing forty like I am. There are guys like Walt
Wilkins and Ray here who are still successful and doing it. He
doesn't seem to be stopping, which is why he's as important as Willie to Austin music. He's just doing his damn thing writing songs
and making records. Doing what you love and continuing is the
measure of success in my opinion. Not many people who are over
seventy are as busy as he is.

I absolutely don't think Ray will be remembered as the "Redneck Mother" guy. People like me before I moved to Texas [might
think that]. I'm from Memphis, and I didn't know Ray Wylie until I
started touring down here. I only knew Jerry Jeff's version of "Redneck Mother." Then I saw Ray perform at Larry Joe Taylor's music
festival [in Stephenville, Texas] because it was one of the first
festivals I played in Texas after I discovered Terri Hendrix, Lloyd
Maines, and Terry Allen. I thought Ray was hilarious. I remember
seeing this gnarly old dude up there playing blues and rock and

roll music for the Texas music festival while everyone did their country thing. Ray will hang on one chord for three songs, and he'll make you laugh all the while.

It didn't take me long to dive into everything else that he's done. He's made so many records and inspired and helped so many musicians. He loves to have people over and show them how to fingerpick in his Ray style, and he'll write it all out. Something I'll always keep is the paper where he wrote out how to fingerpick something that I still haven't learned because it's really hard. I think he'll be remembered as a great teacher to all of us. He's touched a lot of people. Now he's playing with these Texas country dudes and Eric Church, who's this young country dude at the top of the charts. He wants to sing with Ray Wylie and put his name in his song because that makes him cool. I don't know how it would be possible to relate him only to "Redneck Mother." That song's the last thing I think about when I think about his music. He's such a spiritual dude.[6]

Savannah Welch

The Trishas came about because we were performing at that tribute for my dad, [songwriter Kevin Welch, in 2009 at MusicFest in Steamboat Springs, Colorado]. We had our first rehearsals as the

Savannah Welch. Photo by Greg Giannukos.

Trishas at his house in Wimberley, [Texas]. He lives right around the corner on the same street as the Hubbards. I remember Judy being really excited about us getting together, and she came down for our first rehearsal. At the time, Judy and Ray managed Liz and Lincoln, which was Liz Foster in a duo with her then-husband Lincoln Durham. They lived with Ray and Judy for a while when they first moved to town, and Liz used to get up and sing "Whoop and Hollar" with Ray. She was learning harmonica then. So it was a natural choice for him to ask the Trishas to sing on that song.

Judy is one of my dearest, most treasured friends. She's always felt like a big sister. She's been a great supporter in my sobriety. We really connected through that at the beginning. I was not sober when I first met them, but when I did get sober and was seeking support, I knew that I could go to them for that. She's someone I can go to as a voice of reason and a moral compass in general and in my artistic endeavors. She's a nonjudgmental [sounding] board. I know I can go and lay down whatever I need to get off my chest with Judy and Ray.

Sobriety is vital. It was a matter of necessity when I got sober ten years ago. I got to a point where I knew that if it was up to me and my own willpower, I would die. I'm in a different place and have had a lot of healing since then. The plan wasn't to be sober for life or even a number of years. I just thought I needed to clean this up a little bit and pull it back until I got my shit together. Getting my shit together took longer than I thought. By the time I did, I thought, Oh, I'm in a much better place now. I'm not in as much dysfunction. I understand boundaries better, and my pattern of self-destruction and [drinking] is not an option for me. It was a pattern I was able to stop. Drinking wasn't anything I cared about or needed in my life at all. I didn't miss it. I didn't feel a need for it. Also, I had a really solid support system, and Ray and Judy were central to that.[7]

Max Gomez

The "Redneck Mother" bar is currently called the [Motherlode] Saloon in Red River, New Mexico. There's a tiny little shack across from it on a side street, a venue where B. W. Stevenson, Jerry Jeff,

Max Gomez promotional photograph by Kimberly Hays.

Ray, Michael Martin Murphey, and others allegedly all hung out. Now it's an apartment that they rent cheap. I've seen the kids who live there. They ain't got any money. There's a little marquee on the side of the apartment where they would have put up the performers' names. A historian named Steve Heglund has owned the place since then. He probably gave those guys their first gigs. I had dinner the other night with Rick Fowler, Ray, and other folks, and Rick brought up how he and Ray would play Mexican tunes table to table trying to get a job playing for tip money in Red River, New Mexico.

I'm from Taos, New Mexico, and the first gig I got as a kid was performing at this little honky-tonk there called the Old Blinking Light. I played with Michael Hearne. It doesn't take long to realize that Ray Hubbard exists in the music world, and that he wrote "Redneck Mother" and a whole bunch of other great songs that people are covering all the time. I didn't really get to know him until I started playing music in Red River. Ray Wylie was coming to town to play a gig, and I met him and his wife, Judy, passing each other in the hallway of Texas Reds Steakhouse. They're about the nicest people I know in the music business. We were all fast friends who I would call close friends now.

I had my debut record coming out on New West Records at the time. Judy noticed that right away. She invited me to play a few shows opening for Ray. She said to call if I ever had the time and let them know and she'd set it up. I might have sat in and played a couple songs with Ray the night we met in Red River. I think I played a couple of my own songs and then sat in with Ray doing JJ Cale's classic "Crazy Mama." Ray would play it, and the song was simple enough that I could jump up and play with him. They welcomed me in as if I was a peer. They're very friendly and compassionate folks. We're all like extended family.

Ray, Jerry Jeff Walker, Gary P. Nunn's songs had this anthemic sing-along quality. Ray really pioneered that. He's the poor man's poet as far as the things he writes about, the things he's experienced, which is wonderful. His fingerpicking, which is a style based off the way Lightnin' Hopkins fingerpicked and the way Townes Van Zandt studied Lightnin', really draws me to his music. That's a lost art you don't hear anyone else doing except maybe someone doing it at a bluegrass festival, but they play it too fast and I can't even tell. I'll always look up to him just for the fact that he's honed in on that craft and made his own thing.

I studied Robert Johnson and Big Bill Broonzy, but Lightnin' is someone I came across later. He obviously has this folk-country-blues pattern that flows. The rhythm is almost suspended while he's playing lead licks. I'm inspired by the way Lightnin' made records so free. Nobody cues the band worth a damn on some of his most famous recordings. The drummer ends before the bass player and Lightnin' still does another lick. It's like they weren't even paying attention to each other, but it doesn't matter. The essence of what they were doing was so strong that they could screw it up the entire time and the record would still come across. I feel like every studio should take note of that and stop worrying about being perfect.

Townes was more my study in songwriting. I've learned how to pick some ways Townes did like on "If I Needed You." I can pick that note for note, and it's not easy at the level he did. Townes inspires everybody on a songwriting level, and there's no exception over here with me. Townes's songs are so good it's not even fair. You can't even try to understand how he wrote. Most songs are so simple that you can study them with very little effort, but

Townes's songs are so masterful, unique, and original. You'd have to cut them into twelve pieces and study one at a time and then piece them together. By the end, my head would probably explode. I wouldn't call Townes's music the bar. He's above the bar.

Being original isn't impossible. You hear the same excuse from a lot of young songwriters over and over about how everything's already been done and written. I've never been able to understand how anybody could say that and not think it's ridiculous, but if you're trying to come up with something original, you're never gonna do it. If you're just trying to make music and relax and do what you can do, you're gonna do it without even trying. There are a million things and exactly zero things to say about songwriting. Songwriting's an art form I don't believe can be taught. You use the tools that you have to build what you can. It's all dependent on the creator to take the tools in whatever direction they go, whether it's original or not.

Ray has been writing songs recently that have only one chord. They're as simple as can be from a music theory standpoint. He makes a riff and a song out of one root chord. I don't know that I've seen anybody else do that. It's inspiring to see someone changing the rules yet again in our lifetime and for that person to be Ray, who we all know and love. He's here doing it right now. I hadn't even thought about that before, but it's true. He's building on his own unique thing. I don't even know that he'd take credit for creating the tricks he continues to use. In our lives, he's certainly forged the path in his more recent records. I think he'll become a verb. Twenty, thirty years from now we'll be vamping on a blues chord and say, "Yeah, like, let's Ray Wylie Hubbard the thing."[8]

Jack Ingram

Townes Van Zandt, Guy Clark, Jerry Jeff Walker, Willie Nelson, and Ray Wylie Hubbard are in your DNA and culture growing up in Houston, Texas, in the mid-seventies. My entrée to Ray was through Jerry Jeff Walker on ¡Viva Terlingua! when Bob Livingston said, "This song is by Ray Wylie Hubbard." I'm sure Ray wouldn't have drawn it up that way and he's made enough mention of that throughout his life, but that's the way the cards fell. It's funny know-

Jack Ingram, Austin City Limits Music Festival, Austin, Texas, September 19, 2011. Photo by Brian T. Atkinson.

ing him that way before I knew what he was all about. It's almost like he started out in my brain as a mythical superhero.

I got serious about my songwriting in my late teens and early twenties. Coincidentally, Ray got really serious about who he was and what second act he wanted to have at the same time. He's a real songwriting student and a real heart-and-soul songwriter. When he put out *Loco Gringo's Lament*, I went, "Okay, who's this guy?" He knows what he's talking about. I was living in Dallas then and [KHYI] 95.3 The Range played "Conversation with the Devil" all the time. I thought, This is dark, humorous, and all the things that drew me to wanting to be a songwriter in the first place.

I started making shifts in my career. I realized that you can't go with the flow. The flow will take you where it wants. Part of my education in music was learning things before I knew I would need them. I had [Ingram's 1995 album] *Lonesome Questions* and [1995's] *Live at Adair's* in the Top Five on the Americana chart and was sitting with my heroes like Joe Ely, Steve Earle, and John Prine, but I didn't sell any more records. I wasn't having the impact you would think I would have, having a Top Five record. I wanted to have an impact, but I knew I wasn't a good enough songwriter as a twenty-five-year-old kid. I knew that you could make records that could change the trajectory of your career because of people like

Ray. You make a decided effort to aim at a different target.

Ray was this guy who seemed adrift during the Outlaw movement, and then he put out *Loco Gringo's Lament*. The record made him a three-dimensional human songwriter with heart and soul. I wasn't old enough to know the inner workings of the music business when he started doing that, but I did know that he went from a fringe-level guy in Jerry Jeff's outlaw world to being in the conversation when you talk about Tom Waits or the real songwriters from Texas. Man, it gets interesting when you start placing bets on yourself and not relying on perceptions. "Oh, he's the drunk guy. He's the stoner guy." No, man, who are you? Ray wanted to lay that on the line and write personal songs and bet that they're good enough to stand against his heroes. Being a great songwriter's more daunting than being a great hit singer, but I saw Ray Wylie Hubbard do it.

The music dictates who you are and who people think you are. As a songwriter and a fan, I'm always drawn to songs that tell you the truth, allow you to read between the lines, and make up your own story with meat in the verses. It's not just haw-haw-haw blues. I'm drawn to songs that let my imagination go crazy about who Ray Wylie Hubbard is. "Conversation with the Devil" really tells me about his inner struggles and dialogue with himself. However he wants to hide that with his humor is like any good comedian. You can hide it with a punch line, but it's really about telling a story. His songs are interesting to me because you have to figure them out. He's guarded. You have to fight him to get past the sound bites and go, "What makes you cry, dude?"

Asking me to sing on "Dallas After Midnight" [on *Delirium Tremolos*] was the biggest compliment he ever gave me. I was still at a point as a songwriter and artist where I wasn't hedging my bets, but my friends and family sure wished I were. People had the vibe like, "Are you still doing that music thing?" So I was driving from Dallas to Austin one day with a college buddy, and I got a phone call. I picked up the phone and the guy says, "Is this Jack?" "Yeah." "This is Ray Wylie Hubbard." That's like getting a call from Karl Malone if you're in the NBA. "Oh my god." I got off the phone and was like, "Guess who that was, motherfucker? Ray Wylie Hubbard." Ten minutes later and my phone rang again. I'm not kidding. He goes, "I'm looking for Jack Ingram." I said, "This is Jack." "This is Willie Nelson." I was like, "Are you fucking kidding me? Did I rub some genie?" He asked me to play his Fourth of July Picnic. My buddy never asked me if I was doing that music thing ever again.

Anyway, I didn't know that Ray thought anything about me at that point. We probably played festival dates together, but we weren't really friends. He said, "I'm doing this song about a robbery late at night at a liquor store, and I was thinking about all the guys I know who play music. Who out of all them can handle driving the get-away car? Every time I think about it, you're the kind of guy who wouldn't panic or let me down. You wanna come sing this part?" I didn't know I was that guy, but I sure hoped so. I didn't know if anybody bought my bullshit or what they thought about me. I knew Robert Earl Keen didn't like me very much, and that's about it. So for Ray Wylie to give me that, it made me walk a little straighter with pride. It made a big difference.

If Ray had had his way, I would have played Lonesome Pride in *The Last Rites of Lonesome Pride*. He called and said, "Hey, man, I wrote this movie. I want you to play Lonesome Pride." The director made a three-minute trailer to get funding. It was me and Gary Busey, which was a whole trip in itself. He put all that energy into writing a serious script and laid that on me. He knew that I wouldn't let him down, even though I hadn't done much acting. Having someone put that kind of faith in you is everything sometimes. He's not just talking at a party and saying, "That guy's cool." He has real faith. He'll risk his own shit having faith that someone won't let him down.

He puts faith in people I would have written off long ago. He sees the germ of whatever those people want to be and corrals their energy in a way that they want to go. Putting that much thought into who other people want to be is huge. I really do make an effort now to help other artists find what they're looking for because of that faith he had in me and how validating it felt. I would imagine that paying it forward and paying it back came out of recovery for Ray. He's done a remarkable job hanging out in this scene and in those places for a recovering addict. That shows how solid he is with who he is. There's no judgment. He may care about what's going on around him, but he doesn't judge.

Ray wrote himself a new ending to his story. When I think about it analytically, I'm glad he had a chance to do that as the sober Ray Wylie Hubbard. He probably wanted to be that the whole time anyway. The way he looks, acts, and delivers his songs is the way he is. He's mystical. He believes in the mystery and magic of it all. When I hang out with him, I believe in his faith and dedication to that, which allows me to believe even stronger in the same way I write my own life. He makes me believe that if I'm honest with my music, I won't be misconstrued. I can have faith in that as long as I'm doing the work I'm supposed to do. He believes in other people, and he believes in me in a way that's very simple.

Now Ray doesn't have to worry about whether he plays "Redneck Mother" every night. He's absolutely gotten past that. I have faith in my own career that I can go play a show tonight and not play [Ingram's 2005 number one hit] "Wherever You Are." The audience isn't gonna leave completely disgusted with my show. He can play tonight and not play "Redneck Mother," and there might be grumblings from the 10 percent who don't know him, but the people who do won't give a shit if he plays the song. He's always wanted that answer. You can tell that he probably didn't know how to outrun that song way back when, but he has. I would argue that he never actually needed to outrun it in the first place. He should play it with joy and pride. "Redneck Mother" is a fucking great song. Also, how lucky: He wrote a standard. That's what every songwriter wants to do.

I'm about the age Ray was when he started getting really serious about songwriting. I can only imagine if I was truly defined at this point by one song I wrote when I was twenty-four-years old. Jesus Christ. Think about Ray. The past twenty-some years could be argued as the main part of his career besides one song. He's spent all that time defining himself against his own caricature. Imagine if you've never really put out your own record, and you're already starting out as a cartoon. Talk about a difficult row to hoe, buddy. He's inspirational. Ray realized that's where he was and said, "No, I'm not okay with that. I'm gonna write my way out of this comic book." He fucking did.[9]

Coda

Mike Peters (The Alarm)

Left to right: Mike Peters (The Alarm) and Ray Wylie Hubbard, 3TEN ACL Live, August 2017. Hubbard's high-water-mark "Snake Farm" centers around a character named Ramona who cried when Peters's popular Welsh band The Alarm broke up. Photo by Andy Labrow.

I heard about Ray Wylie Hubbard from fans who wrote me about his great song "Snake Farm," which mentions The Alarm in the lyrics. I was really hooked on his music when I heard it and wanted to find out more. I was touched and honored that he name-checked us in "Snake Farm." It's not often that happens in a song, especially in such a cool way. I've included "Snake Farm" on pre-show compilation tapes that have been played over the PA at our gigs. Ray Wylie is a twenty-first-century blues artist who touches people with his eye for detail. He's a human songwriter who conveys the funny side of life, and you get the sense that he's always being true even when writing about someone else.

Ray Wylie came to a The Alarm show at the 3TEN venue in Austin last time. We got to hang out backstage and say hello for a brief while, as he was playing at Antone's. He was so engaging and the real deal, a true musician with a big heart. I was invited to play with him in San Francisco at his show, but our concert ran over, and by the time I called his wife, Judy, Ray was just about to play his encore. Next time we will make it happen. Ray Wylie continues the line that started with Woody Guthrie and runs through Bob Dylan to Willie Nelson and on past Bruce Springsteen and Jack White. He's a true Americana great.[1]

In fond memory of Susanna Clark Atkinson
and John and Scott Fleischauer.—B.T.A.

Rest in Peace, George Reiff

Character Witnesses

TOMMY ALVERSON lives in Arlington, Texas. "Alverson should be the permanent face of the independent Texas Country music movement," The *Dallas Morning News* says. "He embodies all the hallmarks of the sound and the mindset. He's artistically beholden to nobody but himself. Alverson writes songs, but also has no qualms about recording good material from somebody else's pen." Accordingly, Alverson recorded Ray Wyle Hubbard's "Bordertown Girl" on 2004's *Heroes and Friends*.

BOBBY BARE, born April 7, 1935, in Ironton, Ohio, has earned the distinction of being country music's finest songcatcher over the past half century. The Country Music Hall of Fame member introduced several legendary songwriters including Cowboy Jack Clement, Harlan Howard, Billy Joe Shaver, Kris Kristofferson, and Mickey Newbury by recording their songs for the first time. Bare included Ray Wylie Hubbard's "Up Against the Wall Redneck Mother" on his album *Live at Gilly's* (Atlantic Records, 1999). (www.bobbybare.com)

DANNY BARNES, born December 21, 1961, in Temple, Texas, was a founding member of the influential alt-country band Bad Livers in the 1990s. He has since toured with the Dave Matthews Band, Robert Earl Keen, and the Jeff Austin Band. He received the prestigious Steve Martin Prize for Excellence in Banjo and Bluegrass in 2015. "Danny is a real innovator and we want to make sure innovation gets honored over the course of the prize," Martin says. "He plays three-finger and he's also not afraid to strum like an old banjo." (www.dannybarnes.com)

RAY BENSON, born March 16, 1951, in Philadelphia, Pennsylvania, has fronted the Grammy award–winning Western Swing band Asleep at the Wheel for nearly half a century. Iconic 1980s hit maker Huey Lewis's early band Clover frequently split bills with the band in the previous decade. "Ray's a great musician and singer, but he's also a great bandleader," Lewis says. "Being both is pretty rare." The band frames live shows around their signature take on Bobby Troup's "(Get Your Kicks On) Route 66." (www.ray benson.com)

SCOTT H. BIRAM, born April 4, 1974, in Lockhart, Texas, has released nine studio albums from his lo-fi debut *This Is Kingsbury?* (2000) through *The Bad Testament* (2017) for his longtime label Bloodshot Records. Biram's unique one-man band approach matches folk ("Wreck My Car") against fright ("Blood, Sweat, and Murder") as he combines influences including Doc Watson, Lightnin' Hopkins, and Mance Lipscomb with a punk rock attitude. His songs have been covered by Nashville Pussy ("Raisin' Hell Again") and Hank 3 ("Truck Driver"). (wwwscottbiram.com)

TROY CAMPBELL, born in southern Ohio, but a longtime Austin, Texas, resident, rose to prominence as a member of the popular Austin-based band Loose Diamonds in the 1990s. The group released a video for "Downtown" from their collection *Burning Daylight* (1993). The album notched the NAIRD Indie Album of the Year award in 1993. The follow-up *Fresco Fiasco* (1996) was named among that year's Top Ten undiscovered gems by *The New York Times*. The group disbanded in 1996, but Campbell went on to fulfill a higher purpose. He and Danish star Poul Krebs founded House of Songs, an organization that proves music provides a conduit for connecting diverse cultures together. House of Songs now sponsors collaborations in thirteen countries and operates out of Austin, Texas, and Bentonville, Arkansas.

CODY CANADA, born May 25, 1976, in Pampa, Texas, was the lead singer for Texas Red Dirt music pioneers Cross Canadian Ragweed for more than fifteen years. The band found significant commercial success with their albums *Soul Gravy* (2004), *Garage* (2005), and *Mission California* (2007). In 2001, Canada left Cross Canadian Ragweed and formed Cody Canada and the Departed. Ray Wylie Hubbard name-checks Ragweed and their album *Soul Gravy* in his song "Mother Hubbard's Blues." (www.thedeparted.com)

HAYES CARLL shot his career from a cannon with *Trouble in Mind* (2008). The Woodlands, Texas, native's third album was a vibrant vortex backing machetes ("Faulkner Street") with memories ("Knockin' over Whiskeys"), catapulting him from rising talent into an established tunesmith. His song "She Left Me for Jesus" won the Americana Music Association's Song of the Year award (2008). The current Nashville resident, born January 9, 1976, achieved even wider spread success with *KMAG YOYO* (2011) and the reflective *Lovers and Leavers* (2016). (www.hayescarll.com)

Mainstream country music superstar ERIC CHURCH, born May 3, 1977, in Granite Falls, North Carolina, has a deep connection with Ray Wylie Hubbard. "You love your daddy's vinyl, old-time rock and roll," his song "Mr. Misunderstood" goes. "Elvis Costello, Ray Wylie Hubbard, and think Jeff Tweedy / Is one bad mother." *Mr. Misunderstood* won the Country Music Association's Album of the Year award in 2016. Additionally, Church sang on the title track to Hubbard's *Tell The Devil...I'm Gettin' There As Fast As I Can* and cowrote the title track to his *Desperate Man* (2018) with Hubbard.

SLAID CLEAVES's *Still Fighting the War* (2013) spotlights an artist in peak form two decades into his career. Cleaves's effortless collection elegantly delivers vivid snapshots as wildly cinematic ("Rust Belt Fields") as they are carefully chiseled ("Voice of Midnight"). Cleaves, born June 9, 1964, in Washington, DC, but raised in Berwick, Maine, currently lives in Ray Wylie Hubbard's hometown, Wimberley, Texas. He contributed his Kent Finlay cowrite "Lost" to Eight 30 Records' *Dreamer: A Tribute to Kent Finlay* (2015). (www.slaidcleaves.com)

ELIZABETH COOK, born July 17, 1972, in Wildwood, Florida, debuted on the Grand Ole Opry in 2000. She shot her star skyward a decade ago with the Rodney Crowell–produced *Balls* (2007) and has released a half-dozen studio albums altogether, including her most recent *Exodus of Venus* (2016). Cook hosts the morning radio show *Elizabeth Cook's Apron Strings* on SiriusXM's Outlaw Country station. She and Jason Isbell sang Townes Van Zandt's "Pancho and Lefty" and "Tecumseh Valley" on her appearance on *Late Show with David Letterman* in early 2013. (www.elizabeth-cook.com)

NINO COOPER, born in El Paso, Texas, founded the Dirty River Boys with vocalist-guitarist Marco Gutierrez. The band's *Science of Flight* (2012) balances fiery Outlaw Folk originals with one raucous cover (Townes Van Zandt's "Lungs"). They filmed a video for "Raise Some Hell" for CMT's *Concrete Country* and went on to cowrite with Ray Wylie Hubbard "Down by the River," which appeared on *The Dirty River Boys* (2014) and Hubbard's *The Ruffian's Misfortune* (2015). (www.dirtyriverboys.com)

ROGER CREAGER, born July 25, 1971, in Corpus Christi, Texas, released four albums with Dualtone Records, including his debut *Having Fun All Wrong* (1998) and his concert album swan song with the label *Live Across Texas* (2004). Creager followed with *Here It Is* (2008) and *Surrender* (2012) on Thirty Tigers as well as *Road Show* (2014) on Having Fun All Wrong Records. The current Houston resident remains a fixture on the Texas music scene today.

RODNEY CROWELL topped mainstream country music charts a quarter century ago, but in many ways he's always been a workaday songwriter at heart. After all, it was Crowell's writing that elevated him to iconic stature, earned a Grammy Award for "After All This Time" (1990), and notched ASCAP and Americana Music Association lifetime achievement awards (2003 and 2006, respectively). Crowell, born August 7, 1950, in Houston, Texas, earned five consecutive number one *Billboard* country singles with his album *Diamonds and Dirt* (1988). (www.rodneycrowell.com)

RONNIE DUNN, born June 1, 1953, in Coleman, Texas, notched more than a dozen Country Music Association awards, two Grammys, and more than two dozen Academy of Country Music awards as half of the duo Brooks & Dunn. The pair earned twenty number one *Billboard* Country songs, including "My Maria" and "Ain't Nothing 'Bout You," respectively the top country songs in 1996 and 2001. Dunn and Ray Wylie Hubbard cowrote "Bad on Fords," which Dunn recorded with Sammy Hagar on the Red Rocker's *Sammy Hagar and Friends* (2013). (www.ronniedunn.com)

STEVE EARLE, born January 17, 1955, in Fort Monroe, Virginia, but raised near San Antonio, Texas, broke into public consciousness with his seamless debut *Guitar Town* (MCA Records, 1986). Earle might be his generation's defining songwriter and certainly its most diverse. He has recorded classic country (1987's *Exit 0*), folk (1995's *Train a Comin'*), rock (1996's *I Feel Alright*, 2000's *Transcendental Blues*), bluegrass (1999's *The Mountain*), and blues (2015's *Terraplane*). Earle earned a Best Contemporary Folk Album Grammy for *Townes* (2009), a salute to his mentor, the legendary Texas tunesmith Townes Van Zandt. (www.steveearle.com)

TIM EASTON, born April 25, 1966, in Lewiston, New York, but raised in Akron, Ohio, and his early group Haynes Boys's raucous self-titled album rocks ("Jackie") and rolls (the title track) with welterweight fury. High-water marks are simply combustible ("The New Franklin County Woman"). The current East Nashville resident's tenure with New West Records—including *The Truth About Us* (2001), *Break Your Mother's Heart* (2003), *Ammunition* (2006), and *Porcupine* (2009)—produced some of the most memorable Americana music of the early millennium. (www.timeaston.com)

LIZ FOSTER is a member of the Trishas. The band received much critical acclaim for their debut full-length album *High, Wide and Handsome* (2012). Foster cowrote "Train Yard" with Ray Wylie Hubbard.

RADNEY FOSTER, born July 20, 1959, in Del Rio, Texas, first found success with his duo Foster and Lloyd ("Crazy Over You," "Texas in 1880"). Foster launched his solo career with the popular *Del Rio, TX 1959* (1992) and has thrived as both a producer and songwriter for the past two decades with collaborations with the likes of the Randy Rogers Band and mainstream country star Keith Urban. Foster recently released *For You to See the Stars* (2017), an album accompanied with a corresponding short story collection. (www.radneyfoster.com)

RICK FOWLER, born August 4, 1947, in Chicago, Illinois, but raised in Dallas, Texas, played guitar in Three Faces West and Ray Wylie Hubbard & the Cowboy Twinkies. Fowler cowrote "$60 Ford" with Hubbard and "Compromise" with Bob Livingston. Both songs appeared on *Ray Wylie Hubbard & the Cowboy Twinkies* (Warner Bros., 1975).

KINKY FRIEDMAN, born November 1, 1944, in Chicago, Illinois, found cult fame as a satirical songwriter in the 1970s and toured with Bob Dylan that decade. His best known songs include "Get Your Biscuits in the Oven and Your Buns in the Bed," "Ride 'Em Jewboy," "How Can I Tell You I Love You (When You're Sitting on My Face)," and "They Ain't Makin' Jews Like Jesus Anymore." Friedman ran as an Independent Party candidate for Texas governor in 2006. He placed fourth out of six candidates. (www.kinkyfriedman.com)

CHRIS FULLERTON, born December 29, 1985, in Camden, New Jersey, sings country music bold ("Epilepsy Blues") and brave ("Seven Roman Candles"). The current Austin resident immediately turned heads with his debut *Epilepsy Blues*. "Released independently earlier this year but now getting picked up by influential label Eight 30 Records, *Epilepsy Blues* is indeed quite deserving of a wider airing," *No Depression* magazine cofounder Peter Blackstock wrote in the *Austin American-Statesman*. "*Epilepsy Blues* is full of songs that demand to be heard from a brave writer who doesn't back away from the heart of the matter." (www.chrisfullerton.com)

MARY GAUTHIER, born March 11, 1962, in New Orleans, Louisiana, broke through with a vengeance with *Mercy Now* (2005), which included the timeless title track and "I Drink." Legendary songfinder Bobby Bare recorded both songs on *Things Change* (2017). Bare's unflinching video for the latter remains one of the most moving of the past decade. Gauthier, an outspoken recovering addict and alcoholic and openly gay songwriter, recorded the alcoholic lament "Sorry You're Sick" for Eight 30 Records' *Cold and Bitter Tears: A Tribute to Ted Hawkins*. (www.marygauthier.com)

ELIZA GILKYSON, born August 24, 1950, in Los Angeles, California, has been nominated twice for Grammys in the Best Contemporary Folk Album and Best Folk Album categories. The longtime Austin, Texas, resident has recorded more than twenty albums, including the Red House Records high-water marks *Land of Milk and Honey* (2004), *Beautiful World* (2008), and *The Nocturne Diaries* (2014). Ray Wylie Hubbard recorded Gilkyson's "The Beauty Way" on *Delirium Tremolos* (2005). (www.elizagilkyson.com)

MAX GOMEZ released his debut record *Rule the World* on influential label New West Records in 2013. He followed with the five-song EP *Me & Joe* in 2017. "A smart, sharp collection of country songs with a pop touch worthy of Chris Martin, *Me & Joe* sees Gomez getting comfortable in his new surroundings," *Rolling Stone* said, "and getting back to what he enjoys the most: writing music." Such critical acclaim led to Gomez sharing stages with Americana beacons such as James McMurtry, Shawn Mullins, Buddy Miller, Jim Lauderdale, Patty Griffin, and John Hiatt. (www.maxgomezmusic.com)

JON DEE GRAHAM's finest songs find healing within heartbreak ("Codeine," "Beautifully Broken"). The longtime Austin resident, who wrote and played guitar in the groundbreaking bands True Believers and the Skunks, has held a Wednesday-night residency with James McMurtry at the capital city's Continental Club for more than two decades. He was born February 28, 1959, in Eagle Pass, Texas. (www.jondeegraham.com)

WILLIAM CLARK GREEN, born May 19, 1986, in Tyler, Texas, began writing songs while attending Texas Tech University in Lubbock. Green's early albums such as *Dangerous Man* (2008) and *Misunderstood* (2010) showed the young artist rapidly rising in the Texas Red Dirt scene. Green hit his stride with *Rose Queen* (2013) and the hit single "Hangin' Around," a cowrite with Cheatham Street Warehouse owner Kent Finlay that topped the Texas music radio chart. (www.williamclarkgreen.com)

PATTY GRIFFIN, born March 16, 1954, in Old Town, Maine, made a deep impression with her elegant second album, *Flaming Red* (1998). Several musicians including the Dixie Chicks ("Top of the World") have recorded her songs. The longtime Austin, Texas, resident won the Artist of the Year and Album of the Year awards from the Americana Music Association for her album *Children Running Through* (2007). Griffin's *Downtown Church* (2011) won the Grammy award for Best Traditional Gospel album. (www.pattygriffin.com)

BILL HEARNE, born February 11, 1949, began playing music professionally with his future wife, Bonnie Cross, in Austin in 1968. Hearne understood from the start that his forte lies in his interpretive skills instead of writing original songs. His husky Texas baritone burrows into a song's interior with singular warmth and mellowness. "Since I didn't have people to play with when I picked up the guitar at seven years old, I developed a style that incorporated a percussion rhythm while playing lead riffs," Hearne says. "Basically, I tried to be a one-man band." (www.billhearne.com)

MICHAEL HEARNE, born November 3, 1955, in Dallas, Texas, won seven trophies at the New Mexico Music Awards for his critically acclaimed *Sight and Sound* (2001), eleven songs written about eleven different works of art. Hearne frequently writes with iconic tunesmiths Shake Russell and Keith Sykes. He followed with *The High Road to Taos* (2008) and *Red River Dreams* (2016). Hearne has hosted Michael Hearne's Big Barn Dance in Taos, New Mexico since the early 2000s. (www.michaelhearne.com)

TERRI HENDRIX, born February 13, 1968, in San Antonio, Texas, particularly showcases her vast musical diversity on *Cry Till You Laugh* (2010). Bluesman Sonny Terry ("Hula Mary"), Rodney Crowell ("Slow Down"), and jazz icon Ella Fitzgerald all haunt her ninth studio album, which she calls the "yin and yang of life." Hendrix recently took on the ambitious *Project 5*, a collection of four musically disparate albums and a book. She toured Europe with Ray Wylie Hubbard in the 1990s. (www.terrihendrix.com)

JUDY HUBBARD, born June 10, 1957, in Dallas, Texas, married Ray Wylie Hubbard in 1989 and has played many roles in his professional career from manager, tour manager, publicist, and booking agent in years since. The couple resides in Wimberley, Texas, about forty-five minutes south of Austin. Judy has inspired many Ray Wylie Hubbard songs, including "Mother Hubbard's Blues" and "Mother Blues," a vibrant narrative detailing their lives at a time when Judy worked at the well-known Dallas blues club. (www.raywylie.com)

LUCAS HUBBARD, born May 15, 1993, in Dallas, Texas, is Ray Wylie Hubbard's son with Judy Hubbard and has served as his touring guitarist in recent years. He works at the Gibson showroom in Austin, Texas. (www.raywylie.com)

JACK INGRAM, born November 15, 1970, in the Woodlands, Texas, was a popular regional singer-songwriter for more than a decade before skyrocketing his single "Wherever You Are" to number one on the *Billboard* country charts. He's since charted six songs in the Top Forty, including "Love You," "Measure of a Man," and "Barefoot and Crazy." Ingram was named Best New Male Vocalist by the Academy of Country Music in 2008 (despite the fact that he'd been writing and touring for nearly a decade and a half). Ingram's *Midnight Motel* (2016) has garnered significant critical acclaim. "*Midnight Motel* could be called *Backbone*," *Rolling Stone* said. "It's Ingram's first time making a record one hundred percent on his own terms." (www.jackingram.net)

SETH JAMES, born on May 24, 1978, in Forth Worth, Texas, but raised in West Texas, taught himself guitar by listening to Lightnin' Hopkins, Freddie King, and Creedence Clearwater Revival. James entered public consciousness as guitarist in Cody Canada and the Departed from 2010–2013. He launched a solo career after his stint in the Departed and returned to the blues music of his roots. (www.sethjames.com)

JAREN JOHNSTON, born October 4, 1980, in Nashville, Tennessee, has cowritten songs recorded by several country stars including Ronnie Dunn ("Young Buck"), Keith Urban ("You Gonna Fly"), Tim McGraw ("Southern Girl"), and Jake Owen ("Raise 'Em Up"). He's currently a member of the Nashville-based The Cadillac Three, who invited Ray Wylie Hubbard to open their sold-out record release show for *Legacy* (2017) at the Ryman Auditorium in fall 2017. (www.thecadillacthree.com)

CHRIS KNIGHT, born June 24, 1960, in Slaughters, Kentucky, turned heads in Nashville songwriting circles with his early albums *Chris Knight* (1998), *A Pretty Good Guy* (2001), and *The Jealous Kind* (2003). His gritty songs have been recorded by Cross Canadian Ragweed ("Cry Lonely"), Randy Travis ("Highway Junkie"), and Confederate Railroad ("I Don't Want to Hang Out with Me"). John Anderson and Blake Shelton both recorded his most vivid vignette ("It Ain't Easy Being Me"). (www.chrisknight.net)

"SPIDER" JOHN KOERNER, born August 31, 1938, in Rochester, New York, formed the ramshackle folk trio Koerner, Ray & Glover in the early 1960s. The notable group's debut *Blues, Rags and Hollers* (1963) gained nationwide attention after being reissued on legendary Elektra Records the same year it was originally released. Many say Koerner, Ray & Glover were early influences on celebrated songwriter Bob Dylan. Ray Wylie Hubbard paid tribute to Koerner, Ray & Glover with his song "Spider, Snaker, and Little Sun" on *Tell the Devil...I'm Gettin' There As Fast As I Can* (2017). Koerner, Ray & Glover released four more albums, including *Lots More Blues, Rags and Hollers* (1963) and *One Foot in the Groove* (1996). (www.mwt.net/~koerner/index.html)

BEN KWELLER, born June 16, 1981, in San Francisco, California, but raised in Greenville, Texas, earned notoriety with his self-proclaimed "sugar metal" teenage band Radish in the early 1990s. The band released three albums, including *Hello* (1994) and their major label debut *Restraining Bolt* (Mercury Records, 1997). Kweller has released several albums—most notably, *On My Way* (2004) and *Changing Horses* (2009)—as a solo artist. Kweller made headlines during his Austin City Limits Music Festival performance in 2006 when he attempted to stop a severe nosebleed by inserting a tampon thrown onstage by a fan. (www.benkweller.com)

BOB LIVINGSTON, born November 26, 1948, in San Antonio, Texas, has never been a traditional country musician living the honky-tonk life even though he's spent significant time on the roadhouse circuit with Texas's most colorful musicians. Livingston's creative legacy begins as a founding member of the Lost Gonzo Band and continues with his recording with Jerry Jeff Walker, Ray Wylie Hubbard, and Michael Martin Murphey. His album *Gypsy Alibi* was named album of the year at the Texas Music Awards in 2011. (www.boblivingstonmusic.com)

DAVID LOWERY, born September 10, 1960, in San Antonio, Texas, founded the popular indie rock band Camper Van Beethoven as well as the alt-country group Cracker. The latter's gold-selling debut album *Kerosene Hat* (1993) put the band on the map and featured the hit songs "Teen Angst (What the World Needs Now)," "Get Off This," "Euro-Trash Girl," and the MTV staple "Low." Lowery, an outspoken critic of music streaming services for paying low songwriting royalties, is a trained mathematician and has been a lecturer in the University of Georgia's music business program. (www.crackersoul.com)

LLOYD MAINES, born June 28, 1951, in Lubbock, Texas, made his name with the Maines Brothers in the 1970s and went on to perform with Jerry Jeff Walker, Guy Clark, Butch Hancock, Terry Allen, Ray Wylie Hubbard, and several other Texas greats. The multi-instrumentalist played on Americana landmarks such as Uncle Tupelo's *Anodyne* and Wilco's *A.M.* He performs frequently with Terri Hendrix and has been integral in her band and the production of her records for the past two decades. (www.lloydmaines.com)

CARSON McHONE, born March 13, 1992, in Austin, Texas, sang on Ray Wylie Hubbard's "Chick Singer Badass Rockin'," the cleanup position track on his album *The Ruffian's Misfortune*. McHone "writes songs," Hubbard says, "like her life depends on it." She has shared stages with Vince Gill, Ryan Bingham, Charlie Mars, Jerry Jeff Walker, Shakey Graves, and several others. (www.carsonmc honemusic.com)

JAMES McMURTRY, born March 18, 1962, in Fort Worth, Texas, spins stories with a poet's pen ("Ruby and Carlos") and a painter's precision ("Choctaw Bingo"). His latest album *Complicated Game* (2015) echoes high-water marks such as *Just Us Kids* (2008) and *Childish Things* (2005) with literate storytelling ("Long Island Sound") and sharp narratives ("South Dakota"). He released the digital-only single "State of the Union" on his own Dope Records in 2018 and contributed to Eight 30 Records' *Cold and Bitter Tears: A Tribute to Ted Hawkins* ("Big Things") and *Dreamer: A Tribute to Kent Finlay* ("Comfort's Just a Rifle Shot Away") and *The Messenger: A Tribute to Ray Wylie Hubbard.* (www.jamesmc murtry.com)

KELLEY MICKWEE, born in 1979 in Birmingham, Alabama, started out her musical career in the Memphis-based duo Jed and Kelley before joining the Trishas. The band became regionally popular and produced one critically acclaimed album, *High, Wide and Handsome* (2012). Mickwee went on to release her debut solo album *You Used to Live Here* (2014) before she joined Kevin Russell's explosive Shinyribs as a backup singer as the band was taking full flight in the Texas music scene. Shinyribs debuted on *Austin City Limits* television program in 2018. (www.kelleymickwee.com)

GURF MORLIX, born in 1951, in Buffalo, New York, moved to Texas in the mid-1970s and performed with cult legend Blaze Foley. He went on to join Lucinda Williams's band in the early 1980s and produced her albums *Lucinda Williams* (1988) and *Sweet Old World* (1992). In addition to Ray Wylie Hubbard, Morlix has produced Slaid Cleaves, Mary Gauthier, and Robert Earl Keen. He has recorded ten studio albums, including *The Soul and the Heal* (Rootball Records, 2017). Morlix made cameo appearances in Ethan Hawke's 2018 biopic *Blaze*, which starred Ben Dickey as Blaze Foley. (www.gurfmorlix.com)

CORY MORROW, born May 1, 1972, in Houston, Texas, has released nearly a dozen studio albums in the two decades since his debut full-length *The Cory Morrow Band* (1997). Several—including his Pat Green collaboration *Songs We Wish We'd Written* (2001), *Outside the Lines* (2002), *Vagrants & Kings* (2008), and *The Good Fight* (2015)—have reached the Billboard Country chart Top Fifty. His album *Brand New Me* (2010) spotlighted his newfound sobriety and Christian faith. (www.corymorrow.com)

OLGA WILHELMINE MUNDING, born October 18, 1976, in San Francisco, California, was a longtime guitar student of Jessie Mae Hemphill, born October 18, 1923, near Como, Mississippi, and died July 22, 2006, in Memphis, Tennessee. Munding, who has released five albums including *Blues Babe* (2003) and *North Mississippi Christmas* (2012), established the Jessie Mae Hemphill Foundation in 2003 to preserve and archive the African American music of Northern Mississippi. Hemphill was first recorded by blues researcher George Mitchell in 1967 and ethnomusicologist David Evans in 1973, but those field recordings were not released. She launched her recording career with *She-Wolf* (1981) and released several albums, including *Feelin' Good* (1990) and *Heritage of the Blues: Shake It Baby* (2003). Ray Wylie Hubbard's "Jessie Mae" appears on *The Ruffian's Misfortune*. (www.jmhemphill.org; www. laolga.com)

MICHAEL MARTIN MURPHEY, born March 14, 1945, in Dallas, Texas, was a pioneering figure in the Cosmic Country movement in the 1970s. Murphey, who was inducted into the Texas Country Music Hall of Fame in 2009, recorded the hit singles "Wildfire," "A Long Line of Love," "What She Wants," and "Don't Count the Rainy Days." Many consider his album *Geronimo's Cadillac* (A&M Records, 1972), helmed by legendary producer Bob Johnston (Bob Dylan, Leonard Cohen), a Cosmic Country hallmark. (www.michael martinmurphey.com)

CHARLIE MUSSELWHITE, born January 31, 1944, in Kosciusko, Mississippi, made immediate waves with his iconic blues album *Stand Back! Here Comes Charley Musselwhite's Southside Band* on

Vanguard Records (1966). Musselwhite capitalized on the album's success by moving from blues-saturated Chicago to San Francisco, California, where he stood out as the "king of the blues" during the counterculture movement in the late 1960s. Popular musician Ben Harper and Musselwhite recently collaborated on *No Mercy in This Land* (2018), a follow-up to their debut duo album *Get Up!* (2013). Ray Wylie Hubbard's "Mr. Musselwhite's Blues" appears on *The Ruffian's Misfortune*. (www.charliemusselwhite.com).

JACK O'BRIEN, born June 23, 1985, in Brooklyn, New York, but raised in Austin, Texas, serves as singer and bassist for Austin-based psychedelic rock band Bright Light Social Hour, who released their self-titled debut full-length in 2010. O'Brien and his bandmates attended Senator Wendy Davis's filibuster of Texas Senate Bill 5, a measure aimed at adding abortion regulations in Texas. The band broadened their reach when they rushed to their studio that night and by the morning released "Wendy Davis" and an accompanying video made in part with protest footage taken on the band's cell phones. (www.brightlightsocialhour.com)

MIKE PETERS, born February 25, 1959, in Prestatyn, Wales, is best known as the lead singer of The Alarm, which Ray Wylie Hubbard sings about in his song "Snake Farm." The Alarm's highest-charting single in Britain was "Sixty Eight Guns" (1983), which cracked the UK Top Twenty. Their album *Declaration* (1984) peaked in the Top Ten. Such success earned the band opening slots for both U2 and Bob Dylan. The Alarm broke up less than a decade later, and Peters went on to a successful solo career and a stint as the vocalist in Big Country from 2011–2013. (www.thealarm.com)

ROD PICOTT, born November 3, 1964, in New Hampshire but raised in Berwick, Maine, debuted with the seamless *Tiger Tom Dixon's Blues* (2001) and has released nearly a dozen albums, including *Girl from Arkansas* (2004), *Welding Burns* (2011), and the ambitious double album *Out Past the Wires* (2017). The longtime Nashville resident and his childhood friend Slaid Cleaves have collaborated frequently on standout tracks such as "Broke Down" (2000) and "Rust Belt Fields" (2013). Picott contributed "That's What

I'm Gonna Do" to Eight 30 Records' *Floater: A Tribute to the Tributes to Gary Floater* (2018). (www.rodpicott.com)

JEFF PLANKENHORN earned a reputation as one of the most skilled multi-instrumentalists in Central Texas as a frequent sideman for Ray Wyle Hubbard, Joe Ely, and others. He released *Soul Slide* in early 2016. "There is a soulfulness in each song that stirs a flame from the embers of love reclaimed," Ely says. "The stories are universal and in tune. The guitar riffs are wicked but true. This recording is relevant to the times and will be on people's playlists for a long time."

CHRIS ROBINSON, born December 20, 1966, in Marietta, Georgia, founded the popular 1990s rock band the Black Crowes with his brother Rich Robinson. The Black Crowes produced eight studio albums, including their 1990 debut *Shake Your Money Maker* and *The Southern Harmony and Musical Companion* (1992). Following several hiatuses due to unmanageable bickering between the brothers, the Black Crowes officially disbanded in 2015. Chris Robinson has performed with New Earth Mud and the Chris Robinson Brotherhood in years since. (www.chrisrobinsonbrotherhood.com)

RANDY ROGERS, born August 23, 1979, in Cleburne, Texas, cut his teeth at Cheatham Street Warehouse before releasing his debut album *Live at Cheatham Street Warehouse* (2000) and going on to become a highly successful country artist. Indeed, the Randy Rogers Band has charted more than a half-dozen singles, including "Tonight's Not the Night (For Goodbye)" (2005) and "One More Sad Song" (2012). (www.randyrogersband.com)

KEVIN RUSSELL, born May 21, 1967, in Beaumont, Texas, and his colorful narratives ("El Paso," "Lower 48") and nonlinear country blues ("Hooky Junk," "Cranky Mulatto") with Americana favorites the Gourds accurately represented the mystique of Austin, Texas. Russell's energetic soul-funk band Shinyribs has taken Texas music by storm recently with albums such as *I Got Your Medicine* (2017) since the Gourds disbanded indefinitely in 2013. Russell, Jenni Finlay, and Brian T. Atkinson coproduced *Cold and Bitter Tears: The Songs of Ted Hawkins* (Eight 30 Records, 2015).

TOM RUSSELL, born March 5, 1949, in Los Angeles, California, has an eclectic background that includes criminology student, taxi driver, folk artist, art collector, and regular correspondent with late Skid Row poet Charles Bukowski, detailed in the book *Tough Company* (2008). His songs have been recorded by Johnny Cash ("Veteran's Day"), Suzy Bogguss ("Outbound Plane"), Nanci Griffith ("Canadian Whiskey"), Joe Ely ("Gallo de Cielo), and legendary Texas songwriter Doug Sahm ("St. Olav's Gate"). (www.tomrussell.com)

AARON LEE TASJAN, born August 24, 1986, in New Albany, Ohio, has performed with a wide variety of musicians from folk legend Pete Yarrow (Peter, Paul, and Mary) to iconic punk rockers the New York Dolls. Tasjan launched his solo career by opening tours for Ray Wylie Hubbard, and he has released two albums as a solo artist, *In the Blazes* (2015) and *Silver Tears* (2016). Tasjan and fellow Nashville resident Tim Easton recorded "Black Flag Blues" for Eight 30 Records' *Highway Prayer: A Tribute to Adam Carroll* (2016). (www.aaronleetasjan.com)

PAUL THORN, born July 13, 1964, in Kenosha, Wisconsin, but raised in Elvis Presley's hometown, Tupelo, Mississippi, initially gained recognition touring as an opening act for such diverse acts as John Prine, Mark Knopfler, Huey Lewis and the News, and Jerry Jeff Walker. He achieved his highest chart position when his album *Pimps and Preachers* debuted in the Billboard Top 100 in 2010. Thorn's cover of Ray Wylie Hubbard's "Snake Farm" anchors *What the Hell Is Goin' On?* (2012) and received significant airplay on SiriusXM's Outlaw Country. (www.paulthorn.com)

JONATHAN TYLER, born in Dallas, Texas, founded Jonathan Tyler and the Northern Lights in 2007. The band supported its debut *Hot Trottin'* (2007) by opening tours for Cross Canadian Ragweed, the Black Crowes, Leon Russell, Deep Purple, and others. Their follow-up *Pardon Me* (2010) continued rising the band's star, leading to tours with ZZ Top, Robert Randolph and the Family Band, and JJ Grey & Mofro, as well as slots at Bonnaroo Music & Arts Festival, South by Southwest, and Voodoo Fest. (www.jona thantylermusic.com)

JERRY JEFF WALKER, born Ronald Clyde Crosby March 16, 1942, in Oneonta, New York, famously introduced Ray Wylie Hubbard by singing his "Up Against the Wall Redneck Mother" on his landmark album ¡Viva Terlingua! (RCA Records, 1973). Walker is best known for his song "Mr. Bojangles," which has been recorded by Sammy Davis Jr., John Denver, Neil Diamond, Whitney Houston, Elton John, Dolly Parton, Nina Simone, and several dozen more popular singers. (www.jerryjeff.com)

TERRY "BUFFALO" WARE served as guitarist in Ray Wylie Hubbard and the Cowboy Twinkies from 1973 through 1979. Ware formed the Sensational Shoes in Norman, Oklahoma, after the Cowboy Twinkies disbanded. He later released his debut solo album Caffeine Dreams (1981). Ware connected with Hubbard again in 1986, and the duo performed throughout the United States. He played guitar on Hubbard's Lost Train of Thought (1992), Loco Gringo's Lament (1995), and Dangerous Spirits (1997).

SAVANNAH WELCH, born August 4, 1984, in Nashville, Tennessee, is an actress, singer, and multi-instrumentalist in the Trishas. The band released the EP They Call Us the Trishas and a full-length debut High, Wide, and Handsome (2012). (www.thetrishas.com)

WILLIAM ELLIOTT WHITMORE, born May 11, 1978, in Lee County, Iowa, could be labeled the Midwest's Scott H. Biram, as the singers share similar deep country-blues influences and irreverent attitudes. Whitmore has toured with late Soundgarden singer Chris Cornell, Memphis-based rockers Lucero, Frank Turner, and the Low Anthem. He has released eight albums since debuting with The Jarrett Mitchell Demo Album (1999), including his breakthrough Ashes to Dust (2005), Song of the Blackbird (2006) and Radium Death (2015). (www.williamelliottwhitmore.com)

WALT WILKINS's songs—particularly resonant on *Fire, Honey, and Angels* (1999) and *Plenty* (2012)—move both cerebrally and spiritually. Wilkins, born December 29, 1960, in San Antonio, Texas, earned a wider reputation when Pam Tillis recorded his high-water mark "Someone Somewhere Tonight" on her album *Rhinestoned* (2007). "I chose to go full-time on this road twenty-five years ago," the songwriter says. "It's been a spiritual quest, an amazing trip, at turns heartbreaking and transcendent." (www.waltwilkins.com)

JAMIE LIN WILSON, born August 10, 1981, in Houston, Texas, broke into the Texas country scene as a lead singer in the Side-hill Gougers before embarking on a solo career. Her *Dirty Blonde Hair* EP (2010) displayed Wilson's significant songwriting chops, which carried her into work with the Trishas, an all-female singer-songwriter band with Kelley Mickwee, Liz Foster, and Savannah Welch. Wilson has contributed to Eight 30 Records's *Highway Prayer: A Tribute to Adam Carroll* ("Hi-Fi Love"), *Dreamer: A Tribute to Kent Finlay* ("Hill Country"), and *Floater: A Tribute to the tributes to Gary Floater* ("That's When the Eagle Screams"). (www.jamielinwilson.com)

Notes

Prologue

1. For more on Three Faces West, see Rachel Stone, "Ray Wylie Hubbard and Three Faces West," https://oakcliff.advocatemag.com/2012/10/ray-wylie-hubbard-and-three-faces-west/, October 26, 2012 (accessed March 23, 2018).

2. For more on Jerry Jeff Walker's *¡Viva Terlingua!* and his recording of Ray Wylie Hubbard's Outlaw Country anthem "Up Against the Wall Redneck Mother," see Michael H. Little, "Graded on a Curve, Jerry Jeff Walker's *¡Viva Terlingua!,*" www.thevinyldistrict.com/storefront/2015/10/graded-on-a-curve-jerry-jeff-walker-viva-terlingua/, October 7, 2015 (accessed March 23, 2018).

3. Ray Wylie Hubbard, interview with Brian T. Atkinson, November 15, 2017.

4. Margaret Moser, "Snake Charmer: Ray Wylie Hubbard Ain't Afraid of You," *Austin Chronicle*, June 23, 2006.

5. Ray Wylie Hubbard, interview with Brian T. Atkinson, November 15, 2017.

6. Travis Kitchens, "Ray Wylie Hubbard Q&A," http://www.citypaper.com/blogs/noise/bcpnews-qa-ray-wylie-hubbard-talks-dead-thumb-guitar-playing-working-with-willie-nelson-and-more-20150514-story.html, May 14, 2015 (accessed March 23, 2018).

7. Ray Wylie Hubbard, from acceptance speech for receiving the Best Songwriter of the Year award at the 2018 Austin Music Awards, February 28, 2018.

8. Ray Wylie Hubbard, interview with Brian T. Atkinson, November 15, 2017.

9. Moser, "Snake Charmer."

10. Ray Wylie Hubbard, interview with Brian T. Atkinson, November 15, 2017.

Introduction

1. For more on Ray Wylie Hubbard, see Brian T. Atkinson, *I'll Be Here in the Morning: The Songwriting Legacy of Townes Van Zandt* (College Station: Texas A&M University Press, 2012); Rich Koster, *Texas Music* (New York: St. Martin's Griffin, 2000), 40, 43–44, 48; Jason Mellard, *Progressive Country: How the 1970s Transformed the Texan in Popular Culture* (Austin: University of Texas Press, 2013), 82, 83, 85, 111, 205; Jan Reid, *The Improbable Rise of Redneck Rock* (Austin: University of Texas Press, 2004), 105, 128, 358; and Jenni Finlay, "Ray Wylie Hubbard: Grifter,

Ruffian, Messenger," *Pickers and Poets: The Ruthlessly Poetic Singer-Songwriters of Texas* (ed. Craig Clifford and Craig D. Hillis, College Station: Texas A&M University Press, 2016), 101–2.

2. Brian T. Atkinson, "Interview: Ray Wylie Hubbard," *Austin Music*, August 2006, 26.

3. Ringo Starr, "Ringo Starr Loves Snake Farm," www.youtube.com (accessed March 5, 2018).

4. Terri Hendrix, interview with Brian T. Atkinson, September 26, 2017.

5. Ray Wylie Hubbard, *Live at Cibolo Creek Country Club*, Misery Loves Company Records, 1998.

6. Ray Wylie Hubbard, "Ray Wylie Hubbard on Redneck Mother," www.youtube.com (accessed March 5, 2018).

7. Kris Kristofferson, interview with Brian T. Atkinson, September 26, 2009.

8. Gurf Morlix, interview with Brian T. Atkinson, November 29, 2017.

9. Joe Walsh, "Ray Wylie Hubbard, 'Snake Farm' for Joe Walsh's Road Crew (live) Mitchell Pavilion May 2016," www.youtube.com (accessed March 5, 2018).

10. Paul Thorn, interview with Brian T. Atkinson, September 1, 2017.

11. William Elliott Whitmore, interview with Brian T. Atkinson, August 24, 2017.

12. Steve Earle, interview with Brian T. Atkinson, October 23, 2017.

Verse One

1. Ray Wylie Hubbard, interview with Brian T. Atkinson, November 15, 2017.

2. Bobby Bare, interview with Brian T. Atkinson, September 27, 2017; for more on Bobby Bare, see Paul Kingsbury, *The Encyclopedia of Country Music* (Oxford: Oxford University Press, 1998), 28–29; Koster, *Texas Music*, 44; "Bobby Bare Interview with Nashville Music Guide at the Legendary Lunch 2017," www.youtube.com (accessed March 23, 2018); "Your Interview with Bobby Bare," http://nodepression.com/interview/your-interview-bobby-bare (accessed March 23, 2018).

3. For more on the Kerrville Folk Festival, see www.kerrville-music.com (accessed March 24, 2018).

4. Michael Martin Murphey, interview with Brian T. Atkinson, August 30, 2017.

5. For more on Roy Smeck and his guitars, see "Circa 1930 Harmony Roy Smeck Vita-Guitar," www.fretboardjournal.com/columns/catch-day-harmony-roy-smeck-vita-guitar/ (accessed March 23, 2018).

6. Jerry Jeff Walker, interview with Brian T. Atkinson, January 3, 2018.

7. Jerry Jeff Walker, "Jerry Jeff Walker—Interview—11/4/1984—Rock Influence (Official)," www.youtube.com (accessed January 3, 2018).

8. Jerry Jeff Walker, interview with Brian T. Atkinson, January 3, 2018.

9. Jerry Jeff Walker, "Jerry Jeff Walker—Interview—11/4/1984—Rock Influence (Official)," www.youtube.com (accessed January 3, 2018).

10. Jerry Jeff Walker, interview with Brian T. Atkinson, January 3, 2018.

11. Jerry Jeff Walker, "Jerry Jeff Walker Discusses Writing Mr. Bojangles and More with Bruce Robison on *The Next Waltz*," www.youtube.com (accessed January 4, 2018).

12. Michael Hearne, interview with Brian T. Atkinson, February 23, 2018; for more on Michael Hearne's Big Barn Dance, see www.bigbarndance.com (accessed March 24, 2018).

13. Bill Hearne, interview with Brian T. Atkinson, February 27, 2018; for more on Bill and Bonnie Hearne, see www.billhearne.com/wp/ (accessed March 24, 2018); Steve Terrell, "Folk, Country Music Singer, Piano Player Bonnie Hearne Dies at Age 71," *Santa Fe New Mexican*, December 26, 2017.

14. Rick Fowler, interview with Brian T. Atkinson, November 3, 2017; for more on Ray Wylie Hubbard, Rick Fowler, and their Texas Twosome, see Robin Chotzinoff, "Ray Wylie Hubbard," *Edible Austin*, October 26, 2012.

15. Bob Livingston, interview with Brian T. Atkinson, August 21, 2017; for more on Bob Livingston and the Lost Gonzo Band, see www.boblivingstonmusic.com/bio (accessed March 24, 2018).

16. Terry "Buffalo" Ware, interview with Brian T. Atkinson, December 18, 2017; for more on Terry Ware, who currently plays guitar with several artists, including Grammy-nominated Oklahoma-based songwriter John Fullbright, see www.terrybuffaloware.com (accessed March 24, 2018).

17. Tommy Alverson, interview with Brian T. Atkinson, August 24, 2017.

18. Tom Russell, email interview with Brian T. Atkinson, August 22, 2017. For more on Tom Russell, see Atkinson, *I'll Be Here in the Morning*, 56–61.

19. Kinky Friedman, interview with Brian T. Atkinson, October 19, 2017. For more on Kinky Friedman, see Kingsbury, *The Encyclopedia of Country Music*, 184; Gary Hartman, *The History of Texas Music* (College Station: Texas A&M University Press, 2008), 173–74; Koster, *Texas Music*, 8, 42, 62; and Mellard, *Progressive Country*, 56, 78, 83–85, 111, 174.

20. Ray Benson, interview with Brian T. Atkinson, October 10, 2017; for more on Ray Benson and Asleep at the Wheel, see Hartman, *The History of Texas Music*, 112,147; Koster, *Texas Music*, 20, 49, 74; and Mellard, *Progressive Country*, 50, 80–81.

21. For more on Townes Van Zandt, see Robert Earl Hardy, *A Deeper Blue: The Life and Music of Townes Van Zandt* (Denton: University of

North Texas Press, 2008) and *Be Here to Love Me: A Film About Townes Van Zandt* (Palm Pictures, 2004); for more on Townes Van Zandt's influence on his peers and followers, see Atkinson, *I'll Be Here in the Morning*.

22. For more on Lightin' Hopkins and Mance Lipscomb, see Alan Govenar, *Lightnin' Hopkins: His Life and Blues* (Chicago: Chicago Review Press, 2010), and Timothy J. O'Brien and David Ensminger, *Mojo Hand: The Life and Music of Lightnin' Hopkins* (Austin: University of Texas Press, 2013).

23. Steve Earle, interview with Brian T. Atkinson, October 23, 2017; for more on Steve Earle, see Lauren St John, *Hardcore Troubadour: The Life and Near Death of Steve Earle* (New York: Fourth Estate, 2003); Steve Earle, *Doghouse Roses: Stories* (New York: Houghton Mifflin, 2001); Peter Doggett, *Are You Ready for the Country: Elvis, Dylan, Parsons, and the Roots of Country Rock* (New York: Penguin Books, 2000), 359, 413, 418, 451, 453, 454–55, 480, 496; Jason Mellard, " 'Gettin' Tough': Steve Earle's America," *Pickers and Poets: The Ruthlessly Poetic Singer-Songwriters of Texas,* ed. Craig Clifford and Craig D. Hillis (College Station: Texas A&M University Press, 2016), 161–65; and Koster, *Texas Music,* 69, 71, 72, 73, 75, 222.

Verse Two

1. Ray Wylie Hubbard, interview with Brian T. Atkinson, November 15, 2017.

Chorus

1. Ray Wylie Hubbard, interview with Brian T. Atkinson, November 15, 2017.

2. Troy Campbell, interview with Brian T. Atkinson, January 12, 2018; for more on Troy Campbell and Loose Diamonds, see Don McLeese, "Troy Campbell—Loose from the Diamonds," *No Depression,* June 30, 1999; for more on the House of Songs, see www.thehouseofsongs.com (accessed March 24, 2018).

3. Jon Dee Graham, interview with Brian T. Atkinson, December 20, 2017; for more on Jon Dee Graham and his punk rock band the Skunks, see Brian T. Atkinson and Jenni Finlay, *Kent Finlay, Dreamer: The Musical Legacy Behind Cheatham Street Warehouse* (College Station: Texas A&M University Press, 2016), 123–25, 241; for more on Jon Dee Graham, see www.jondeegraham.com (accessed March 24, 2018).

4. Danny Barnes, interview with Brian T. Atkinson, November 20, 2017; for more on Danny Barnes and Bad Livers, see Alex Steininger, "Interview: Danny Barnes on Bad Livers, Minor Dings, and Danny Barnes," https://www.inmusicwetrust/articles/39h01.html (accessed March 23, 2018); for more on Danny Barnes, see www.dannybarnes.com (accessed March 24, 2018) and www.eight30records.com (accessed March 24, 2018).

5. Lloyd Maines, interview with Brian T. Atkinson, December 11, 2017; for more on Lloyd Maines, see www.lloydmaines.com (accessed March 24, 2018).

6. For more on Leadbelly and Woody Guthrie, see Woody Guthrie and Leadbelly, *Folkways: The Original Vision: Songs of Woody Guthrie and Lead Belly* (Folkways, 2005).

7. Terri Hendrix, interview with Brian T. Atkinson, September 26, 2017; for more on Terri Hendrix, see Brian T. Atkinson, "Roll On: Terri Hendrix," *Pickers and Poets*, 209–11, *Atkinson, I'll Be Here in the Morning*, 187–92, and Atkinson and Finlay, *Kent Finlay, Dreamer*, 164–67.

8. James McMurtry, interview with Brian T. Atkinson, January 4, 2018; for more on James McMurtry, see Atkinson, *I'll Be Here in the Morning*, 102–5, Atkinson and Finlay, *Kent Finlay, Dreamer*, 174–76, and Brian T. Atkinson, "James McMurtry Is a Craftsman of *Complicated* Stories," www.cmtedge.com, March 4, 2015 (accessed March 23, 2018).

9. Gurf Morlix, interview with Brian T. Atkinson, November 29, 2017; for more on Gurf Morlix, see Kathy Sands-Boehmer, "Q and A with Gurf Morlix," http://nodepression.com/interview/q-and-gurf-morlix, February 18, 2013 (accessed March 23, 2018).

10. Rod Picott, interview with Brian T. Atkinson, August 2, 2017; for more on Rod Picott, see Brian T. Atkinson, "Rod Picott Follows a *Crooked* Road," www.cmtedge.com, February 12, 2014 (accessed March 23, 2018).

11. Slaid Cleaves, interview with Brian T. Atkinson, November 9, 2017; for more on Slaid Cleaves, see Atkinson and Finlay, *Kent Finlay, Dreamer*, 185–87, and Brian T. Atkinson, "Slaid Cleaves Seasons His Songs with Love and War," www.cmtedge.com, June 19, 2013 (accessed March 23, 2018).

12. Mary Gauthier, interview with Brian T. Atkinson, November 22, 2017.

13. Mary Gauthier, interview with Brian T. Atkinson, December 1, 2017.

14. Mary Gauthier, interview with Brian T. Atkinson, November 22, 2017; for more on Mary Gauthier, see Kelly McCartney, "Five Questions: Mary Gauthier," http://nodepression.com/interview/five-questions-mary-gauthier, September 11, 2014 (accessed March 23, 2018); "Sarah Silverman Interviews Mary Gauthier on I Love You, America," www.youtube.com, November 3, 2017 (accessed March 23, 2018); and "Healing the Emotional Wounds of War Through Song," www.cbsnews.com, March 21, 2018 (accessed March 23, 2018).

15. Eliza Gilkyson, interview with Brian T. Atkinson, December 31, 2017; for more on Eliza Gilkyson, see Brian T. Atkinson, "Eliza Gilkyson Elicits Songs From Late Night Thoughts," www.cmtedge.com, April 1, 2014 (accessed March 23, 2018).

16. Patty Griffin, interview with Brian T. Atkinson, January 9, 2018;

for more on Patty Griffin, see NPR Staff, "Patty Griffin, Self-Made 'Servant of Love,' on the Strange Gift of Age," www.npr.org, September 20, 2015 (accessed March 23, 2018).

17. Chris Knight, interview with Brian T. Atkinson, September 23, 2018; for more on Chris Knight, see Brian T. Atkinson, "Chris Knight: Trailer II," https://americansongwriter.com/2009/09/chris-knight-trailer-ii/, September 15, 2009 (accessed March 23, 2018); and Grant Alden, "Chris Knight—The River's Own," http://nodepression.com/article/chris-knight-rivers-own, December 31, 1997 (accessed March 23, 2018).

18. For more on George Reiff's memorial concert, see Peter Blackstock, "Big Names Will Gather for Musical Memorial to Honor George Reiff," https://www.statesman.com/NEWS/20171201/Big-names-will-gather-for-musical-memorial-to-honor-George-Reiff, December 1, 2017 (accessed January 25, 2018); and Lynne Margolis, "Austin Gives Beloved Player/Producer George Reiff a Fitting Memorial," https://americansongwriter.com/2017/12/austin-gives-beloved-player-producer-george-reiff-fitting-memorial/, December 19, 2017 (accessed January 25, 2018).

19. Kevin Russell, interview with Brian T. Atkinson, December 22, 2017; for more on Kevin Russell, see Atkinson, *I'll Be Here in the Morning*, 182–86; Brian T. Atkinson, "Q&A: Kevin Russell of Shinyribs," http://lonestarmusicmagazine.com/qa-kevin-russell-shinyribs/, October 13, 2015 (accessed March 23, 2018); and Brian T. Atkinson, "ACL Music Festival: 10 Highlights," www.cmtedge.com, October 07, 2013 (accessed March 23, 2018).

20. Rodney Crowell, interview with Brian T. Atkinson, January 30, 2018; for more on Rodney Crowell, see Atkinson, *I'll Be Here in the Morning*, 31–36; Brian T. Atkinson, "Rodney Crowell Peels Back Layers in Tarpaper Sky," www.cmtedge.com, April 14, 2014 (accessed March 23, 2018); and Brian T. Atkinson, "Rodney Crowell: The Outsider," https://glidemagazine.com/2423/rodney-crowell/, September 13, 2005 (accessed March 23, 2018).

21. Radney Foster, interview with Brian T. Atkinson, February 24, 2018; for more on Radney Foster, see Atkinson and Finlay, *Kent Finlay, Dreamer*, 155–56, Brian T. Atkinson, "Radney Foster Faces the Muse, Finds a New Album," www.cmtedge.com, May 15, 2014 (accessed March 23, 2018).

Verse Three

1. Ray Wylie Hubbard, interview with Brian T. Atkinson, November 15, 2018.

2. Hayes Carll, interview with Brian T. Atkinson, November 8, 2018. For more on Hayes Carll, see Atkinson, *I'll Be Here in the Morning*, xvi–xvii; Brian T. Atkinson, "Townes Van Zandt's Sixth Annual Wake, Old Quarter (Galveston, TX), January 1, 2003," *No Depression*, March–

April 2003, 21; for more on Hayes Carll's dexterity as a live performer, see Brian T. Atkinson, "Hayes Carll, The Continental Club, Austin, TX, May 12," *Maverick Country*, August–September 2006, 25–26; and Brian T. Atkinson, "Role Models: Fred Eaglesmith," *American Songwriter*, November–December 2007, 114; for more on Hayes Carll's development as a songwriter, see Brian T. Atkinson, "4 To Watch For," *Paste*, December–January 2004, 70; Brian T. Atkinson, "Hayes Carll: Everybody's Talkin'," *No Depression*, March–April 2005, 61; Brian T. Atkinson, "Hayes Carll Q&A," *Texas Music*, Spring 2008, 22, 25–27; Brian T. Atkinson, "CD Review: Hayes Carll, Featured in iTunes This Week," www.austin360.com, March 28, 2008 (accessed March 23, 2018); Brian T. Atkinson, "Everything Is Relative in Holiday Song," *Austin American-Statesman*, December 27, 2009, G2; and Brian T. Atkinson, "Hayes Carll: *KMAG YOYO* Review," *Lone Star Music*, January–February 2011, 45.

3. Jeff Plankenhorn, interview with Brian T. Atkinson, March 1, 2018. For more on Jeff Plankenhorn, see Staff, "Jeff Plankenhorn," www.austinsongwriter.com/profiles/jeff-plankenhorn/ (accessed March 23, 2018).

4. Aaron Lee Tasjan, interview with Brian T. Atkinson, September 20, 2017. For more on Aaron Lee Tasjan, see Juli Thanki, "Aaron Lee Tasjan and Tim Easton Team Up for 'Black Flag Blues," https://www.tennessean.com/story/entertainment/music/2016/10/10/aaron-lee-tasjan-tim-easton-team-up-black-flag-blues/91851504/, October 10, 2016 (accessed March 23, 2018).

5. Tim Easton, interview with Brian T. Atkinson, September 20, 2017; for more on Tim Easton, see Brian T. Atkinson, "Tim Easton Plays It Cool in East Nashville," www.cmtedge.com, August 27, 2013 (accessed March 23, 2017).

6. Elizabeth Cook, email interview with Brian T. Atkinson, October 19, 2017. For more on SiriusXM, see www.siriusxm.com.

7. For more on Eric Church and Ray Wylie Hubbard, see John Freeman, "Hear Ray Wylie Hubbard's New Song with Eric Church, Lucinda Williams: Texas Legend Shares Video for 'Tell the Devil I'm Getting There as Fast as I Can,' the Title Track from His New Album," www.rollingstone.com, May 31, 2017 (accessed March 23, 2018); and Angela Stefano, "Watch Eric Church Perform with Ray Wylie Hubbard at Texas Heritage Songwriters' Hall of Fame Induction," http://theboot.com/ray-wylie-hubbard-eric-church-texas-heritage-songwriters-hall-of-fame/, February 26, 2018 (accessed March 23, 2018).

8. Jaren Johnston, interview with Brian T. Atkinson, January 9, 2018; for more on the Cadillac Three, see Paul Sexton, "Interview: The Cadillac Three—Southern Comforters," www.countrymusicmag.com, April 25, 2017 (accessed March 23, 2018).

9. Eric Church, interview with Brian T. Atkinson, July 23, 2018. For more on Eric Church and Ray Wiley Hubbard Performing Hub-

bard's "Screw You, We're from Texas" on February 3, 2017 at American Airlines Center in Dallas, Texas, see "Eric Church and Ray Wylie Hubbard—Screw You We're From Texas," https://www.youtube.com/watch?v=hZ8IJAZwl84 (accessed July 20, 2018); for more on Eric Church's "Mr. Misunderstood," which name-drops Ray Wylie Hubbard, see "Eric Church—Mr. Misunderstood," https://www.youtube.com/watch?v=rOuF3k_-asA (accessed July 20, 2018); for more on Eric Church and Ray Wylie Hubbard's cowrite "Desperate Man," see Joseph Hudak, "Eric Church Steals Music, Airdrops It to Fans in 'Desperate Man' Video," https://www.rollingstone.com/music/music-country/eric-church-steals-music-airdrops-it-to-fans-in-desperate-man-video-700610/ (accessed July 20, 2018).

10. Ronnie Dunn, text message conversation with Brian T. Atkinson, January 22, 2018; for more on Brooks and Dunn, see *Rolling Stone* staff, "Ronnie Dunn Talks New Song with Kix Brooks, Duet with Reba: Legendary Singer Tells How He and His Longtime Musical Partner Reunited for 'Damn Drunk' and Reveals New Duet on Today's Ram Report," www.rollingstone.com, August 5, 2016 (accessed March 23, 2018); CMT Staff, "CMT's Exclusive Interviews: Brooks & Dunn Talk About Their Split," www.cmt.com, August 12, 2009 (accessed March 23, 2018); Danielle Anderson, Kix Brooks Talks Being Back on Stage with Ronnie Dunn: 'It's Like Riding a Bicycle!'" www.people.com, July 7, 2017 (accessed March 23, 2018); and Chuck Dauphin, "Brooks & Dunn's 15 Best Songs: Critic's Picks," www.billboard.com, September 5, 2017 (accessed March 24, 2018).

11. Chris Robinson, interview with Brian T. Atkinson, October 7, 2018; for more on Chris Robinson and the Black Crowes, see Andy Greene, "Chris Robinson on Why He's Ready to Sing Black Crowes Songs Again: The Singer Talks Reviving His Former Band's Catalog on the Road with New Group As the Crow Flies, and Discusses His Split with Brother Rich," www.rollingstone.com, January 9, 2018 (accessed March 23, 2018); Andy Kahn, "Chris Robinson Discusses The Black Crowes, Chris Cornell, The CRB & More," www.jambase.com, November 13, 2017; Staff, "Chris Robinson Wants to Make Music Not Get the Black Crowes into the Rock and Hall of Fame: Musician Also Talks Meeting Icons Joe Cocker, Gregg Allman, and Crosby, Stills, Nash & Young," www.howardstern.com, May 16, 2017 (accessed March 24, 2018); and Staff, "Rich Robinson Continues Feud with His Brother Chris in New Rolling Stone Interview," www.relix.com, February 8, 2018.

12. Paul Thorn, interview with Brian T. Atkinson, September 1, 2018.

13. Brian T. Atkinson, "Paul Thorn Spreads a Soulful, Positive Message," www.cmtedge.com, August 8, 2014 (accessed March 23, 2018).

14. Paul Thorn, interview with Brian T. Atkinson, September 1, 2018.

15. David Lowery, interview with Brian T. Atkinson, December 1, 2018; for more on David Lowery, see www.davidlowery.com.

16. Cody Canada, interview with Brian T. Atkinson, September 3, 2017; for more on Cody Canada, see Atkinson and Finlay, *Kent Finlay, Dreamer*, 197–99; and www.thedepartedmusic.com (accessed March 24, 2018).

17. William Clark Green, interview with Brian T. Atkinson, January 19, 2018; for more on William Clark Green, see Atkinson and Finlay, *Kent Finlay, Dreamer*, 202–4.

18. Roger Creager, interview with Brian T. Atkinson, January 25, 2018; for more on Roger Creager, see www.rogercreager.com (accessed March 24, 2018).

19. Cory Morrow, interview with Brian T. Atkinson, February 13, 2018; for more on Cory Morrow and sobriety, see Eric Woods, "Saved and Sober Cory Morrow Celebrates *Brand New Me* CD," www.lubbock-online.com, September 24, 2010 (accessed March 23, 2018); for more on Cory Morrow and his Christian faith, see John Goodspeed, "Cory Morrow Brings Faith into his Music," www.expressnews.com, October 15, 2015 (accessed March 23, 2018).

20. Randy Rogers, interview with Brian T. Atkinson, January 5, 2018; for more on Randy Rogers, see Atkinson and Finlay, *Kent Finlay, Dreamer*, 191–96.

21. Nino Cooper, interview with Brian T. Atkinson, October 11, 2014; Brian T. Atkinson, "The Dirty River Boys Draw on El Paso Roots," www.cmtedge.com, October 15, 2014 (accessed March 23, 2018).

22. Brian T. Atkinson, "The Dirty River Boys Go with the Flow," www.cmtedge.com, June 10, 2010 (accessed March 23, 2018).

23. Jonathan Tyler, interview with Brian T. Atkinson, September 22, 2017; for more on Jonathan Tyler & the Northern Lights, see Brian T. Atkinson, "On the Horizon: Jonathan Tyler & the Northern Lights," www.americansongwriter.com, June 2, 2010 (accessed March 23, 2018).

24. Scott H. Biram, interview with Brian T. Atkinson, October 23, 2017; for more on Scott H. Biram, see Atkinson and Finlay, *Kent Finlay, Dreamer*, 215–16; Brian T. Atkinson, "Scott H. Biram: A Crash Course in Perseverance," www.nodepression.com, April 30, 2004 (accessed March 23, 2018).

25. William Elliott Whitmore, interview with Brian T. Atkinson, January 24, 2018; for more on William Elliott Whitmore, see Brian T. Atkinson, "William Elliott Whitmore Brings Radium Death to Life," www.cmtedge.com, March 31, 2015 (accessed March 23, 2018).

26. Chris Fullerton, interview with Brian T. Atkinson, December 1, 2017; for more on Chris Fullerton, see Peter Blackstock, "Chris Fullerton Balances Beauty, Damage on Brilliant *Epilepsy Blues*," www.mystatesman.com, December 4, 2017 (accessed March 23, 2018); Doug Freeman, "Chris Fullerton, *Epilepsy Blues* (Eight 30)," www.austinchronicle.com, September 1, 2017 (accessed March 23, 2018); and www.eight30records.com (accessed March 24, 2018).

27. Carson McHone, interview with Brian T. Atkinson, October 13, 2017; for more on Carson McHone, see "Chick Singer Badass Rockin' by Ray Wylie Hubbard (with Carson McHone)," www.youtube.com, April 21, 2015 (accessed March 23, 2018).

28. Jack O'Brien, interview with Brian T. Atkinson, August 27, 2017; for more on Bright Light Social Hour, see www.brightlightsocialhour.com (accessed March 24, 2018).

29. Ben Kweller, interview with Brian T. Atkinson, January 30, 2018; for more on Ben Kweller, see Andy Langer, "A Former Boy Wonder Takes Charge of His Career," www.newyorktimes.com, January 28, 2012 (accessed March 23, 2018); and Alex Young, "Interview: Ben Kweller," www.consequenceofsound.net, July 10, 2009 (accessed March 23, 2018).

Bridge

1. Ray Wylie Hubbard, interview with Brian T. Atkinson, March 24, 2018.

2. Charlie Musselwhite, interview with Brian T. Atkinson, February 28, 2018; for more on Charlie Musselwhite, see Marty Gunther, "Featured Interview—Charlie Musselwhite," www.bluesblastmagazine.com, March 31, 2014 (accessed March 23, 2018); and Dave Lawrence, "Charlie Musselwhite Complete 2015 Interview," www.youtube.com, December 15, 2015 (accessed March 23, 2018).

3. "Spider" John Koerner, interview with Brian T. Atkinson, February 27, 2018; for more on Koerner, Ray & Glover, see "Koerner, Ray, and Glover," www.redhouserecords.com (accessed March 23, 2018)

4. Olga Wilhelmine Munding, interview with Brian T. Atkinson, March 21, 2018; for more on Jessie Mae Hemphill, see Staff, "Jessie Mae Hemphill Obituary: Electric Guitar Songs with a Blues Ambience and Hypnotic Beat," www.theguardian.com, August 8, 2006 (accessed March 24, 2018), and Staff, "Jessie Mae Hemphill Obituary: Jessie Mae Hemphill, Guitarist, Percussionist, and Singer: Born Como, Mississippi 18 October 1923; Married 1941 L. D. Brooks (deceased); Died Memphis, Tennessee 22 July, 2006," www.independent.co.uk, August 10, 2006 (accessed March 24, 2018); for more on the Cat Power controversy surrounding Jessie Mae Hemphill, see Andy Tennille, "Matador Records Skips Important Credit on Cat Power's *Jukebox*," *SF Weekly*, April 9, 2008.

Verse Four

1. Judy Hubbard, interview with Brian T. Atkinson, March 6, 2018. Judy Hubbard effectively restarted Ray Wylie Hubbard's career as his management and muse since the couple married in the late 1980s.

2. Lucas Hubbard, interview with Brian T. Atkinson, February 14, 2018. Lucas Hubbard currently serves as lead guitarist in Ray Wylie Hubbard's touring band.

3. Seth James, interview with Brian T. Atkinson, March 2, 2018; for more on Seth James, see www.sethjames.com (accessed March 24, 2018).

4. Jamie Lin Wilson, interview with Brian T. Atkinson, February 21, 2018; for more on Jamie Lin Wilson, see Atkinson and Finlay, *Kent Finlay, Dreamer*, 222–23; and Amy McCarthy, "Jamie Lin Wilson, Hi-Fi Love [Exclusive Premiere]," www.theboot.com, October 11, 2016 (accessed March 23, 2018); for more on the Trishas, see Brian T. Atkinson, "Trishas Figure It Out As They Go Along," *Austin American-Statesman*, January 28, 2010, D9; Brian T. Atkinson, "The Trishas: High, Wide, and Handsome," *Lone Star Music*, August 1, 2012.

5. Liz Foster, interview with Brian T. Atkinson, December 8, 2017.

6. Kelley Mickwee, interview with Brian T. Atkinson, November 2, 2017.

7. Savannah Welch, interview with Brian T. Atkinson, March 2, 2018.

8. Max Gomez, interview with Brian T. Atkinson, October 24, 2017. For more on Max Gomez, see Brian T. Atkinson, "Max Gomez Takes on the World with Debut Album," www.cmtedge.com, February 18, 2013 (accessed March 23, 2018); and Jeff Gage, "Eclectic Songwriter Max Gomez Talks Creating Revival, Melodic New EP: New Mexico-Based Performer Gets Focused on 'Me & Joe,' His First Release in Three Years," www.rollingstone.com, November 6, 2017 (accessed March 23, 2018).

9. Jack Ingram, interview with Brian T. Atkinson, January 20, 2018; for more on Jack Ingram, see Atkinson, *I'll Be Here in the Morning*, 198–204; Atkinson and Finlay, *Kent Finlay, Dreamer*, 228–31; and Andy Langer, "Jack Out of the Box: Can Former Frat-Boy Fave Jack Ingram Finally Find His Place Among the Great Texas Songwriters?" www.texasmonthly.com, September 2016 (accessed March 24, 2018).

Coda

1. Mike Peters, email interview, October 4, 2017; for more on The Alarm, see Ray Wylie Hubbard's "Snake Farm," *Snake Farm*, Sustain Records, 2006; and www.thealarm.com (accessed March 24, 2018).

Selected Discography

A Selected Discography for Ray Wylie Hubbard

Ray Wylie Hubbard & the Cowboy Twinkies, Warner Bros., 1975
Off the Wall, Lone Star Records, 1978
Something About the Night, Renegade Records, 1979
Caught in the Act, Misery Loves Company Records, 1984
Lost Train of Thought, Misery Loves Company Records, 1992
Loco Gringo's Lament, Deja Disc Records, 1994
Dangerous Spirits, Rounder/Philo Records, 1997
Live at Cibolo Creek Country Club, Misery Loves Company Records,
   1998
Crusades of the Restless Knights, Rounder/Philo Records, 1999
Eternal and Lowdown, Rounder/Philo Records, 2001
Growl, Rounder/Philo Records, 2003
Delirum Tremolos, Rounder/Philo Records, 2005
Snake Farm, Bordello Records, 2006
A: Enlightenment, B: Endarkenment (Hint: There Is No C), Bordello
   Records, 2010
The Grifter's Hymnal, Bordello Records, 2012
The Ruffian's Misfortune, Bordello Records, 2015
Tell the Devil . . . I'm Gettin' There As Fast As I Can, Bordello Records,
   2017

INDEX